W9-AFS-243

Praise for
The Principal's Guide to
SCHOOL BUDGETING

The checklists provided within this book, along with the case studies, provide opportunities for college students to develop budgets and to critique resource use within K–12 schools to improve utilization of resources, with increased K–12 student achievement in mind. This book continually offers reminders to build school budgets upon the needs of K–12 students to improve academic achievement for all.

—Dr. Elizabeth Crane, Adjunct faculty
Eastern Kentucky University
Richmond, KY

The Principal's Guide to School Budgeting *enables understanding of the dynamics of school finance and school budgeting in practical and thoughtful ways. It is a "must have" resource.*

—Dr. Theresa E. Saunders, Assistant Professor
Eastern Michigan University
Ypsilanti, MI

This book offers a series of practical examples, case studies, and reflective questions that the reader could use to delve deeper into his/her own understanding of the information being shared. The authors provide practical suggestions and tips for implementing the ideas and resources/ charts that can be used to help guide the reader through the process.

—Dr. LaQuita Outlaw, Principal—Grades 6–8
Bay Shore Middle School
Bay Shore, NY

This is an excellent book for any aspiring educational leader. The authors have extensive experience which they have used to create an interesting description of how an ethical school leader can bring all stakeholders of a school community together to develop a common vision, prioritize the most important goals for a school, and then use the school's fiscal and human resources to improve learning for all students.

—Dr. Michael Fanning, Associate Professor
School of Continuing Education
California State University, East Bay
Hayward, CA

Dedicated to Xavier Barrera and the late Louise Moser.
Both mentors helped shape us into effective school leaders.

—The Boys

THE PRINCIPAL'S GUIDE TO

SCHOOL BUDGETING

Third Edition

RICHARD D. SORENSON
LLOYD M. GOLDSMITH

CORWIN
A SAGE Publishing Company

FOR INFORMATION:

Corwin

A SAGE Company

2455 Teller Road

Thousand Oaks, California 91320

(800) 233-9936

www.corwin.com

SAGE Publications Ltd.

1 Oliver's Yard

55 City Road

London, EC1Y 1SP

United Kingdom

SAGE Publications India Pvt. Ltd.

B 1/I 1 Mohan Cooperative Industrial Area

Mathura Road, New Delhi 110 044

India

SAGE Publications Asia-Pacific Pte. Ltd.

3 Church Street

#10-04 Samsung Hub

Singapore 049483

Publisher: Arnis Burvikovs

Development Editor: Desirée A. Bartlett

Editorial Assistants: Kaitlyn Irwin and Mia Rodriguez

Production Editor: Amy Schroller

Copy Editor: Erin Livingston

Typesetter: Hurix Digital

Proofreader: Dennis W. Webb

Indexer: Sheia Bodell

Cover Designer: Scott Van Atta

Marketing Manager: Nicole Franks

Copyright © 2018 by Corwin

All rights reserved. When forms and sample documents are included, their use is authorized only by educators, local school sites, and/or noncommercial or nonprofit entities that have purchased the book. Except for that usage, no part of this book may be reproduced or utilized in any form or by any means, electronic or mechanical, including photocopying, recording, or by any information storage and retrieval system, without permission in writing from the publisher.

All trademarks depicted within this book, including trademarks appearing as part of a screenshot, figure, or other image, are included solely for the purpose of illustration and are the property of their respective holders. The use of the trademarks in no way indicates any relationship with, or endorsement by, the holders of said trademarks.

Printed in the United States of America

Library of Congress Cataloging-in-Publication Data

Names: Sorenson, Richard D., author. | Goldsmith, Lloyd Milton, author.

Title: The principal's guide to school budgeting / Richard D. Sorenson, Lloyd Milton Goldsmith.

Description: Third edition. | Thousand Oaks, California : Corwin, [2018] | Includes bibliographical references and index.

Identifiers: LCCN 2017032471 | ISBN 9781506389455 (pbk. : alk. paper)

Subjects: LCSH: School budgets—United States.

Classification: LCC LB2830.2 .S67 2018 | DDC 371.2/06--dc23 LC record available at https://lccn.loc.gov/2017032471

This book is printed on acid-free paper.

SUSTAINABLE FORESTRY INITIATIVE

Certified Chain of Custody

Promoting Sustainable Forestry

www.sfiprogram.org

SFI-01268

SFI label applies to text stock

17 18 19 20 21 10 9 8 7 6 5 4 3 2 1

DISCLAIMER: This book may direct you to access third-party content via Web links, QR codes, or other scannable technologies, which are provided for your reference by the author(s). Corwin makes no guarantee that such third-party content will be available for your use and encourages you to review the terms and conditions of such third-party content. Corwin takes no responsibility and assumes no liability for your use of any third-party content, nor does Corwin approve, sponsor, endorse, verify, or certify such third-party content.

Contents

Preface

Noah Purifoy was a "junkyard genius" who assembled artistic sculptures from three tons of rubble salvaged from the 1965 Watts riots in Los Angeles. Noah took multiple pieces of junk and created powerful messages in art. While the authors of this newly revised text would never claim to be budgeting geniuses, we do believe we've assembled and created powerful messages in the form of budgeting ideas, practices, and processes, making this edition an even more valuable resource for practicing and prospective school leaders. So, welcome to the newly revised third edition of *The Principal's Guide to School Budgeting*, a national best-selling text.

The third edition is purposefully written for practicing and aspiring public and private school administrators who want to enhance their instructional, technical, and managerial skills not only as the school's leader but also as the school's visionary, planning coordinator, and budgeting manager. The authors provide the reader with an essential understanding of the interwoven relationship between two independent yet distinctly connected accountability systems—academic and fiscal.

School leaders—from a financial and budgetary perspective—are responsible for understanding the equity issues and fiscal consequences associated with school budgeting as well as the relationship between educational goal development and resource allocation management. The authors provide school leaders with an overview of school budgeting practices within a collaborative decision-making context. Using school-oriented situations and the national standards for administrators as they relate to school leadership and budgeting, the reader acquires the necessary skills to plan and develop a budget; allocate, expend, and monitor funds; manage and evaluate budget reports; and prepare school action or improvement plans aligned with a fiscal accountability system.

To improve the book's usefulness as a desk resource, it has been purposely organized into brief, single-topic–focused chapters. Each chapter begins with an appropriate quote and general overview and includes numerous visuals, tables, and relevant activities, such as utilizing accounting codes, projecting student populations, conducting a needs assessment, implementing a budget calendar, and building, defending, and amending a budget.

New enhancements to this third edition include an overview of how national and state reform practices are affecting school allocations, the inclusion of the newly adopted Professional Standards for Educational Leaders (PSEL), updated statistical information and relevant budgetary materials and vignettes, a technology overview and how it affects budgetary practices in this digital age, a new section on school fraud and credit card abuse, crowdfunding, and how school funds can be misappropriated if the school leader is not readily focused and engaged in the budgetary process. Additionally, technology-oriented/budgeting screenshots are included within this new edition. Finally, real-life school and budgeting applications and/or situations can be found throughout the newly revised text:

• Chapter 1, "The Budget–Vision Relationship and the National Standards," presents and reviews the PSEL in relation to the correlation between budget and vision and the planning, knowledge, and skills necessary to be an effective school leader, and the three keys to ethics in school leadership.

• Chapter 2, "Culture, Data, Conflict Resolution, and Celebrating Success," reflects upon the importance of school culture, data-driven decision making, and types of data and assessment as related to academic planning and school budgeting as well as the importance of conflict resolution and celebrating success.

• Chapter 3, "A Model for Integrating Vision, Planning, and Budgeting," showcases an eight-component model related to budget and vision implementation and concludes with a real-life planning metaphor that correlates with the elements of an educational action plan.

• Chapter 4, "Understanding the Budgeting Process," examines the delineation between school finance and school budgeting, the basics of school finance, sources of school funding, and essential steps to budgetary success. This chapter also examines budgeting in this era of fiscal constraint and conservative funding. Specifically, aspects of this chapter provide the reader with detailed information and budgetary facts as to how states are coping with continued state funding cuts (long after the Great Recession); how these trends are, sadly, politically inspired and motivated; and how school leaders can still find hope by developing an optimistic work environment that places students first and foremost in instructional and budgetary planning efforts.

- Chapter 5, "Effective, Efficient, and Essential Budgeting Practices," examines the budget plan, expenditure accountability and control, budgetary systems, analyses of school action and budget plans, generated sources of income, fraud and embezzlement, moral and ethical behaviors, and accounting and auditing procedures.

- Chapter 6, "Building the School Budget," reflects upon the budgeting process and those responsible for building the budget, coding applications, the concept of projecting student enrollment, and major budgeting processes, issues, and considerations. This chapter also contains three student-centered case studies.

Special features of the book include the following:

- discussion questions
- case study applications and problems
- experiential exercises
- electronic budgetary screenshots
- budgeting checklist for administrators
- selected templates and forms
- references and resources

School budgeting is a daunting process for many school leaders because most are not bookkeepers, accountants, or financial planners. Many have received minimal training in the budgeting process. This process involves not only computerized accounting procedures and programs but also vision and goal development, instructional planning, and decision making. This can intimidate even the best educational leaders due to their lack of understanding of school-based budgeting and its integrative approaches, which can explain the willingness of some leaders to ignore, avoid, or pass on certain budgetary and planning responsibilities to others. For these reasons alone, the newly revised third edition of *The Principal's Guide to School Budgeting* has been written by two former school administrators with a combined 85 years of experience in the public school arena and who, moreover, have extensive practical experience working with site-based decision-making committees in writing instructional goals and objectives, in the development of school and district budgets, and in defending instructional and budget outcomes to superintendents and school boards.

The Principal's Guide to School Budgeting, third edition, is not designed to be an exhaustive study of the budget and planning subject, nor is it designed to merely provide a basic understanding of the topic. Instead, the contents provide the necessary information and tools needed to incorporate the ideas set forth into real school applications. As a result, readers will be able to take the integrated budget, vision, and planning concepts presented and incorporate them in a practical and relevant manner in their own school settings.

Comment: The authors have made every effort to provide accurate and up-to-date internet, technological, and digital information throughout the text. However, technology, the internet, and digitally posted information are continuously changing. Therefore, it is inevitable that certain websites and other technology-oriented sources, resources, and materials listed within this text will change or become obsolete.

Acknowledgments

We would like to express our appreciation to several individuals who contributed to the development of our book in terms of the first, second, and third editions of *The Principal's Guide to School Budgeting*. So many people have influenced our lives and careers as school administrators and university professors. To those special individuals and friends, we publicly extend our respect and gratitude. A special acknowledgment is extended to the fine folk at Corwin, especially Arnis E. Burvikovs, our second and third edition editor, and Lizzie Brenkus, our first edition editor, both of whom believed in us and took our written project and helped us fulfill another goal in our professional lives. Also, we are appreciative of the guidance and help we received for this edition from Desirée A. Bartlett, senior associate editor; Kaitlyn Irwin, editorial assistant; and Amy Schroller, production editor.

First, I would like to thank my spouse and children: Donna, my loving wife and best friend of 42 years and the mother of our two adult children—Lisa (a school counselor) and Ryan (an exercise physiologist). Of course, I would be remiss in not recognizing our fine son-in-law, Sam (a petroleum engineer), and our three grandchildren, Savannah Grace, Nehemiah Timothy, and Amelia Harper. Hook 'em horns, kiddos!

Second, this book has been strengthened by the contributions of my dear friend and former colleague—Alice Frick, school finance wizard extraordinaire—and two very special research assistants: Adriana E. Spencer and Mary F. Sholtis. These three individuals—Alice, Adriana, and Mary—provided me with invaluable advice and assistance. Adriana and Mary, as did my wife, conducted exceptional research for me, and they actively and accurately followed my credo: "Dig, and dig deep!" Thank you, ladies!

Third, gratitude is extended to Ysleta Independent School District (YISD) employees: Brenda Chacon, associate superintendent of elementary schools; Lynly Leeper, certified public accountant (CPA) and chief financial officer (CFO); Mary Haynie, registered Texas school business administrator (RTSBA), comptroller—division of finance; Maria A. Ontiveros, budget director—budget department; and the remainder of those within the finance division at YISD who were so helpful with the school budget technologies and screenshots within Chapter 6. Also, much appreciation is extended to Rob Kennedy-Jensen with Tyler Technologies, Inc. for his due diligence in securing permission for our usage of said screenshots.

Finally, for allowing me to try out all of my budgeting "stuff," a special note of appreciation is extended to all of the graduate students in the Educational Leadership and Foundations Department at The University of Texas at El Paso. Serving you has always been an honor and a privilege.

Dedicated to the memory of my loving father, Belton Dwane Sorenson (1928–2017), United States Marine and U.S. Army Command Sergeant Major.

—RDS

I would like to thank Mary, my wife and confidant, for having patience with me through this process. I want to thank my colleagues, Dr. Karen Maxwell and Dr. Bruce Scott, for their invaluable support and advice. A special thanks to my colleagues on the Texas Council of Professors of Educational Administration executive board for their friendship and support. I thank Bob and Montie Spaulding for being spiritual advisors to me for most of my life, helping me to keep first things first. I also want to acknowledge and thank all the congregants at the Freedom Fellowship inner-city outreach for teaching me so much about life and giving.

—LMG

Publisher's Acknowledgments

Corwin gratefully acknowledges the contributions of the following reviewers:

Dr. Elizabeth Crane,
Adjunct faculty
Eastern Kentucky University
Richmond, KY

Dr. Michael Fanning,
Associate Professor
School of Continuing Education,
California State University,
East Bay
Hayward, CA

Dr. Ann Hassenpflug, Professor
University of Akron
Akron, OH

Dr. LaQuita Outlaw,
Principal—Grades 6–8
Bay Shore Middle School
Bay Shore, NY

Dr. Theresa E. Saunders, Assistant Professor
Eastern Michigan University
Ypsilanti, MI

About the Authors

Richard D. Sorenson, professor emeritus, is the former director of the Principal Preparation Program and chairperson of the Educational Leadership and Foundations Department at The University of Texas at El Paso (UTEP). He earned his doctorate from Texas A&M University at Corpus Christi in the area of educational leadership. Dr. Sorenson served public schools for 25 years as a social studies teacher, principal, and associate superintendent for human resources.

Dr. Sorenson works with graduate students at UTEP in the area of school-based budgeting, personnel, educational law, and leadership development. He was named The University of Texas at El Paso College of Education Professor of the Year (2005), and he is an active writer with numerous professional journal publications. Dr. Sorenson has also authored textbooks, teacher resource guides, and workbooks in the area of the elementary and secondary social studies curricula. He has been actively involved in numerous professional organizations, including the Texas Elementary Principals and Supervisors Association (TEPSA) and the Texas Association of Secondary School Principals (TASSP), for which he conducted annual new-principal academy seminars.

Dr. Sorenson has been married to his wife, Donna, for the past 42 years and has two adult children, Lisa (a school counselor with the Cypress-Fairbanks Independent School District in Houston, Texas) and Ryan (an exercise physiologist in El Paso, Texas); a wonderful son-in-law, Sam (a petroleum engineer in Houston, Texas); and three grandchildren: Savannah Grace, Nehemiah Timothy, and Amelia Harper—all of whom are the pride and joy of his life.

Dr. Sorenson makes time each day to exercise, walking 5–10 miles, all depending on how industrious he feels! Rick and Donna reside in El Paso, Texas, on the U.S./Mexico border, with their home facing the majestic Franklin Mountains.

Lloyd M. Goldsmith earned his EdD in educational leadership from Baylor University. He is a professor at Abilene Christian University at Dallas, where he teaches doctoral courses in leadership theory. He also serves as an admission officer. Dr. Goldsmith teaches school budgeting, instructional leadership, and leadership theory. He served public schools for 29 years as an elementary science teacher, middle school assistant principal, and elementary school principal.

Dr. Goldsmith and a fellow chemistry professor are in their 16th year of codirecting a program facilitating high school chemistry teachers in developing effective instructional strategies. Dr. Goldsmith has served on several state committees for the Texas Education Agency. He served two terms as president of the Texas Council of Professors of Educational Administration. His research interests relate to effective principal practices and leadership preparation.

Dr. Goldsmith enjoys teaching in his church's inner-city outreach ministry, where he helps equip those living in poverty to better handle life's challenges. He is active in the works of the Ben Richey Boys Ranch.

Dr. Goldsmith has been married to his wife, Mary, for the past 31 years and has three adult children—Abigail, Eleanor, and Nelson. He also has three grandchildren by Abigail and son-in-law, Andrew. Abigail directs a preschool. Eleanor teaches second grade in a Title 1 school where Dr. Goldsmith began his own teaching career. Nelson is a licensed professional building inspector. Dr. Goldsmith's wife, Mary, recently retired from teaching high school biology for 41 years. Lola, his chocolate lab, is royally spoiled and walks the good doctor daily. Life is good!

Introduction

Budgeting and accounting intimidate many individuals, whether it is at work or at home. In this book, the reader examines numerous budgeting processes that connect each to the national Professional Standards for Educational Leaders (PSEL). However, before delving into school budgeting, the authors encourage you, the reader, to examine each of the resources available at the conclusion of the text. A description of each resource (A–C) is detailed below.

Resource A—Selected Forms

Resource A provides the reader with a couple of selected forms, the Budget Development Spreadsheet and the Strategy Page, designed to aid in completing Case Study Application #3 at the conclusion of Chapter 6: The Budget Development Project.

Resource B—Experiential Exercises

• The Budgeting Codes Activity

This activity within the pages of Resource B provides the reader with four scenarios by which the budget accounting codes can be learned and incorporated.

• Accounting Codes Reference Sheet

This reference sheets permits the reader to utilize the coding structure as applied to the previously noted Budget Codes Activity as well as other learning activities specific to Chapter 6.

Resource C—Budgeting Checklist for School Administrators

This checklist ensures that the reader has a successful budgetary year by identifying bookkeeping tasks and responsibilities, budget manager tasks and responsibilities, fundraising and crowdfunding considerations, site-based team and budget development indicators, and important budgetary questions—all worthy of perusal.

1

The Budget–Vision Relationship and the National Standards

You do not lead by hitting people over the head—that's assault, not leadership.

—Dwight David Eisenhower (Thinkexist, 2017)

School Leadership: Innovative, Courageous, and Visionary

School leaders face the challenge of improving student academic achievement in a time of contracting resources and a host of other challenges, including the following:

- maximizing scarce resources
- making budget adjustments without adversely impacting student achievement
- fiscal efficiency
- stretching human capital
- serving an increasingly poor student population

- providing individual instruction more quickly and cheaply
- using funding as a lever to spur innovation
- aligning goals and strategies with funding
- providing teachers and principals what they need, how they need it, when they need it
- meeting the high expectations held by top-performing nations in reading and mathematics
- increasing parental involvement (Center for Public Education, 2009)

Innovative, courageous, and visionary leadership combined with fresh ideas enables educators to conquer these and other challenges in schools. School leaders would do well to remember a leadership lesson from General Eisenhower, who led the American armed forces to victory in Europe in World War II. As a military officer, he realized that assault was not leadership. General Eisenhower's advice is worth remembering in the heat of budget battles.

School Budgeting, School Vision

Budgetary and visionary leadership: these are two issues school leaders must confront on a daily basis. The relationship between school budgeting and vision is as intertwined as is love with marriage. In both cases, you can't have one without the other (Iger, 1998). These two forces, budget and vision, come with their own accountability systems. The former is fiscal; the latter is academic. Technology gives rise to greater and more complicated accounting procedures. Leaders can become overwhelmed when trying to make sense of a sea of data being spewed from a variety of sources. With all of these and other demands, what is a school leader to do? A different approach to the situation is required. Lead; don't assault.

School budgeting is certainly about spreadsheets, reports, tracking the expenditure of funds, and the completing of a myriad of accounting forms (see Chapter 6). It is easy to get caught up in the accounting dimension of budgeting and neglect its companion—vision. It is the integration of vision within the school budgeting process that transforms school budgeting from merely number crunching to purpose-driven expenditures supporting academic success for all students. An articulated and shared vision creates the environment necessary for planning for academic success and for all students to flourish.

Figure 1.1   The Integrated Budget Train

> The school leader is in the locomotive leading the cars of vision, planning, and budgeting."Yes you can! Yes you can! Yes you can!"comes rolling back from the locomotive for all to hear.

SOURCE: Kathy Myrick, illustrator.

Principals must rethink their approach to school budgeting. School budgeting must not be thought of as merely an accounting responsibility. Leaders must leave the primary accounting responsibility to certified public accountants (CPAs) and the business office. These folks must be allowed to provide the technical expertise and support necessary to meet the regulatory requirements associated with state and federal fiscal accountability standards. Principal leadership skills must carry the school budgeting process to the next level. This is achieved by integrating the school vision with the budgeting and academic processes for the purpose of achieving academic success for all students.

Imagine a train heading down a track, as depicted in Figure 1.1. The track is time; the train is the school. The locomotive represents the school leader. This individual leads the local motivation to create a shared vision for the school. The remaining cars are the school's vision and budget and planning process. The movement of the train down the track is the school year. Like the locomotive, the leader is key to moving the school "down the track." Bringing the cars of vision, budget, and planning is essential—so essential, in fact, they are recognized and supported in the Professional Standards for Educational Leaders (PSEL).

The Professional Standards for Educational Leaders

The PSEL is a logical place to commence a discussion of the relationship between leaders and school budgeting and planning. The PSEL replaced the Interstate School Leaders Licensure Consortium (ISLLC) 2008 standards. Table 1.1 provides a correlation between these two sets of standards. Sometimes in the heat of the school budgeting and planning battle, the PSEL can appear distant to leaders and stakeholders. That should not be the case. Rather, these standards provide leaders with a firm foundation for exploring and growing leadership development and practice.

A brief examination of the PSEL provides an overview of the authors' assertion that all standards address budget issues and do indeed speak loudly to leaders and other stakeholders engaged in

Table 1.1   Side-by-Side Correlation of the ISLLC Standards and the PSEL

ISLLC Standards	PSEL
1. Vision	1. Mission, Vision, and Core Values 10. School Improvement
2. School Culture and Instructional Program	4. Curriculum, Instruction, and Assessment 5. Community of Care and Support for Students 6. Professional Capacity of School Personnel 7. Professional Community for Teachers and Staff
3. Operations, Management, and Resources	5. Community of Care and Support for Students 6. Professional Capacity of School Personnel 9. Operations and Management
4. Collaboration With Faculty and Community	8. Meaningful Engagement of Families and Community
5. Ethics	2. Ethics and Professional Norms 3. Equity and Cultural Responsiveness
6. Political, Social, Legal, Cultural Context	3. Equity and Cultural Responsiveness 8. Meaningful Engagement of Families and Community

SOURCE: Hansen (2016). Prepared for the National Association of Elementary School Principals by Courtney Rowland with the American Institute for Research, Center for Great Teachers and Leaders. Used with permission.

the budgeting process. The lofty goals of these national standards *are* connected to the reality of leading schools. These standards are crucial in making a difference in student success as well as in providing for student well-being and learning and "outlining foundational principles of leadership to help ensure that each child is well-educated and prepared for the 21st century" (National Policy Board for Educational Administration [NPBEA], 2015, p. 2). Future-oriented standards provide guidance in the fast-changing global arena where educational leaders reside. The PSEL standards demand active, not passive, leadership. These standards assume that leaders are collaborative and inclusive in leading their schools. However, leadership is stronger and more effective when other stakeholders are involved, such as teachers, counselors, and paraprofessionals. This collaborative leadership demands cultivating and improving leadership growth in all stakeholders. The PSEL "reflect the importance of cultivating leadership capacity in others" (NPBEA, 2015, p. 4).

The PSEL provide a clarion call for collaboration between all stakeholders within the school and its community. The standards are "a compass that guides the direction of practice directly as well as indirectly through the work of policy makers, professional associations, and supporting institutions" (NPBEA, 2015, p. 4).

Steven Covey (2004), in his book, *The Seven Habits of Highly Effective People,* encouraged leaders to "begin with the end in mind." In essence, that is exactly what the PSEL call on school leaders to do, as every standard promotes *each* student's academic success and well-being. *Each* means all students, 100%. *Each* also implies individual attention to all students. Who wants a child or grandchild to not meet with academic success? Can school leaders walk down their school's hallways and look at students and determine which ones they do not want to meet with success? What moral choice do school leaders have but to "promote *each* student's academic success and well-being"? This *"each* student" dimension of the PSEL demands a train trip for planning big and promoting success. It requires another visit to two longtime friends—school budgeting and vision—and an examination of their often-overlooked relationship in the planning process.

The PSEL are examined through a school budgeting lens in an effort to explore how the national leadership standards address the school budgeting process. This examination provides school leaders with guiding principles for school budgeting.

Initially, a leader might be criticized for taking such a Utopian train trip. Critics will accuse the leader of not living in the real world. School leaders will suffer through the criticism and cynicism of these sarcastic and skeptical voices because they understand that every student meeting with success is, by its very nature, a Utopian goal. Visiting Utopia provides us with a perfect vision for our schools. It is imperative to begin with this perfect vision. To begin planning for academic success for *each* student with a vision that is less than ideal dooms a leader and team in their quest for academic success for *each* student.

The PSEL define the practice for educational leaders. They offer guidance for professional practice as well as inform how educational leaders are "prepared, hired, developed, supervised and evaluated" (NPBEA, 2015, p. 2). The PSEL provide greater emphasis on student learning and provide strong guidance to guarantee that each student is prepared for success in the 21st century. The PSEL clarify and offer greater specificity for educational leaders.

While in Utopia devising a plan for academic success for *each* student, give primary consideration to the interrelationship between school budgeting and vision. While neither of these concepts is new, it could be argued that school leaders have not given due consideration to the significance of the symbiotic relationship they have on the academic success of students and schools. It is essential to consider budgeting and vision simultaneously in the planning process in order to increase our understanding of their influence on each other and the fulfillment of the national standard's clarion call for "academic success and well-being for *each* student." It is imperative that the discussion of school budgeting and vision begin with an introductory overview of each PSEL. It is also essential that this overview of the standards be accomplished through a school budgeting and vision lens. The language of the PSEL is explored further in the ensuing chapters.

An Introduction of the PSEL Through a Budget–Vision Lens

A macro-view of the PSEL provides an appropriate introduction to these standards and their elements. The PSEL influence how leaders perceive the manifestation of campus leadership behavior. The "Yesterday and Today" side-by-side comparison (beginning on p. 11) of previous leadership expectations (Yesterday) with that of the PSEL leadership expectations (Today) for each standard allows for a cursory examination of the change in leadership behavior. In other words, it allows us to delineate where we have been (Yesterday) to where we are going (Today) in campus leadership. The "Key Differences Between ISLLC Standards and the PSEL" feature provides a cursory examination of the differences between the two standard sets.

PSEL 1: Mission, Vision, and Core Values

Effective educational leaders develop, advocate, and enact a shared mission, vision, and core values of high-quality education and academic success and well-being of *each* student.

PSEL 1: Mission, Vision, and Core Values, like each of the standards, includes the phrase "success and well-being of *each* student." This phrase requires leaders to approach budgeting and vision with the expectation *each* student will meet with success, not only those students who come to school prepared and nurtured by their families but also those who come with little nurturing and minimal preparation. Leaders might do well to stop and reread the previous statement and allow the significance of it to sink in. "Success and well-being of *each* student" does not allow leaders or other stakeholders to rationalize or explain away their responsibility to have *each* student meet with success. The focus is no longer on organizational effectiveness; rather, it seeks success for each student.

Kouzes and Posner (2007) identified five practices of strong leaders. One of those practices was inspiring a shared vision that would guide all of the organization's stakeholders. Leaders are those who have the obligation to help stakeholders visualize goals and outcomes. Likewise, leaders must help those they lead by providing a positive example. This requires leaders to keep their word on commitments they make with others. Doing so moves the organization forward.

Budgeting, vision, and academic success are intertwined with each other in the planning process. They are not isolated variables operating independently in a school's culture. When leaders accept this coupling of budgeting and vision and understand their combined effect on academic achievement, budgeting expands from a fiscal responsibility to a fiscal vision opportunity that in turn drives planning for academic success for each student.

PSEL 1: Mission, Vision, and Core Values is at the very core of this book's purpose in that it calls for the melding of mission, vision, and core values within the budgeting process. Not only must a school leader facilitate the development, articulation, and implementation of a school vision, the leader must also be a steward of that vision. Stewardship is the administration and management of the financial affairs of another. A school leader ensures that the school's resources are allocated in a manner that supports the school's vision. The school's budget does not belong to the principal or any other leader. It belongs to all the school's stakeholders.

It belongs to the public who sacrifice through the payment of taxes thus providing the budget revenues.

The Council of Chief State School Officers (CCSSO) provides a succinct summary of the key differences between the ISLLC and PSEL standards (CCSSO, 2016). This comparison assists in understanding the changes between the old standards and the new ones.

KEY DIFFERENCES BETWEEN THE ISLLC STANDARDS AND THE PSEL

The PSEL shift from a focus on organizational effectiveness to the success of each student. These standards provide specific guidance for areas in which an effective leader sets goals, including equity and social justice. There is a new focus on the core values defining the school's culture that goes beyond simply the mission and vision that drive improvement. Finally, effective leaders are expected to model and pursue these changes in all aspects of their leadership.

SOURCES: ISLLC (2008), PSEL (2015).

Yesterday and Today—Mission, Vision, and Core Values

The "Yesterday and Today: Where We've Been and Where We're Going" feature provides a further opportunity to explore the leadership shift from the ISLLC standards to the PSEL (Just Ask Publications and Professional Development, 2017). Marcia Baldanza, creator of the "Yesterday and Today: Where We've Been and Where We're Going" feature, points us to the past and present as well as toward the leadership behavior we need today. Many schools have accomplished the leadership shift from *Yesterday* to *Today*; other schools have not and still others are in the process of change. Some principals have become *Today* (instructional) leaders while others remain *Yesterday* (custodial) leaders or somewhere in between.

In *Yesterday* schools, principals focused attention on the school facilities and ensured that the school was managed in an orderly fashion, with students sitting quietly at desks. Principals spent little time or energy in instructional practices or encouraging a culture of continuous improvement or a student-centered education. The vision and mission were ignored or, at best, posted somewhere in the building, never to be reviewed or discussed.

In *Today* schools, principals focus on student learning and achievement. Principals delegate managerial and other routine duties to supplementary individuals. Principals tout the vision and mission statements frequently so all stakeholders know and understand the vision, mission, and core values.

Examine the Yesterday and Today table for *PSEL 1: Mission, Vision, and Core Values*. Ponder where you and the school stakeholders are on mission, vision, and core values today compared to yesterday.

Yesterday and Today
Where We've Been and Where We're Going **PSEL 1: Mission, Vision, and Core Values**
Effective educational leaders develop, advocate, and enact a shared mission, vision, and core values of high-quality education and academic success and well-being of *each* student.

Yesterday	Today
Leader-shaped and leader-dependent culture and expectations	Collaborate with stakeholders to develop and promote data-driven vision, mission, and core values of and commitment to success for each student
Leader-developed goals explained to staff, progress check at the end of year	Translate the vision into measurable actions; monitor, evaluate, and adjust as needed
Oversight of facilities, processes, and operations	Identify, model, and support instructional and organizational practices that contribute to success
Focus on safe, orderly, well-managed district, schools, and classrooms	Articulate, advocate, and cultivate core values for • child-centered education • high expectations and student support • equity, inclusiveness, and social justice • openness, caring, and trust • culture of continuous improvement

SOURCE: Just Ask Publications and Professional Development (2017).

PSEL 2: Ethics and Professional Norms

Effective educational leaders act ethically and according to professional norms to promote *each* student's academic success and well-being.

PSEL 2: Ethics and Professional Norms is essential in growing the integrated budget–vision–planning process. It is noteworthy that this standard immediately follows *PSEL 1: Mission, Vision, and Core Values*, which established the importance of having a school vision. Core values and ethics must be melded in order to be an ethical, professional leader.

The *Ethics and Professional Norms* standard is a reminder that character does in fact matter. Principals must examine personal motives and their treatment of others as well as how they carry out their personal and professional missions. Leaders must decide what they are not willing to do in order to achieve personal and school goals.

Integrity, fairness, and ethical behavior are a trio of concepts school leaders struggle to define. Former United States Supreme Court Justice Potter Stewart, commenting in the *Jacobellis v. Ohio* case concerning the issue of pornography, stated he could not attempt to define pornography and yet acknowledged, "But I know it when I see it" (Linder, n. d.). Like Stewart, educators know integrity, fairness, and ethical behavior when observed but struggle to define this trio of terms.

This trio can be analyzed utilizing the works of Plato, John Locke, Immanuel Kant, Niccolo Machiavelli, and others, but that might seem detached from the day-to-day challenges school leaders face. Leaders must depend on their personal judgment and experiences in determining how to react to given situations (see the fraud and embezzlement issues as discussed in Chapter 5, along with "Case Study Application #2: Fiscal Issues and the New Principal" in Chapter 4 and "Case Study Application #2: Sex, Money, and a Tangled Web Woven" in Chapter 5). Readers should take time from their busy schedules to consider integrity, fairness, and ethical behavior. After all, the in-the-face demands of academic accountability, student discipline, per-pupil expenditure, and a host of other demands provide for a variety of excuses for bypassing an examination of these terms. Cooper (2012) suggests that school leaders often make administrative decisions using rationality and systematic reflection in a piecemeal fashion. Cooper asserts that leaders are ad hoc problem solvers, not comprehensive moral philosophers who only resort to the next level of generality and abstraction when a repertoire of practical moral rules fail to assist in reaching a decision. Sound familiar?

Examining Three Key Terms—The Trio

It is important to examine *PSEL 2: Ethics and Professional Norms* in the light of budgeting and vision and to pay close attention to the three key terms found in this standard—*integrity, fairness,* and *ethics* (see Table 1.2).

Integrity. Integrity, the first of the trio of ethical terms, is an important dimension of leadership. Leaders who value integrity are not only interested in results but are also interested in relationships. This is easily illustrated in the world of high-stakes student assessment. Each year, educators are under increasing pressure to meet a mandated level of academic performance for their students. The consequences for not achieving these defined goals are increasing. The temptation from a variety of schemes for school leaders to manipulate these data is also increasing.

Principals must not only consider integrity within the sphere of academic goals. They must also consider the integrity of their relationships with all of the school's stakeholders to be successful. For integrity to exist, leaders must show genuine concern for others and their personal goals. When concern and integrity exist, trust flourishes and further empowers the leader to lead the school toward fulfilling its shared vision.

Stories abound in which school leaders succumb to temptation and misrepresent themselves, inappropriately use school funds, or manipulate data (see "Fraud and Embezzlement: How the Money Vanishes" in Chapter 5 p. 180). When this is discovered, these leaders lose their reputation and effectiveness along with their dignity. It takes a lifetime to build a good reputation and only a minute to lose it. A superintendent from a school of 33,000 students retired from her job with three years remaining on her contract as a result of a controversy associated with recommending a contract to be offered to a firm for the delivery of services to the school district. At issue was her failure to advise the board that she had worked as a consultant for the firm for several years (Borja, 2005).

Table 1.2   Key Terms in PSEL 2: Ethics and Professional Norms

Integrity	Soundness of and adherence to moral principle and character
Fairness	Free from bias, dishonesty, or injustice
Ethics	A system of moral principles

SOURCE: Stein (1967).

High-stakes testing is a prime area for leaders to be tempted to cheat by manipulating data. Variables such as test security, student exemptions, and test preparation become factors. In a highly publicized case, systematic cheating was uncovered in Atlanta's public school system. Forty-four schools and at least 178 educators, including the superintendent, were involved in this alleged cheating incident (Severson, 2011). Cizek (1999) compiled a list of euphemisms that have been used by educators in attempts to soften the term *cheating*. Sadly, two of the more creative euphemisms were *falsely reporting success* and *achievement similarities not attributable to chance*.

Samuel Johnson, one of the most quoted moralist from the 18th century, said, "Integrity without knowledge is weak and useless, and knowledge without integrity is dangerous and dreadful" (Brainy Quote, 2001–2017a). Integrity alone will not allow a school leader to meet with success. Principals must understand every facet of a school and its students. Principals must have a command of the school's vision and its budget. If a leader lacks integrity, the school is at risk; doubt and fear will replace integrity. People will revert to the selfish nature of man, and the common good of the learning community will be forgotten.

Fairness. Once again, school leaders risk their effectiveness when they separate vision from the budget, especially when it comes to fairness. It is essential to consider both budget and vision as integral parts of the planning process to completely understand the complex nature of fairness.

Fairness, the second of the trio of key terms, does not mean ensuring everyone gets the same amount of something or the same treatment. Fairness is when everyone receives what is needed in order to successfully accomplish his or her goals. Some students will need one cup of patience while others will require two, three, or even four cups of patience to reach their goals. Still others will need different resources dedicated to them to ensure their academic success, thus the continued clarion call for Title 1 funds for disadvantaged students in high-poverty schools. Another example is students with learning disabilities who might need greater special education resources in order to reach their instructional goals than those without disabilities.

When principals accept the fact that vision is what drives the budget and shared vision is designed to help all students achieve their potential, then they begin to understand that fairness requires resources to be allocated on the basis of need in order to obtain academic goals. Fairness is not dividing the financial pie into equal pieces. For example, the New Jersey School Board Association (NJSBA, 2007) reports that the New Jersey per-pupil expenditure for students in special education was $16,081, compared to $10,050 for general education. The financial pie was not divided into equal pieces. Instead, it was apportioned based on meeting the individual needs of students.

Schools perish when a lack of vision exists. When money is thrown at problems, human nature takes over to ensure "give me my fair share." This usually translates into "get all I can get." In the absence of an understanding of the budget–vision relationship in the planning process, greed takes control and the good of the learning community is abandoned.

Unfortunately, fairness does not become a part of a school's social fabric overnight. It cannot be ordered or microwaved into existence. Instead, the leader must keep the budget–vision relationship in front of the team and make inroads into fairness as opportunities arise. Through persistence, fairness will become valued as part of the school's culture and will manifest itself in ethical behavior.

Ethics. Ethical behavior is an essential part of the school leader's persona. Fairness, integrity, and equity are employed to best conduct the school's business. School leaders must act in an ethical manner when handling discipline problems, implementing state-mandated accountability testing, managing school budgets, consulting with parents, supervising faculty and staff, and in a host of other situations.

Principle of Benefit Maximization

A continued examination of the national standards with regard to their implication on budgeting and vision reveals how appropriate it is to consider the principle of benefit maximization. This principle requires principals to make choices that provide the greatest good for the most people. When developing a school vision, the process must be one of inclusiveness. Shared vision is about meaningfully involving everyone, not only those with the greatest political clout or the loudest voices in the vision development process. The principal must help craft and share a school vision that not only provides each student with the opportunity to meet with success but also a vision that is truly shared by all stakeholders. The PSEL's mantra to "promote *each* student's academic success and well-being" reminds us that *each* means all students will meet with success.

The principle of benefit maximization also applies to the budgeting process. Budgets must provide the greatest good for the most students. This means tough decisions must be made. Tough decisions are not always popular decisions. But tough decisions made with integrity and fairness and in an ethical manner will propel schools toward the fulfillment of a school's vision. It is essential that the school budget be considered in tandem with the school vision.

The budget is an essential tool in turning the vision into reality. When the budget process is divorced from the vision process, the likelihood of the vision being fulfilled dramatically decreases. Bracey (2002) provides a vivid illustration of what can happen when the budget process and the academic vision process are divorced. In his book, *The War Against America's Public Schools*, Bracey details the 21st-century attack on public school via privatization (see Chapter 4 of this book) and writes about a group of superintendents enthusiastically embracing a new efficiency model that changed them from scholars into managers. Bracey concludes his chiding of this particular efficiency model by writing, "Of course, one might wonder why, instead of studying ways to save money on toilet paper, superintendents didn't investigate why their charges dipped it in water and slung it at the walls" (p. 37).

Considering the toilet paper problem from a purely accounting perspective, the focus is only on the financial cost associated with providing the toilet paper for student use and neglects the possible academic issues at play in the misuse of the toilet paper. By only considering the financial issue associated with the use or misuse of the toilet paper, leaders wipe out the opportunity to get to the academic bottom of the toilet paper cost problem in terms of its cost to the school's vision to have all students meet with academic success. By including the academic perspective in conjunction with the budget perspective, hence the budget–vision connection, the toilet paper problem is then also considered as a potential indication of an academic failure to meet the needs of all students. Bottom line: Budgeting and vision must be considered simultaneously if schools are to reach their goal of 100% student success.

The Golden Rule Principle

A second principle to consider in the examination of ethics is the Golden Rule. Many might mistakenly limit the Golden Rule to the teachings of Jesus; however, there is some version of the Golden Rule in five of the world's major religions. The universal truth found in the Golden Rule is important to consider in our ethical treatment of others. It requires principals to treat all people with equal value. People are entitled to equal opportunity. Principals must value all people and respect their educational goals. People must not be considered as merely assets to be used to achieve the school vision.

Finally, leaders must respect individuals' rights to make their own choices. When including the Golden Rule as part of the code of ethics, principals are more apt to integrate the budget process with the vision. The end result: Leaders are less likely to see people as objects to be manipulated to achieve selfish purposes.

KEY DIFFERENCES BETWEEN THE ISLLC STANDARDS AND THE PSEL

PSEL 2 goes beyond the ISLLC standards by making a clear call to action for leaders to model ethical and professional behaviors—especially trust, collaboration, and perseverance. Effective leaders are expected to do their jobs well while providing moral direction for the school and staff. Finally, there is a clear emphasis on placing children at the center of education and accepting responsibility for their academic success.

SOURCES: ISLLC (2008), CCSSO (2016), PSEL (2015).

Yesterday and Today—Ethics and Professional Norms

The introduction to this PSEL is the longest. It is the author's contention that ethics and professional norms undergird all of the PSEL; hence, the longer introduction. In *Today* schools, principals and other campus stakeholders must focus on ethics and professional norms. Ponder where you and other stakeholders are in following the ethics and professional norms on your campus.

Yesterday and Today
Where We've Been and Where We're Going
PSEL 2: Ethics and Professional Norms

Effective educational leaders act ethically and according to professional norms to promote *each* student's academic success and well-being.

Yesterday	Today
Accomplish tasks in isolation	Act ethically and professionally in all aspects of school leadership
Determine areas for improvement and sets goals without input from others	Promote the norms of fairness, integrity, transparency, trust, collaboration, perseverance, learning, and continuous improvement
	(Continued)

(Continued)	
Operate school smoothly and without notice: Students' performance not seen as the responsibility of school but the result of family background	Place children at the center of education and accept responsibility for each student's academic success and well-being
Conform to implied or set standards of conduct without free expression	Safeguard the values of democracy, individual freedom and responsibility, equity, social justice, community, and diversity
Run a safe environment without complaint	Provide moral direction for the school and promote professional behavior

SOURCE: © 2017. Just ASK Publications & Professional Development. All rights reserved.

PSEL 3: Equity and Cultural Responsiveness

> Effective educational leaders strive for equality of educational opportunity and culturally responsive practices to promote *each* student's academic success and well-being.

Culturally responsive behavior leadership is essential for today's campus leaders. Leadership is no longer limited to teaching; it requires the entire school environment to be responsive to the instructional needs to all students in general and minoritized students specially (Khalifa, Gooden, & Davis, 2016). A large body of literature focuses on culturally responsive academic instruction. Campus leaders and other stakeholders can assist in equity and cultural responsiveness by increasing their cultural knowledge, enhancing staff members' cultural self-awareness, validating others' culture, increasing cultural relevance, establishing cultural validity, and emphasizing cultural equity (Banks & Obiakor, 2015).

Striving for equity of educational opportunity and cultural responsiveness requires campus leadership. This requires principals to prioritize and budget time and resources to support academic achievement and "act as social activists who advocate for societal change to make their communities 'a better place to live'" (Johnson, 2007, p. 53).

> ## KEY DIFFERENCES BETWEEN THE ISLLC STANDARDS AND THE PSEL
>
> *PSEL 3: Equity and Cultural Responsiveness* requires leaders to ensure equity and cultural responsiveness for each student by encouraging perceptions of student diversity as an asset for teaching and learning, confronting and altering institutional biases rather than simply recognizing them, and serving as a true advocate for equity and cultural responsiveness in all aspects of leadership. In addition, the standard emphasizes preparing students to be productive in a diverse, global society rather than focusing only on improving their academic or social outcomes.
>
> SOURCES: CCSSO (2016), ISLLC (2008), PSEL (2015).

Yesterday and Today—Equity and Cultural Responsiveness

In *Today* schools, principals and other campus stakeholders must focus on equity and cultural responsiveness. Ponder where you and the other school stakeholders are in establishing equity and cultural responsiveness on your campus.

Yesterday and Today	
Where We've Been and Where We're Going	
PSEL 3: Equity and Cultural Responsiveness	
Effective educational leaders strive for equity of educational opportunity and culturally responsive practices to promote *each* student's academic success and well-being.	
Yesterday	*Today*
Treat students as groups and not as individuals	Treat each student fairly, respectfully, and with understanding of culture and context
Recognize and reward conformity among students and teachers	Recognize student's strengths, diversity, culture as assets for teaching and learning
Allow tenure to manage teaching assignments, regardless of skill	Ensure that each student has access to effective teachers, learning opportunities, and academic and social support
	(Continued)

(Continued)	
Implement leader-developed and leader-dependent policies on discipline	Develop policies that address misconduct in a positive, fair, and unbiased manner
Identify with and support the mainstream practices	Confront and alter institutional biases and act with cultural competence and responsiveness
Assign students to a college or vocational track early and schedule accordingly	Prepare students to live productively and contribute to diverse cultural contexts of global society

SOURCE: © 2017. Just ASK Publications & Professional Development. All rights reserved.

PSEL 4: Curriculum, Instruction, and Assessment

> Effective educational leaders develop and support intellectually rigorous and coherent systems of curriculum, instruction, and assessment to promote *each* student's academic success and well-being.

Curriculum, instruction and assessment are at the heart of school leader responsibilities. Newman, Smith, Allensworth, and Bryk (2001) recognized the importance of a strong instructional program. They coined the term *instructional program coherence*, defining it as "a set of interrelated programs for students and staff that are guided by a common framework for curriculum, instruction, assessment, and learning climate and that are pursued over a sustained period" (p. 297). The authors, as former principals, observed many instructional improvement programs come and go. School stakeholders frequently became jaded and skeptical of the next new curriculum plan. Regardless of how many instructional programs are adopted, they often fail because they are frequently uncoordinated, short lived, or limited in scope.

Instructional technology continues to evolve. It seems as if when a new technology is implemented, it immediately needs to be updated or even replaced, be it hardware, software, or faculty and staff training. Although not peer reviewed, the blog, *14 Things That Are Obsolete in 21st Century Schools*, managed by Ingvi Omarsson (2017), an elementary teacher in Iceland, informally illustrates the rapid change in instructional technology teachers experience throughout the globe.

SOURCE: Omarsson (2017).

1. Computer rooms

2. Isolated classrooms

3. Schools that don't have Wi-Fi

4. Banning phones and tablets

5. Tech director with an administrator access

6. Teachers that don't share what they do

7. Schools that don't have Facebook or Twitter

8. Unhealthy cafeteria food

9. Starting school at 8 o'clock for teenagers

10. Buying poster, website, and pamphlet design for the school

11. Traditional libraries

12. All students get the same class because they are born in the same year

13. One–*professional development*–workshop-fits-all

14. Standardized tests to measure the quality of education

It is essential that all stakeholders possess ownership of the school's action or improvement plan and recognize the importance of allocating community resources to achieve the desired academic results that are in line with the school's vision and mission. The community is literally investing its resources in its children and is expecting a return on its investment in the form of educated, enlightened, and productive individuals. When schools fail to produce this product, the community resources must be reallocated to address this failure in the form of welfare, juvenile detention, and adult prison programs. The failure of schools to meet student needs creates a domino effect that is felt throughout the community. Failure to meet the campus goals for students creates an intensely competitive environment for the community resources, as other public institutions vying for the same limited public resources must meet the shortcomings of school programs.

An example of added costs to the public occurs when education is not successful is found in the prison system. The 2003 Literacy Behind Bars Survey revealed that 41% of prisoners in state and federal prisons had their high school diploma or equivalent. This compares to 85% to 88% of the general population. This survey, the most comprehensive assessment of educational backgrounds of prisoners in 10 years, also reported overall prison inmates with GED/high school equivalency certificates had higher literacy scores than those with high school diplomas (Greenberg, Dunleavy, & Kutner, 2007).

Keeping a person in prison costs more than two and a half times the amount it takes to educate a child. The average per-pupil expenditure for students in U.S. public elementary and secondary schools in 2013–2014 was $12,335 (U.S. Census Bureau, 2016). Utah, at $6,555, spent the least per pupil in educating children. New York spent $20,610 per pupil, making it the largest spender per pupil (U.S. Census Bureau, 2016). The Vera Institute for Justice reported in 2012 that the average cost to taxpayers to keep a prisoner incarcerated was $31,286 (Henrichson & Delaney, 2012). On average, the cost of keeping an individual in prison is $18,736 more per year than the average per-pupil cost for students in public schools.

The cost to the public for unsuccessful schools is also reflected in the median earning of adults based on educational attainment. The U.S. Bureau of Labor Statistics (2011) reported that the more educated a person, the greater the person's income is likely to be. Conversely, the earlier a person drops out of school, the lower the person's income is.

The unemployment rate for workers with a high school diploma is 87.5% greater than for workers with a bachelor's degree (U.S. Bureau of Labor Statistics, 2016). This relationship between educational attainment and income is shown in Figure 1.2. The cost to society for students not meeting with academic success is staggering. Assuming a 40-year work career and not adjusting for inflation, the worker with a bachelor's degree will earn $1,396,480 more in a work career than the student who left school with less than a high school education.

Figure 1.2   Unemployment Rate and Earnings for Educational
Attainment

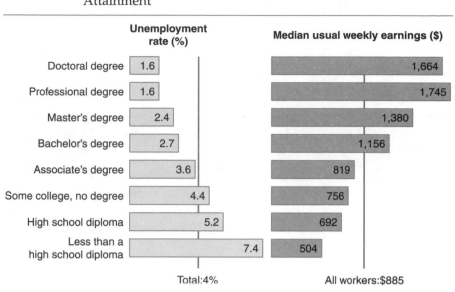

SOURCE: U.S. Bureau of Labor Statistics (2016).

When schools fail to achieve the PSEL's call for academic success for each student, then schools can expect other systems to compete with them for public resources. It is imperative for students to meet with academic success not only to become greater producers for society but also to lessen the need for other institutions such as prisons and welfare programs; this, in turn, increases the availability of funds to enrich the services provided by public education.

KEY DIFFERENCES BETWEEN THE ISLLC STANDARDS AND THE PSEL

PSEL 4: Curriculum, Instruction, and Assessment incorporates broad references to leadership expectations, such as supervising instruction, monitoring, and evaluating and supporting rigorous and coherent curriculum. PSEL 4 and its elements suggest specific indicators of how to do this well, such as how to promote effective instructional practices. Also, PSEL 4 goes further than the ISLLC standards when addressing assessments by stating that effective leaders employ valid assessments.

SOURCES: CCSSO (2016), ISLLC (2008), PSEL (2015).

Yesterday and Today—Curriculum, Instruction, and Assessment

In a *Today* school, principals and other campus stakeholders must focus on curriculum, instruction, and assessment. Ponder where you and the other school stakeholders are on implementing curriculum, instruction, and assessment at your school.

Yesterday and Today	
Where We've Been and Where We're Going	
PSEL 4: Curriculum, Instruction, and Assessment	
Effective educational leaders develop and support intellectually rigorous and coherent systems of curriculum, instruction, and assessment to promote *each* student's academic success and well-being.	
Yesterday	*Today*
Set and maintain expectations for conduct	Set and maintain high expectations for student learning
Teach the scope and sequence of adopted text	Align curriculum, instruction, and assessment to academic standards
Instruct once to whole group using teacher's edition as lesson plan	Ensure instructional practice is <ul><li>consistent with child development and intellectually challenging</li><li>authentic to student needs</li><li>differentiated</li><li>personalized</li></ul>
Use computers in lab settings to play learning games	Promote effective use of technology in the service of teaching and learning
Administer end-of-unit or chapter test and/or teacher-developed exam	Employ valid assessments
Use data as a one-time event for report cards and promotion/graduation	Use data to monitor student progress and improve instruction

SOURCE: © 2017. Just ASK Publications & Professional Development. All rights reserved.

PSEL 5: Community of Care and Support for Students

Effective educational leaders cultivate an inclusive, caring, and supportive school community that promotes the academic success and well-being of *each* student.

Schools must have a strong community to support the students under its care. This does not happen unless leaders intentionally promote and shepherd the stakeholders within the school and its broader community. Gordon and Louis (2009) affirmed the importance of the democratic assumptions that underpin public education in the United States and the importance of involving as many stakeholders as possible to impact student achievement in a positive manner. Hence, openness and sharing increases the potential to solve problems in learning communities.

Trust between parents and school is important in growing a healthy school community. Lewis and Weigert (1985) noted that trust requires ongoing and frequent interactions with all stakeholders within the school. Parents' and other stakeholders' social interactions within the school provide the environment for developing trust (Adams, Forsyth, & Mitchell, 2009, p. 4). If the various school stakeholders fail to have frequent and meaningful interaction with each other, they cannot expect to grow the trust needed for healthy environment. Campus leaders must invest time and energy in developing the conditions necessary to develop a healthy community of care and support for the students and their parents. On a note of caution, schools that are doing well academically may not feel the need or urgency to recruit community members and parents, since their campus is functioning well; they do not want to risk outside stakeholders taking the school off of its academic course (Gordon & Louis, 2009).

KEY DIFFERENCES BETWEEN ISLLC STANDARDS AND THE PSEL

PSEL 5: Community of Care and Support for Students extends the ISLLC standards' global view of school culture and student learning by providing specific actions for leaders to take to improve school community. PSEL 5 places strong emphasis on supports for students and creating a trusting environment that mirrors the culture of the community while ensuring that all students feel accepted, valued, cared for, and encouraged.

SOURCES: CCSSO (2016), ISLLC (2008), PSEL (2015).

Yesterday and Today—Community of Care and Support for Students

In a *Today* school, principals and other campus stakeholders must focus on community of care and support for students. Ponder where you and the other school stakeholders are at in establishing a community of care and support of students at your school.

Yesterday and Today	
Where We've Been and Where We're Going	
PSEL 5: Community of Care and Support for Students	
Effective educational leaders cultivate an inclusive, caring, and supportive school community that promotes the academic success and well-being of *each* student.	
Yesterday	*Today*
Establish a safe and orderly environment	Build and maintain safe, caring, healthy school environment that meets academic, social, emotional, physical needs of each student
Create a purposeful and businesslike environment	Create and sustain environment where each student is known, accepted, valued, trusted, respected, cared for, and encouraged to be an active and responsible member of community
Seek alternative placements for students needing support. Extracurricular activities limited to high school music and sports	Provide coherent support systems, services, and extracurricular accommodations for each student
Provide guidance and advice for academics and college-bound students only	Promote relationships that value and support academic learning and positive social/emotional development
Ensure that students are free from physical harm	Cultivate and reinforce student engagement in school and positive school conduct
Use a sink or swim approach to English language learners. Different cultures are expected to adapt and conform	Infuse learning environment with cultures and languages of community

SOURCE: 2017. Just ASK Publications & Professional Development. All rights reserved.

PSEL 6: Professional Capacity of School Personnel

Effective educational leaders develop the professional capacity and practice of school personnel to promote *each* student's academic success and well-being.

Educators are operating in a new era of teacher evaluation. It is important for school leaders to address the professional capacity of all school personnel. Growing professional capacity is a deliberate endeavor; it must not be a haphazard endeavor (Hallinger & Heck, 2010). Principals working as instructional leaders are at the very core of solid teacher practice. Principals who effectively use a sound teacher evaluation system promote a professional learning community that fosters effective teaching and learning (Childress, 2014). This requires principals to provide human capital, social capital, cultural capital, and financial capital as well as informational resources (Lai, 2014).

Development of professional capacity of educators remains an ongoing challenge. Darling-Hammond and McLaughlin (1995) addressed professional development concerns over two decades ago. Three professional development designs were suggested: (1) opportunities for teacher inquiry and collaboration, (2) strategies to reflect teachers' questions and concerns, and (3) access to successful models of (new) practice.

Darling-Hammond and McLaughlin (1995) also offered ideas as both learners and teachers. Three suggestions were provided: (1) engage teachers in partial tasks and provide opportunities to observe, assess, and reflect on the new practices; (2) be participant driven and grounded in enquiry, reflection, and experimentation; and (3) provide support through modeling, coaching, and the collective solving of problems.

Darling-Hammond and McLaughlin's (1995) suggestion for policies that support professional development identify needs that many of the readers still experience on their campuses over two decades later. The ISLLC standards as well as the PSEL 6 remain an ongoing challenge not only for the campus instructional leader but for all campus stakeholders.

KEY DIFFERENCES BETWEEN THE ISLLC STANDARDS AND THE PSEL

PSEL 6: Professional Capacity of School Personnel breaks one function within ISLLC Standard 2 into nine elements that provide specific actions leaders can take to develop staff capacity. PSEL 6 emphasizes the importance of providing continuous professional and personal improvement supports for teachers, not simply focusing on improving professional capacity. The standard specifically mentions the need to promote a healthy work–life balance for both the educational leader and staff members.

SOURCES: CCSSO (2016), ISLLC (2008), PSEL (2015).

In a *Today* school, principals and other campus stakeholders must focus on the professional capacity of school personnel. Ponder where you and the other school stakeholders are growing the professional capacity of your school's personnel on your campus.

Yesterday and Today—Professional Capacity of School Personnel

Yesterday and Today	
Where We've Been and Where We're Going **PSEL 6: Professional Capacity of School Personnel**	
Effective educational leaders develop the professional capacity and practice of school personnel to promote *each* student's academic success and well-being.	
Yesterday	*Today*
Assign staff from district pool	Recruit, hire, support, develop, and retain effective and caring teachers
Replace staff as vacancies occur. Assign "buddy" teacher to impart culture	Plan for and manage staff turnover and succession. Provide opportunities for effective induction and mentoring
Provide district- or school-determined staff development at predetermined times	Differentiate opportunities for faculty learning and apply knowledge of adult learning and development
Observe and evaluate teachers annually with little feedback and little dialogue	Deliver actionable feedback about instruction through valid, research-anchored systems of supervision and evaluation
Select veteran teachers to lead and serve on committees with little input from others affected	Develop the capacity, opportunities, and support for teacher and school community leadership
Offer assistance after hospitalization or significant illness or loss	Promote the personal and professional health, well-being, and work–life balance of faculty, staff, and self

SOURCE: © 2017. Just ASK Publications & Professional Development. All rights reserved.

PSEL 7: Professional Community for Teachers and Staff

Effective educational leaders foster a professional community of teachers and other professional staff to promote *each* student's academic success and well-being.

Growing a professional community is a deliberate endeavor; it must not be a haphazard endeavor (Hallinger & Heck, 2010). It is essential for principals to promote a professional learning community that fosters effective teaching and learning. This requires leaders to provide human capital, social capital, cultural capital, financial capital as well as informational resources.

Developing and offering professional development for faculty and staff provides an opportunity to grow the school's capacity to improve teaching and learning. This in turn empowers PSEL 6's charge to "foster continuous improvement of individual and collective instructional capacity to achieve outcomes envisioned for each student." *Foster* is a well-selected word for this PSEL. *Foster* encourages. *Foster* supports. *Foster* stimulates. *Foster* cultivates and nurtures. *Foster* strengthens and enriches.

It is the responsibility of the school leader to nurture and develop the school's learning culture, be it the faculty, staff, or student body (Hoy & Miskel, 2012). This is a responsibility that cannot and must not be delegated. It is within the school's culture that the traditions, values, and beliefs of the various stakeholders are manifested (Deal & Peterson, 2009). School leaders must seize the opportunity to define and shape the professional learning community. Leaders must be certain not to lead with reckless behavior. It is important to get teachers and other professional staff on board. If principals, teachers, and staff see the importance of a professional learning community, it will thrive.

What leaders, through time and labor, value will be inculcated in the school's culture. If principals value the importance of a professional learning community for teachers and staff, it will become part of the school's culture. Principals are likely to hear someone say, "At this school, we put our money where our mouth is when it comes to growing our professional learning community."

Resources must be aligned with the school's vision during the planning process if the school's culture and instructional program are to be conducive to student learning and staff development. Anything less than aligning the budget with the vision bastardizes the process.

One final point about professional community—some long-term faculty and staff have acquired substantial institutional memory. Some of these individuals are burned out. They have stayed past their time of effectiveness for various reasons. Others have lots of institutional knowledge they kept to themselves. Still others know where the bodies are buried. In the cartoon, Oliver is one who knows where the bodies are buried.

And then there's Oliver. He's been with the school longer than anyone - you know where all the bodies are burried, eh Ollie? Keep up the good work!

We laugh at the Oliver cartoon in part because many, if not most of us, have experienced interactions with long-term employees, be they faculty or staff. We cautiously laugh because *trust* is involved. Long-term school employees, be they administrators, teachers, paraprofessionals, custodians, or others, know where the bodies are buried. Interestingly, the 1941 Hollywood classic film *Citizen Kane* is credited to be the first known source of "knows where the bodies are buried" (YARN, 2005–2017). A long-term employee who holds a position of trust in a school acquires knowledge of many secrets, secrets that powerful employees would rather be kept buried. In other words, a long-term employee knowledgeable of secrets can and will use those secrets to secure something of value. This behavior points us back to Oliver; he, like thousands of other long-term employees, knows where the bodies are buried. One must always be waiting for the other shoe to drop; something will happen but it is usually bad.

KEY DIFFERENCES BETWEEN THE ISLLC STANDARDS AND THE PSEL

PSEL 7: Professional Community for Teachers and Staff addresses two functions within ISLLC Standard 2 by breaking them into eight elements that provide specific actions leaders can take to develop a professional community for teachers and staff. PSEL 7 and its elements emphasize the school leader's role in supporting effective professional learning opportunities that are collaborative, job embedded, and faculty initiated in order to promote capacity.

SOURCES: CCSSO (2016), ISLLC (2008), PSEL (2015).

Yesterday and Today—Professional Community for Teachers and Staff

In a *Today* school, principals and other campus stakeholders must focus on the professional community for teachers and staff. Ponder where you and the other stakeholders are at in growing a professional community for teachers and staff.

Yesterday and Today
Where We've Been and Where We're Going
PSEL 7: Professional Community for Teachers and Staff

Effective educational leaders foster a professional community of teachers and other professional staff to promote *each* student's academic success and well-being.

Yesterday	Today
Use calendar day and times for workshops	Develop conditions that promote effective professional development, practice, and learning
Post mission statement in main office	Empower and entrust staff with collective responsibility for meeting mission, vision, and core values
Help students be responsible for their failures or not meeting goals and credit teaching for success	Promote mutual accountability for each student's success

(Continued)

(Continued)	
Assign teacher "buddies" for school support and seek district support for poor performance	Develop and support working relationships to promote improved capacity and practice
Consult an expert to provide workshops or in-service meetings	Design and implement job-embedded other professional learning opportunities
Implement district-initiated programs and projects	Encourage faculty-initiated improvement programs and practices

SOURCE: © 2017. Just ASK Publications & Professional Development. All rights reserved.

PSEL 8: Meaningful Engagement of Families and Community

Effective educational leaders cultivate and engage families and the community in meaningful, reciprocal, and mutually beneficial ways to promote *each* student's academic success and well-being.

Some three decades ago or more, *Beyond The Bake Sale: An Educators Guide To Working With Parents* (Henderson, Marburger, & Ooms, 1986) was published. The authors' superintendent made this book a required study for all administrators. The superintendent recognized the importance of involving families and the community in a meaningful way. Through the superintendent's leadership, campus leadership increased their engagement with their communities and families. Henderson and colleagues (1986) identified five family and community roles in schools:

1. **Partners:** Parents performing basic obligations for their child's education and social development.

2. **Collaborators and problem solvers:** Parents reinforcing the school efforts with their child and helping to solve problems.

3. **Audience:** Parents attending and appreciating the school's (and their child's) performance and productions.

4. **Supporters:** Parents providing volunteer assistance to teachers, the parent organization, and other parents.

5. **Advisors and/or co-decision makers:** Parents providing input on school policy and programs through membership in ad hoc or permanent governance bodies. (p. 3)

Henderson et al. even included self-assessment checklists for (1) key characteristics of your school, (2) key characteristics of families in your school, (3) assessing the family–school relationship, and (4) assessing the parent–teacher relationship.

Twenty-three years later, Warren, Hong, Rubin, and Uy's (2009) "Beyond the Bake Sale" approach is significantly different from their predecessor's approach. These researchers went beyond the campus to include a community-based relational approach to fostering parent engagement in schools. A comparison between the 1986 "bake sale" and the 2009 "bake sale" illustrates the differences between the traditional school community-centered model (Henderson et al., 1986) and the community-based model (Warren et al., 2009). See Table 1.3.

The community-based bake sale and partnerships with business often come to mind first when one envisions engagements of family and community with schools. Most likely, partnerships with universities come to mind second. Generally, partnerships with businesses focus on student achievement and school improvement. This manifests itself in many ways, including equipment donations and the donating of funds to encourage higher attendance rates as well as providing tutors (Warren et al., 2009).

Universities also partner with schools to provide professional development that focuses on student achievement. Likewise, schools form service-learning partnerships to address academic needs and environmental concerns within the community. These partnerships strengthen communities by involving citizens and empowering families (Ferlazzo, 2011).

Table 1.3   A Comparison of School-Centered and Community-Based Models

Traditional School-Centered Model	Community-Based Model
Activity based	Relationship based
Parents as individuals	Parents as members of community/collective
Workshops that provide information	Training for leadership development and personal growth
School-to-parent communication	Mutual exchange of relational power

SOURCE: Warren et al. (2009, p. 245).

> ### KEY DIFFERENCES BETWEEN THE ISLLC STANDARDS AND THE PSEL
>
> *PSEL 8: Meaningful Engagement of Families and Community* focuses on building productive relationships that lead to increased student learning and an improved school rather than concentrating only on family and community engagement. It encourages two-way communication and maintaining a presence in the community as specific ways to collect meaningful data and input.
>
> SOURCES: CCSSO (2016), ISLLC (2008), PSEL (2015).

Yesterday and Today—Meaningful Engagement of Families and Community

In a *Today* school, principals and other campus stakeholders must focus on meaningful engagement of families and community. Ponder where you and the other school stakeholders are at in growing and supporting meaningful engagement of families and community.

Yesterday and Today	
Where We've Been and Where We're Going **PSEL 8: Meaningful Engagement of Families and Community**	
Effective educational leaders engage families and the community in meaningful, reciprocal, and mutually beneficial ways to promote *each* student's academic success and well-being.	
Yesterday	*Today*
Are businesslike, purposeful, directive	Are approachable, accessible, and welcoming
Invite parents to open house and conferences	Create and sustain productive relationships to benefit students
Communicate by informing, educating, and telling	Engage in regular two-way communication with families and communities about school
Share prepared remarks for parent–teacher association meetings. Presence limited to supervision of staff and students	Maintain a presence and create a means for partnerships to promote student learning and school improvement
Distinguish school as a place for students and teachers	Develop and provide school as a resource

Focus on the business of schooling students	Advocate publicly for the importance of education
Solicit volunteers to work in the schools	Build and sustain partnerships with public and private sectors

SOURCE: © 2017. Just ASK Publications & Professional Development. All rights reserved.

PSEL 9: Operations and Management

Effective educational leaders manage school operations and resources to promote *each* student's academic success and well-being.

A casual glance at this PSEL standard could be deceptive. Reading the words *operations and management* might conjure a mental model of cleaning the building, sending notes to and from the classroom and the office, and assigning faculty load based on teacher preference. This mental model for operations and management is likely to have a weak connection to teaching and learning at best—and no connection at worse. This is no longer the case; PSEL 9 is much more than an old mental model of operations and management typically assigned to noninstructional items. In fact, this standard speaks directly to the premise of this book. Element D reads "[Effective leaders] are responsible, ethical, and accountable stewards of the school's monetary and non-monetary resources, engaging in effective budgeting and accounting practices" (NPBEA, 2015, p. 23) and embodies the Sorenson-Goldsmith Integrated Budget Model as detailed in Chapter 3. This standard readily relates to school leaders serving as accountable stewards when it comes to budgetary management. School leaders must engage in effective, efficient, and essential budgetary processes and practices (see Chapters 5 and 6).

PSEL 9: Operations and Management also addresses the importance of developing and managing the relationships with feeder schools in meeting enrollment, curricular, instructional, and budgetary matters. A wide range of strategies can be developed and implemented to strengthen the ties with feeder schools. These strategies include collaborating with each feeder school to receive permission to provide recruitment information such as introductory letter or develop a section on the school's website targeting feeder school families (Independent School Management, 2017).

PSEL 9 requires "productive relationships with the central office and school board" (NPBEA, 2015, p. 23). The Center for Public Education noted that effective board members develop solid collaborative working relationships with the various stakeholders based on respect and collegiality as well as a commitment to student success (Center for Public Education, 2009).

KEY DIFFERENCES BETWEEN THE ISLLC STANDARDS AND THE PSEL

PSEL 9: Operations and Management addresses the leader's need to develop a broad perspective that goes beyond management and operations. It anchors leaders to work with an end in mind for every action (e.g., "to promote the mission and vision of the school" and "to improve quality and efficiency"). The standard maintains consistency with other PSEL elements by focusing on each student's learning needs. In addition, the importance of developing and managing productive relationships—rather than simply perceiving management and operations as a list of things to accomplish—is emphasized.

SOURCES: CCSSO (2016), ISLLC (2008), PSEL (2015).

In a *Today* school, principals and other campus stakeholders must focus on operations and management. Ponder where you and the other stakeholders are at in developing and implementing solid, efficient operations and management.

Yesterday and Today—Operations and Management

Yesterday and Today Where We've Been and Where We're Going PSEL 9: Operations and Management	
Effective educational leaders manage school operations and resources to promote *each* student's academic success and well-being.	
Yesterday	*Today*
Keep buildings clean, safe, and running efficiently	Institute, manage, and monitor operations and systems to promote school vision
Teachers are assigned/scheduled based on preference and students are placed into tracks (college or not)	Manage resources and schedules to optimize professional capacity to address each student's learning needs
Classrooms are entered and messages are routinely delivered over the intercom	Protect teachers' and other staff members' work and learning from disruption

Intercom and walkie-talkies are used to communicate internally, phone calls and newsletters are used for external communications	Employ technology to improve overall operations and communication
Head counts and pretests in fall lead to adjustments in facility and curriculum	Develop and manage relationships with feeder schools for enrollment management and instructional articulation
Contact with supervisors is related to information needs. Little if any contact with school board is present	Develop and manage productive relationships with the central office and school board

SOURCE: © 2017. Just ASK Publications & Professional Development. All rights reserved.

PSEL 10: School Improvement

Effective educational leaders act as agents of continuous improvement to promote *each* student's academic success and well-being.

For the last two decades, there has been a clarion call for continuous improvement in instruction, technology, communication, and data analysis, to list a few (Halverson, Prichett, Grigg, & Thomas, 2005). Continuous improvement depends heavily on the interactions between teachers as well as those interactions with the principal. Time is an important factor in school improvement (see Sorenson, Goldsmith, & DeMatthews, 2016). The more time school leaders invest on instructional leadership, the greater increase in instruction. The more time teachers are engaged with the principal in the instructional leadership role, the more likely positive improvement will occur in the instructional practice for those teachers (Halverson et al., 2005).

The Carnegie Foundation for the Advancement of Teaching published a white paper, *Continuous Improvement in Education* (Park, Hironaka, Carver, & Norgstrum, 2013). Six overarching themes were identified. A direct public school connection has been added to each of these overarching items.

Leadership and strategy. Leaders of continuous improvement schools bring a mindset to their work. Unlike the Lone Ranger, these leaders do not believe in silver bullets as a strategy for school improvement. Rather, they focus on establishing disciplined processes for developing, testing, evaluating, and improving the school's core work streams and programs for building capacity to engage in instructional leadership.

Communication and engagement. Effective communications and strategies are essential for engaging all stakeholders in the school. Many schools employ systems thinking that brings about greater collaboration between the school's stakeholders. This, in turn, allows the faculty and staff to identify and address root causes to the problems their school faces.

Organizational infrastructure. Schools must employ continuous improvement of instruction. This requires the development of structures across core processes and specific goals. Schools must identify a central organization that coordinates the work of the various groups.

Systems thinking. Using systems thinking, schools employing continuous improvement can establish structures around specific goals or processes that encourage interactions across their campuses.

Methodology. Methodology is a must in using continuous improvement. Factors such as purpose focus on inquiry and improvement must be targeted. Some schools use the inquiry process for strategic planning purposes; other schools use an improvement process. Both processes must be constructed around student data to improve instruction.

Data collection and analysis. Tracking campus data informs schools on the progress they are making toward campus goals. Data monitoring is essential. It is critical that schools collect outcome data while tracking student performance using local and state-level assessments. A challenge for many, if not most, schools is to develop a solid, efficient data-collection process.

Capacity building. Campuses must invest in faculty and staff training. This must become part of the school's culture. Not to do so is likely to impede continuous improvement.

KEY DIFFERENCES BETWEEN THE ISLLC STANDARDS AND THE PSEL

PSEL 10: School Improvement unpacks a single function within ISLLC Standard 1 into thirteen elements that promote continuous learning and improvement. This standard emphasizes the importance of focusing improvement efforts on achieving the vision, fulfilling the mission, and promoting core values. The 13 elements of PSEL 10 align with multiple ISLLC functions and are woven throughout the other PSEL, providing insight into the competencies the PSEL developers expect of effective leaders.

SOURCES: CCSSO (2016), ISLLC (2008), PSEL (2015).

Yesterday and Today—School Improvement

In a *Today* school, principals and other campus stakeholders must focus on school improvement. Ponder where you and the other stakeholders are at in implementing school improvement on your campus

Yesterday and Today	
Where We've Been and Where We're Going **PSEL 10: School Improvement**	
Effective educational leaders act as agents of continuous improvement to promote *each* student's academic success and well-being.	
Yesterday	*Today*
Establish goals at the start of year and visit them again at the end of the year	Use methods of continuous improvement to fulfill the mission and promote core values
Solicit staff to assist with plan compliance	Promote readiness for improvement by building mutual commitment and accountability
Share plan with staff and assume buy-in	Develop knowledge, skills, and motivation to succeed in improvement efforts
System goals and strategies are set at the district level and flow to the school; the school leader tells these to the staff and evaluates them at end of the year	Engage with others in ongoing evidence-based inquiry, strategic goal setting, planning, implementation, and evaluation
Manage multiple improvement efforts, even if they are seemingly at odds	Adopt a systems perspective and promote coherence among improvement efforts
Implement what was asked by district leadership and departments	Manage uncertainty, risk, competing initiatives, and politics of change with courage and perseverance.

SOURCE: © 2017. Just ASK Publications & Professional Development. All rights reserved.

Final Thoughts

School budgeting and vision must be considered simultaneously in the planning process in order for schools to increase their likelihood of achieving the PSEL's Utopian goal of promoting *each* student's academic success and well-being.

The trick for school leaders is to incorporate the generalities of the national standards into practical steps to achieve the ideal of academic success for all students. This chapter at times might appear to be "Pollyannaish." Some of the examples and metaphors could illicit a "pie in the sky" reaction from you, the reader. However, it is essential to begin the integrated budget planning process with a "pie in the sky" perspective. To do otherwise would immediately lower expectations to less than 100% of the students obtaining academic success. Achieving 99.9% is not good enough. If 99.9% were good enough, then 12 babies would be given to the wrong parents each day, two planes landing daily at O'Hare International Airport would be unsafe, and 291 pacemaker operations would be performed incorrectly this year (Snopes, 2017). The PSEL standards introduction sets the stage for further exploration of the standards and how they impact academic and leadership performance as well as campus budgeting matters.

Discussion Questions

1. Which three PSEL influence the budget–vision relationship the most in your employment situation? Defend your choices.

2. Do you agree or disagree with the author's contention we "must visit Utopia" in creating a vision for our schools or is this just fluff? Support your response.

3. What are your initial thoughts on the author's contention that budgeting and vision must be integrated in the planning process in order to promote the "academic success and well-being of *each* student" phrase in each PSEL standard?

4. A *Yesterday and Today* box provided a comparison between old leadership behavior and new leadership behavior associated for each of the 10 PSEL standards. The behaviors on the left side of the *Yesterday and Today* box refer to *Yesterday* behaviors. The behaviors on the right side of the box refer to *Today* behaviors. Provide one example of a *Yesterday and Today* behavior change from where you've been to where you're going on your campus for each of the 10 PSEL. If there is not an example of such a behavior change for a PSEL on your campus, identify a change that would be positive for your campus.

5. Select any two of the 10 key differences between ISLLC standards and the PSEL boxes. Share three insights you gained on the two key differences you selected.

Case Study Application:
Belle Plain Middle School

The application of a case study or case studies is presented at the conclusion of each chapter to provide applicable and relevant workplace scenarios so the reader can apply, in a practical manner, the knowledge acquired through textual readings.

Belle Plain Middle School (BPMS) is composed of approximately 1,000 students in Grades 6 through 8. The school is 40% Anglo, 25% Hispanic, 25% African American, 5% Asian American, and 5% Other. Of these students, 60% qualify for free or reduced lunch, 12% of the students are identified as limited-English-proficient; the campus mobility rate is 30%.

The facility is 25 years old and is in an average state of repair. The neighborhood around the school is composed of modest homes of a similar age to the school. Many homes are in good repair and evidence pride in ownership. Most of the nearby businesses are independently owned small businesses. There is the typical scattering of franchised fast-food restaurants.

The majority of parents of the students at BPMS are employed in blue-collar jobs. A recently constructed subdivision of upper-middle-class homes in the attendance zone has created the potential of changing the campus demographics. The supermajority of students who reside in the new subdivision are either being homeschooled or are enrolled in a private school 20 minutes away because of parent concerns about the academic integrity of BPMS. The parents from this subdivision who have enrolled their children in the school want to meet with the principal about becoming more involved in the school and in their children's education.

The BPMS faculty is divided into two groups. The Old Pros are those teachers who have an average experience of more than 15 years at the school. The Greenhorns are faculty and staff that have less than five years of experience at the school. The latter group has a high turnover rate. There is tension between the two faculty groups as well as a certain amount of distrust. The Old Pros perceive the Greenhorns as short on experience and long on idealism. The Greenhorns perceive the Old Pros as jaded and insensitive to the needs of the students. They also accuse the Old Pros of being unwilling to attempt innovative strategies to meet student needs because of professional bias.

A total of 65% of all students passed the state reading test. The passing rate for Hispanics and African Americans was 52%; limited-English-proficient students had a 47% passing rate. Percentages who passed the state mathematics test were 71% of all students: 59% of the Hispanic students, 61% of the African American students, and 53% of the limited-English-proficient students.

The percentage of students identified as needing special education services is 17% above the state average. The percentage of Hispanic students in special education is 53% higher than the Anglo rate.

You are the new principal on the campus. You are the third principal in five years. The selection process for hiring you was substantially different from that employed with previous principals. The superintendent secured a search committee comprised of parents, teachers, staff, and community members.

A successful effort was made to involve individuals of all ethnic and socioeconomic groups. The superintendent screened the initial applicant list and submitted the names of five individuals for the committee to interview and make a recommendation to him. The two male and three female finalists are ethnically diverse. Like you, all of the finalists were from outside the school district.

The superintendent and board have set a priority of turning BPMS around. You have been promised a 12% increase in your campus budget for the next three years. The campus has also been allotted two additional faculty positions to be determined by you in a collaborative effort with the faculty and staff.

The previous two principals gave lip service to involving teachers and staff in making academic plans for the students. A campus academic improvement plan was developed each year but was never referred to during the school year. The previous principals usually made some modifications to the previous year's plan and ran it by the faculty for a quick vote before sending it to the superintendent.

Teachers have little or no knowledge about the campus budget. They are not aware of what financial resources are available to the campus. Currently, the primary way of securing financial resources is to ask the principal and wait until a response is received.

Three years ago, the parent–teacher organization was abandoned for lack of attendance. The superintendent has informed you the two Hispanic board members receive frequent complaints that Hispanic parents do not feel welcome or valued on the campus. A recent parent survey compiled by the central administration indicates, among other things, many of the Old Pros believe their students are not performing well because the children do not try hard enough and the parents do not care.

Application Directions

The PSEL are to be incorporated within your responses to the application questions. Download the PSEL to have easy access to each standard and their elements. This will assist you in developing deeper responses in the case study as well as deepening your understanding of the PSEL.

Use the BPMS Case Study Application Worksheet to house your responses to the case study. The case study worksheet provides a graphic organizer for your responses. The first column identifies a PSEL. The second column, *Action to Address a BPMS Need*, is where you will put the need(s) you identify in the case study. Should you not be able to identify an action to address a BPMS need, use the third column, *Additional Information Needed to Strengthen or Make a Recommendation*.

Download a copy of the Belle Plain Middle School Case Study Application Worksheet. The worksheet can be downloaded at http://resources.corwin.com/schoolbudget. You can also easily replicate this worksheet using the table feature in Word. A copy of the worksheet follows.

Belle Plain Middle School Case Study Application Worksheet		
PSEL	*Action to Address a BPMS Need*	*Identify Additional Information Needed to Strengthen or Make a Recommendation*
1: Mission, Vision, and Core Values		
2: Ethics and Professional Norms		
3: Equity and Cultural Responsiveness		
4: Curriculum, Instruction, and Assessment		
5: Community of Care and Support for Students		
6: Professional Capacity of School Personnel		
7: Professional Community for Teachers and Staff		
8: Meaningful Encouragement of Families and Community		
9: Operations and Management		
10: School Improvement		

Personal Leadership Growth Improvement Plan

The Personal Leadership Growth and Improvement (PLGI) Plan provides an opportunity to take a closer self-examination of your leadership skills. Review the PSEL. Select *one* effective leader expectation from each PSEL. Copy and paste it in the cell labeled *Identified PSEL Expectation to Strengthen Your Leadership Skills* column. Finally, in the third column, *Bulleted Actions to Strengthen Your Leadership Skills,* identify two bulleted actions for each PSEL element in the second column that would strengthen your leadership skills. You, the reader, are encouraged to refer back to your PLGI Plan as you progress through this book. Readers are encouraged to modify their PLGI Plan data input as you progress through this book. As you read and learn more about yourself and the PSEL, it is natural to amend the information in the cells as needed. By doing so, you are modeling continuous improvement in leadership growth and skills development. The PLGI Plan should be incorporated in your annual performance review. Doing so demonstrates your commitment to go beyond what is required.

Download a copy of the PLGI Plan worksheet. The worksheet can be downloaded at http://resources.corwin.com/schoolbudget. You can also easily replicate the worksheet using the table feature in Word. A copy of the worksheet follows.

Personal Leadership Growth Improvement Plan		
PSEL	*Identified PSEL Expectation to Strengthen Your Leadership Skills*	*Bulleted Actions to Strengthen Your Leadership Skills*
1: Mission, Vision, and Core Values		
2: Ethics and Professional Norms		
3: Equity and Cultural Responsiveness		
4: Curriculum, Instruction, and Assessment		
5: Community of Care and Support for Students		
6: Professional Capacity of School Personnel		
7: Professional Community for Teachers and Staff		
8: Meaningful Encouragement of Families and Community		
9: Operations and Management		
10: School Improvement		

2

Culture, Data, Conflict Resolution, and Celebrating Success

Anyone could carve a goose were it not for the bones.

—T. S. Eliot, 1935, *Murder in the Cathedral*

Carving a Budget Aligned With a School's Vision and Mission

Our Utopian trip in Chapter 1 provided a clear view of the ideal learning environment school leaders seek. Unfortunately, no one lives in an ideal world. Instead, the world is filled with many challenges such as shortages of financial and physical resources, and schools serve an ever-growing and increasingly diverse student population. In an opinion column, George Will commented on the challenges of constructing the federal government budget when he penned, "'Anyone,' said T. S. Eliot, 'could carve a goose were it not for the bones.' Anyone could write a sensible federal budget, were it not for the bones—the sturdy skeleton of existing programs defended by muscular interests" (Will, 2005). The same can be said about the integrated school budget process. When school leaders become serious about aligning the school budget with the school vision, they can expect to encounter the sturdy skeletons of existing programs as they carve a budget aligned with the school's vision and mission. The bones of programs near and dear to some stakeholders will not necessarily be germane to attaining the school's vision and mission. Besides the bones of existing programs, school leaders can also expect bones of impaired vision from stakeholders who either do not understand or choose not to accept the academic success for all as exemplified in Ron Edmonds's remark uttered more than 30 years ago:

> We can, whenever we want, successfully teach all children whose schooling is of interest to us. We already know more than we need to do that. Whether or not we do it must depend on how we feel about the fact that we haven't so far. (Edmonds, 1979, p. 56)

The challenge for any school leader and stakeholders is growing a culture that supports the school's vision and mission. An examination of the importance of school culture, data, conflict resolution, and celebrating success in the integrated budget model is in order.

Culture

The importance of a school culture receptive to the integrated budget model purported in this book cannot be overemphasized. Wilkins and Patterson (1985) wrote, "Culture consists of the conclusions a group of people draws from its experience. An organization's [school's] culture consists largely of what people believe about what works and what does not" (p. 5). Integrating the budget and vision into a single process cannot flourish unless it is woven into the fabric of the school's culture. The integrated budget model requires a school culture receptive to collaboration. Schools, which possess a collegial spirit, share values, beliefs, and traditions are more apt to spawn the required collaborative environment that in turn increases enthusiasm, energy, and motivation (Green, 2013; Lunenburg & Irby, 2006). This integration must be valued by the school's culture, since it frequently influences people's opinions and behaviors while serving as the vehicle to turn dreams into reality.

School culture was touched upon in Chapter 1 with the examination of the *Professional Standards for Educational Leaders (PSEL) 3: Equity and Cultural Responsiveness*. This national standard calls on education leaders to "strive for equity of educational opportunity and culturally responsive practices to promote *each* student's academic success and well-being." This national standard warrants closer examination because the integrated budget process cannot exist with any degree of usefulness unless it is inculcated into the school's culture.

Green (2013) defined culture as "the shared values, beliefs, assumptions, rituals, traditions, norms, attitudes and behaviors of the faculty and staff. It is the tie that binds all elements of the school" (p. 92). The community is the school. Green's use of the adjective *shared* in defining culture is of importance when considering it with the PSEL 3 edict encouraging education leaders to "strive for equity of educational opportunity and culturally responsive practices." *Shared* is a *we* thing. *Shared* implies that all stakeholders in the school possess common core values. *Promote* requires school leaders to take the initiative to advocate, nourish, and sustain the school culture in such a manner that meets the edict of *PSEL 3: Equity and Cultural Responsiveness*.

A brief examination of school culture's three elements—values, beliefs, and attitudes—makes a case for the integration of budget and vision a part of every school's culture. This examination is conducted within the PSEL obligation to advocate, nourish, and sustain the school culture.

Values

Values are those ideals leaders hold near and dear. They are the ideals leaders deem important. Values shape the practice of teachers and staff (Nash, 1996). For the integrated budget approach to become inculcated within a school's culture, stakeholders must understand how this approach helps them fulfill their personal mission as well as the school's mission. It is essential for leaders to model their values (Shaw, 2012). Leaders advocate for the integrated approach to budgeting when they support it, plead its case, and assist the stakeholders in understanding it. Leaders nurture it by discussing it in formal and informal team meetings and by sharing it with parents and community members. Leaders sustain it by never allowing the integrated budget approach to be removed from the stakeholder's conscience.

Beliefs

Beliefs are what leaders hold to be true. The integrated relationship among budget, vision, and planning must become something stakeholders hold to be true. Gradually, through time and effort and by consistently keeping the integrated budget process at the center of school planning, events will unfold and stories will develop that will become part of the school's heritage. Stories will be rooted in cherished accomplishments that occur through the integrated budgetary process. Rituals will manifest themselves as ceremonies. Deal and Kennedy (1982) purport that ceremonies are to culture what movies are to scripts. They afford the players an opportunity to act out their beliefs. Ceremonies become ongoing events that sustain the integrated budget approach in the school culture.

SAD SACK SCHOOL

Good, bad, or ugly, schools have a culture. The authors observed a school with a poisonous culture. A strong level of distrust existed among this school's stakeholders. Teachers didn't trust the principal. The principal didn't trust the teachers. Friction was high between professionals and paraprofessionals. No sense of community existed. The campus ran amuck. If there was a mission statement, it was likely "Take care of yourself." Throughout the campus, an air of failure and defeat prevailed. Distrust had replaced trust. Rumors replaced constructive conversation. Data were abused and used to abuse. The school was in a hopeless downward spiral.

This school did not set out to become what it had become. Undoubtedly, the school at one time was quite different. It appeared that time, difficult problems, and tough situations combined with weak leadership and lacking a plan to address the school's challenges led to the poisonous culture. It was obvious that the stakeholders were not satisfied with their situation but they couldn't overcome their sense of helplessness and frustration. Their negativity generated more negativity, spinning into a bottomless downward spiral.

However, despite this desperate situation, glimmers of hope existed in a couple of areas within this school. This story illustrates the impact of an unhealthy culture on schools. The story also offers hope for those who are trapped in unhealthy cultures. This story is for those who are hunkered down in bunkers of positive thought in an unhealthy culture. Culture can be changed! Culture changes when hunkered-down groups purposefully seek change. Change agents identify the root causes of discontent and start addressing these root causes, gradually dismantling the negativity.

Two excellent sources related to the topic of culture are Chapter 4 in *The Principal's Guide to Time Management: Instructional Leadership in the Digital Age* (Sorenson, Goldsmith, & DeMatthews, 2016) and Chapter 6 in *The Principal's Guide to Curriculum Leadership* (Sorenson, Goldsmith, Méndez, & Maxwell, 2011). These sources are instructionally and culturally based texts designed for school leaders and written in the principal's voice!

Attitudes

Attitudes are how leaders feel about things. Did a parent or caregiver ever tell you "Watch your attitude!"? This statement usually had "that" tone in it, letting you know that your attitude was not appreciated for whatever reason. You learned as a child that there were ways things were done around your home. In healthy homes, parents communicated with the family members to collaboratively develop a shared family culture respecting all of its members. In unhealthy homes, dysfunctional behavior had family members in contentious relationships. Eventually, some unhealthy families seek intervention to improve the family. Other unhealthy families never seek intervention and either dissolve or remain contentious.

Schools are a lot like families. Over time, a school's stakeholders realize that their school cannot function at its best unless they develop a healthy culture. The integrated budget approach is at the core of a healthy school's planning process. The more the integrated budget process is used in planning, the more deep-seated it becomes as part of the school's culture, and the organization's health improves. Deal and Peterson (1998) aptly observed that a certain attitude develops: this is the way things are done in the school, this is how we celebrate, and this is how we appreciate each other. It takes time for ideas like these to become part of the school's culture. Ebullient leaders never tire in their effort to advocate and nurture the budget–vision–planning relationship for it to be incorporated as a part of the culture. Leaders must never cease in their efforts; they must constantly strive to sustain them as part of the school's culture.

Data

Lorna Earl's school and data observation over 25 years ago remains astute:

> We live in a culture that has come to value and depend on statistical information to inform our decisions. At the same time, we are likely to misunderstand and misuse those statistics

because we are "statistically illiterate" and consequently have no idea what the numbers mean. (Earl, 1995, p. 62)

Schools, at times, appear to be drowning in data. State testing data have a prominent role not only in state accountability policies but also in federal accountability policies. Celio and Harvey (2005), along with others, suggest that schools are awash in data. Leaders must ensure high-quality data are used in decision making. School leaders must work with school stakeholders in analyzing data, identifying solutions, and implementing those solutions. Time must be allocated for data gathering and analysis. Data analysis is essential to effective, efficient, and essential budget building processes (see Chapters 5 and 6).

Ronka, Lachat, Slaughter, and Meltzer (2009) noted the importance of schools "to navigate a sea of data ranging from reading assessment, [to] norm-referenced data, as well as diagnostic, state and local data" (p. 18). The plethora of data sources and questions requires an organized approach to data analysis. Ronka et al. (2009) also employed an essential question approach to data use. Examining data collaboratively encouraged the faculty and staff to become more involved in data analysis. This in turn quickly improved the team's ability to identify and employ the different data types to address the questions at hand. This essential-questions approach proved highly effective in building data literacy. Questions included the following:

- How do student outcomes differ by demographics, programs, and schools?
- To what extent did specific programs, interventions, and services improve outcomes?
- What is the longitudinal progress of a specific cohort of students?
- What are the characteristics of students who achieve proficiency and those who do not?
- Where are we making the most progress in closing achievement gaps?
- How do absence and mobility affect assessment results?
- How do student grades correlate with state assessment results and other measures?

Data-Driven Decision Making

The Sorenson-Goldsmith Integrated Budget Model (Figure 3.1, p. 85) is introduced in Chapter 3. The third and fourth components of this model involve data gathering and data analysis. Before getting the proverbial cart before the horse, the authors are compelled to call attention to data gathering and analysis before introducing their model. It's okay to look ahead in Chapter 3 and take a peek at the budget model.

Effective use of data changes a school's culture. Data expose bias and ignorance; they provide "Aha!" moments as well as debunking ineffective practices. In short, data gathering and analysis are a catalyst for changing a school's culture for the good.

The authors have personal experience in using data to expose ineffective teaching practices. Ineffective practices, left alone and unchallenged, become encoded within a school's culture. To be fair, school leaders must not think ineffective practices are deliberately adopted with the intent to harm or limit student achievement or potential. This said, whether ineffective instructional practices are unintentional or intentional, the results are the same—low performance for students *and* teachers, low expectations, and a drag on the school's culture.

Both authors had the opportunity to affect school culture by using data to end the practice of ability grouping into academically segregated classrooms. Providing our faculties with longitudinal as well as disaggregated student achievement data made it apparent to the stakeholders that this teaching practice was only widening the gap between the various subpopulations on their campuses. This data "Aha!" could not be refuted by anecdotal arguments offered by those clinging to this failed instructional strategy. The dismantling of ability groups began, albeit with strong resistance from a group dedicated to the ability-grouping mantra. A data decision-making culture planted a foothold in the school's culture.

As time passed (cultural change doesn't happen overnight), both campuses matured in incorporating data within the decision-making process. Stakeholders seeking additional data sources evidenced this. As the use of data-driven decisions increased on the campus, so did the level of teacher expectations for all students. No longer were faculty and staff content with whole-school academic performance data. There was an expectation for data to be disaggregated into the appropriate subpopulations. Data analysis sparked imaginations as interventions were formulated to improve the performance of subpopulations not meeting campus expectations.

As data gathering and analysis continued their mercurial rise in the school's culture, so did the concept of continuous incremental improvement. No longer would faculty, staff, parents, and community members be satisfied with maintaining the status quo. The school was now committed to continuous improvement.

One example of continuous improvement was in the area of student achievement. One teacher group that had been using data-driven decision making for several years was consistently witnessing its students' mastery on the state reading examination fall between the 90% to 100% passing rate. This teacher group took its data analysis to the next level. These teachers began examining not only *if* their students passed the reading exam but also *how well* they passed the exam. This led to a higher self-imposed level of expectation for student achievement. The academic goal would no longer be limited to the state's mandated passing score on the exam but on how well the students scored above the state's required reading exam score. How sweet it is—incremental improvement.

This story is not over. The faculty and staff did not stop at this level of data analysis. They drilled their data analysis of student subpopulation performance down to the reading objective level. They even added an analysis of student wrong answers on the exam questions. This analysis determined where and how the teachers refined their delivery of instruction to help the students master the reading curriculum. When faculty, staff, parents, and the community value data-driven decision making, watch out! The sky's the limit on where academic success will go at that school.

Barriers to the Use of Data

The previous data story had a happy ending. But happy endings don't occur without hard work. Barriers block data use in schools. Stakeholders must be diligent in their quest to gather and analyze data required in the third and fourth components of the Sorenson-Goldsmith Integrated Budget Model. Likewise, stakeholders must not allow personal bias on a subject matter interfere with identifying subjects needing improvement.

Holcomb (2004) identifies six reasons why data are little used and why it is a challenge to motivate people to be data driven. Holcomb's data use barriers are

- lack of proper training in involving others in decision making and in the appropriate use of decision making,
- lack of time,
- feast or famine (fearing that there are no data or panicking over too much: "What are we going to do with all these data?"),
- fear of evaluation (fearing that the data are going to be used against individuals or schools),

- fear of exposure (the fear that even though your colleagues believe you are a good teacher, the data might expose you as a fraud), and
- confusing a technical problem with a cultural problem.

School leaders and faculties all have witnessed Holcomb's data barriers and, like the authors, have personally experienced them.

Developing an awareness of these data barriers is necessary to address data concerns. Holcomb (2004) postulates that collecting data for the sake of collecting data is an exercise in futility "unless it engages people by connecting to the deep and authentic passion for teaching and learning" (p. xxi).

How does a school break down its data barriers? Johnson (2002) effectively describes five stages in the change process for creating stakeholders who value the incorporation of data gathering and analysis into the decision-making process. Briefly, those steps are as follows:

1. *Building the leadership and data teams.* Building leadership and data skills must be incorporated in the reform process. Training is provided on the skills needed to collect and analyze data.

2. *Killing the myth/building dissatisfaction.* Data are used to reveal false beliefs about educational practices, such as having low expectations for certain groups of students.

3. *Creating a culture of inquiry.* The school values provocative questioning and responses that use data to inspire the school change process.

4. *Creating a vision and plan for your school.* This stage requires a long-term collaborative planning process that will result in positive change. It involves establishing priorities, allocating resources, and assigning responsibilities.

5. *Monitoring progress.* Monitoring becomes a part of the school culture.

This concludes an early peek into the Sorenson-Goldsmith Integrated Budget Model (p. 85).

Both Holcomb's and Johnson's books are superior resources in providing the technical expertise necessary in implementing the third and fourth components of the Sorenson-Goldsmith Integrated

Budget Model, introduced in the next chapter. Data gathering and data analysis are challenging components of this model. Be patient with yourself and others as data skills are acquired and honed.

W. Edwards Deming believed that "quality comes not from inspection but from improvement of the process" (Walton, 1986, p. 60). Leaders improve the process when they improve the quality of the data used in decision making. Good decision making is only as good as the data used in formulating the decisions. The challenge for school leaders today is to sift through mountains of information to construct informed decisions. The dilemma faced in this process is that schools are about the business of students, and students' needs cannot always be easily described, plotted, and analyzed on spreadsheets.

Recent federal legislation as well as state legislation aimed at increasing education accountability requires school leaders to use new data sources. Laffee (2002) writes, "The tools of education—intuition, teaching philosophy, personal experience—do not seem to be enough anymore. Virtually every state has put into place an assessment system intended to measure and validate student achievement and school performance" (p. 6). School leaders need to not only possess the three skills Laffee references; they must go beyond them.

Data Types

Today's school leader must employ a variety of data types. Disaggregated data, longitudinal data, perception data, qualitative data, and quantitative data are five data types (see Table 2.1). Each data type provides its own unique assistance in developing an integrated budget.

Disaggregated Data

Disaggregated data are data broken down by specific student subgroups such as current grade, race, previous achievements, gender, and socioeconomic status. Disaggregated data provide leaders with an additional level of specificity needed to identify the academic needs of students. A fictitious academic example of the Langtry B. Jensen (LBJ) Middle School is provided to illustrate the importance of disaggregated data. Table 2.2 displays student achievement disaggregated by grade, race, and economic status. For the sake of brevity, we truncated the display to only two years of data and limited it to two narrow areas of the curriculum.

Instead of examining student achievement data from a whole-school population perspective, school leaders now have the opportunity to examine student academic performance by ethnicity

Table 2.1   Types of Data

Data Type	Definition
Disaggregated	Data are broken down by specific student subgroups, such as current grade, race, previous achievements, gender, and socioeconomic status.
Longitudinal	Data are measured consistently from year to year to track progress, growth, and change over time. True longitudinal studies eliminate any students who were not present and were not tested in each of the years of the study.
Perception	Data are used to inform educators about parent, student, and staff perceptions about the learning environment, which could also reveal areas in need of improvement.
Qualitative	Data are based on information gathered from one-on-one interviews, focus groups, or general observations over time (as opposed to quantitative data).
Quantitative	Data are based on "hard numbers" such as enrollment figures, dropout rates, and test scores (as opposed to qualitative data).

SOURCE: American Association of School Administrators (2002).

as well as socioeconomic status. For example, when examining the first-year seventh-grade reading scores, it is noticed the campus had a passing rate of 83%, which was 1% higher than the state-passing rate of 82%. The initial reaction might be one of academic smugness, believing we were performing above the state average in seventh-grade reading. But by employing disaggregated data, the leader and faculty recognize problems exist in the reading program. Whites passed at the rate of 93%, Hispanics at 77%, and the low-socioeconomic-status group at 72%. The 16 to 21 percentage points lower performance of the latter two subpopulations provides us with priority and academic direction as to where we need to intervene. The use of disaggregated data assisted the leader and the faculty in identifying an instructional delivery problem that would not have been identified had it not been for the use of disaggregated data.

Longitudinal Data

Longitudinal data are data measured consistently from year to year to track progress, growth, and change over time. True longitudinal studies eliminate any students who were not present and tested in each of the years of the study. Turning to Table 2.2, it becomes obvious that not only does it contain disaggregated

Table 2.2   LBJ Middle School State Academic Performance

	State	District	Campus	African American	Hispanic	White	Low socioeconomic status
Met State Standard: Grade 6							
Reading							
Second Year	87	83	86	*	84	89	82
First Year	80	76	83		80	88	74
Mathematics							
Second Year	78	65	80	*	77	84	73
First Year	71	61	65		64	68	53
Met State Standard: Grade 7							
Reading							
Second Year	83	79	94	*	92	98	94
First Year	82	78	83		77	93	72
Mathematics							
Second Year	71	60	71	*	69	76	69
First Year	63	52	57		52	69	43
Met State Standard: Grade 8							
Reading							
Second Year	90	88	94	*	89	99	84
First Year	84	79	86		83	93	75
Mathematics							
Second Year	67	57	83	*	76	92	72
First Year	62	50	48		44	55	38

NOTE: All numbers are percentages.

* = Less than 10 students

data, it also contains longitudinal data. Once again, for the sake of brevity, this example contains only two years of data. In an actual school situation, we would want five or so years of data, if at all possible. As we examined these data for both years, we identified significant improvement in several areas. One example is the sixth-grade mathematics scores for low-socioeconomic students. In the first year, 53% of the students passed the mathematics test compared to 73% in the second year. This was an increase of 20 percentage points. Another way to examine these data is to return to the low-socioeconomic sixth-grade students' mathematics score in the first year of 53% and compare it to the low-socioeconomic seventh-grade students' mathematics scores of the second year of 69%. By comparing the scores in this manner, the leader and team are following relatively the same group of students over a two-year period. This analysis reveals a growth of 16 percentage points between the first and second year in this same-group comparison. Using sophisticated software, school leaders readily construct longitudinal comparisons of same groups from year to year, which, in turn, provides guidance to areas of curriculum and instruction requiring intervention.

Perception Data

Perception data are data that inform educators about parent, student, and staff perceptions regarding the learning environment, which could also reveal areas in need of improvement. An example of perception data collection is a parent survey conducted by the school planning committee at LBJ Middle School. Table 2.3 contains a summary of the responses to 3 of 35 questions in the LBJ Parent Survey. Parents were asked to respond to the questions by circling a number on a scale of 1 to 4 (1 = strongly agree, 2 = agree, 3 = disagree, 4 = strongly disagree). The results for two years are included in Table 2.3. It should be noted 61% of the parents responded to the survey in the first year and 62% responded in the second year.

Since Table 2.3 contains more than one year of survey results, not only are there perception data but there are also longitudinal and quantitative data. One observation that can be drawn from these data is that parents have a more positive perception of the mathematics program in the second year than they did in the first year. Go another step further and return to Table 2.3 and note during this same time period, there was also a corresponding significant improvement in student performance in mathematics. Could these two data observations be linked?

Table 2.3   LBJ Middle School Parent Survey Results (Abridged)

Question	Response	First Year, %	Second Year, %
If I were given a voucher and could enroll my child at any other middle school, I would still enroll my child at LBJ Middle School.	1	82	92
	2	2	2
	3	3	4
	4		2
The reading program at LBJ Middle School is a good program for my child.	1	77	89
	2	4	8
	3	7	3
	4	12	0
The mathematics program at LBJ Middle School is a good program for my child.	1	66	82
	2	4	3
	3	10	8
	4	20	7

Qualitative Data

Qualitative data are data based on information gathered from one-on-one interviews, focus groups, or general observations over time (as opposed to quantitative data). One example of qualitative data is when a school district brings in focus groups to discuss a controversial topic such as sex education. The district compiles the comments from the sessions and uses them in conjunction with information from other sources to revise its sex education program.

Quantitative Data

Quantitative data are data based on "hard numbers," such as enrollment figures, dropout rates, and test scores (as opposed to qualitative data). Referencing to Table 2.2, one realizes it contains the reporting of test scores. This means that these data are quantitative data. Two earlier examinations revealed that the data in Table 2.2 were also disaggregated data as well as longitudinal data. Data can meet the definition of more than one data category.

Assessment

There are two basic types of assessment: formative and summative. Formative assessment is "assessment in which learning is measured at several points during a teaching/learning phase, with the primary intention of obtaining information to guide the further teaching or learning steps. Formative assessments include questioning, comments on a presentation or interviewing" (American Association of School Administrators [AASA], 2002, p. 68). An example of formative assessment is a pretest given in an academic area such as algebra, reading comprehension, or keyboarding skills. This information would then be used to drive the instructional strategy and the development of lesson plans.

The second type of assessment is summative. Summative assessment is "an assessment at the end of a period of education or training that sums up how a student has performed" (AASA, 2002, p. 70). An example of summative assessment is a benchmark test given in mathematics, reading, science, or other subjects to determine individual student mastery of taught objectives. Formative and summative assessment, when planned properly, can yield all five types of data discussed earlier. Formative and summative data used in conjunction with each other are invaluable in making program adjustments.

Acknowledging Opportunities for Growth and Development

Schools have grown in complexity and require sophisticated assessment and data analysis. The immediate cause of this phenomenon, according to Elmore (2002), is quite simple. A powerful idea dominating policy discourse about schools stipulates that students must be held to higher academic achievement expectations and school leaders must be held accountable for ensuring that all students meet or exceed such expectations. This perspective, and multiple others, subsequently dictates "numerous, simultaneous, and systematic changes in organizing, teaching, and administering schools" (Hoy & Miskel, 2012, p. 292). Such emerging viewpoints, demands, and expectations have dictated the absolute need for school leaders to be active participants in continuous and varied professional development opportunities. Data analysis is at the heart of this process.

For school leaders to be successful leaders—whether it be envisioning school reform initiatives, planning programmatic changes, developing a school budget, or advancing opportunities for increased student achievement—they must understand the once-standard, one-shot in-service workshop model is no longer acceptable. What is known and what research supports is that professional development must be entrenched in practice, research-based, collaborative, standards-aligned, assessment-driven, and accountability-focused procedures—all of which serve to increase the capacity, knowledge, and skills of administrators to improve their leadership practices and performances (National Staff Development Council, 2001). Educators must recognize that student learning can only be enhanced by the professional growth and development of school leaders (Desimone, Porter, Garet, Yoon, & Birman, 2002). Educators must take this a step further by creating a professional learning community. DuFour and Eaker (1998) require our society to acknowledge that our postindustrial knowledge-based society no longer educates the populace by employing a traditional education model. Those who have yet to make this transition must do so post haste.

Staff development, like other facets of a school, must be data driven. Needs assessment surveys from the faculty analyzed in conjunction with data from other sources (such as student achievement data) increased the effectiveness of the training, resulting in increased performance of both the employees and students.

An example of data-driven staff development took place in a school having a high percentage of students who were not meeting with success in writing as measured by the state's assessment program. A review of the testing data by the site-based decision-making (SBDM) committee revealed that this problem was evident throughout all the assessed grades (see Chapter 3 and Chapter 5). The SBDM committee surveyed the teachers and discovered that the writing teachers felt inadequately trained to teach writing within the parameters of the curriculum and assessment program. The committee also discovered that writing was only a priority for the language arts teachers in the grades that were tested by the state. Other teachers felt no ownership in teaching writing across the curriculum.

The SBDM committee conducted a review of potential writing workshops and selected one they deemed most appropriate for their students based on an analysis of the disaggregated achievement data. The committee also surveyed teachers throughout the district and developed a writing-across-the-curriculum plan that was supported by the faculty.

The SBDM committee ensured that these two strategies were incorporated in the school action plan. Funding was secured to bring in the writing consultants as well as to secure the required materials for the teachers. Likewise, the training received priority on the staff development calendar.

Referring to Figure 2.1, evidence of the alignment of the three elements of vision, planning, and budget exists. Vision manifested itself in the school's vision to have all students meet with academic success. Planning occurred through data gathering, data analysis, and the needs prioritization conducted by the school's SBDM committee. Budgeting was present through the commitment of fiscal resources, time, and personnel. The writing project definitely resided in the success zone. Data support this conclusion in that three years later, the school's scores in writing made significant increases, going from significantly below state average to above state average.

UNDERGROUND RESISTANCE

The members of LBJ Middle School's SBDM committee have grown in their understanding of the use and importance of a variety of data sources in campus planning. Unfortunately, not everyone at LBJ shares the enthusiasm for increasing the use of data-driven decision making. LaKisha Galore and Stan Barrier are vocal in their effort to diminish data analysis at LBJ. Their mantra is, "You can find data to prove anything." Ms. Galore and Mr. Barrier are creating a growing pocket of resistance to data-based decision making.

Pause and Consider

- What, if anything, should be done to address Ms. Galore and Mr. Barrier's campaign against data-based decision making?
- What could the LBJ SBDM committee do to proactively carry data analysis to the next level at LBJ?

Conflict Resolution

Conflict will always exist in the school budgeting process. Each of the various stakeholders has special interests and agendas that are near and dear to their hearts. At times, passion and tempers can flair in the heat of the school budgeting process. Words can be spoken that speakers later wish they had not spoken. Joey Cope, a practicing attorney and mediator, has worked many years in assisting others in resolving their conflicts in a peaceful, civil manner. Cope's "Principal Peace Primer," originally introduced in *The Principal's Guide to Managing School Personnel* (Sorenson & Goldsmith, 2009), is an essential tool for principals and other school leaders in resolving conflicts on their campuses—including those in the school budgeting process.

Personnel and Conflict Resolution

Strange, isn't it? We often think effective school leadership produces a calm and reasonable environment in which students, faculty, staff, and parents, superintendents, and board members glide serenely to their proper places with smiles on their faces. Problems will occasionally surface. But those will be dispatched with a well-discerned command from you, the school leader.

Instead, you feel barricaded in your office with the hope somehow, someway, peace is going to break out all around you. In the meantime, the better part of valor seems to be to play defense, develop no-nonsense policies, and to speak with intense volume and great authority in the hope those around you will either rally to your side or cower in your presence.

It doesn't have to be like that. And often, it isn't like that when you're able to get a clear view of what conflict is and how it can be managed. To get started, it may be a little easier to define *peace*. Peace is what we really want in our lives.

Peace is not an absence of war; it is a virtue, a state of mind, a disposition for benevolence, confidence, and justice (Brainy Quote, 2001–2017b).

What!?! Benevolence, confidence, and justice!?! No, we want *real* peace. Serenity, calm, paradise. People doing what they are supposed to and leaving us and each other alone. That's peace, right?

Actually, Dutch philosopher Baruch Spinoza had it right when he noted that peace was not the absence of war or conflict. Peace occurs in the midst of conflict.

The truth be told, the effective school leader *needs* conflict.

The Negative Things About Conflict

At your next faculty meeting, ask the assembled academic warriors, "How many of you *like* conflict?"

If your crowd is typical, you'll see only a few, if any hands go up. Most of those who respond affirmatively will be your campus clowns who just want attention. In all likelihood, when confronted with conflict, the jokester is the first one to offer a glib remark and then disappear. The other group is composed of those who could best be called troublemakers. They feel they have power. When we were young, we called them bullies.

Most people will refrain from raising their hands because they share negative views of conflict. Wilmot and Hocker (2007) propose a list that resonates with all of us (see Tables 2.4 and 2.5).

For those who choose to manage conflict in a positive way, these approaches set the stage for using disagreement and difficulty as a way to transform problems and people. An analogy of how conflict can build up your school and those who work and study there is seen in physical exercise and its benefit to the body.

Table 2.4   Negative Views of Conflict

1. Harmony is normal and conflict is abnormal.

2. Conflicts and disagreements are the same phenomenon.

3. Conflict is a result of personal pathology.

4. Conflict should never be escalated.

5. Conflict interaction should be polite and orderly.

6. Anger is the predominant emotion in conflict interaction.

7. There is one right way to resolve differences.

SOURCE: Wilmot & Hocker (2007, pp. 34–36).

Table 2.5   Positive Approaches to Conflict

1. Conflict is inevitable; therefore, the constructive way to approach conflict is as a fact of life.

2. Conflict serves the function of "bringing problems to the table."

3. Conflict often helps people join together and clarify their goals.

4. Conflict can function to clear out resentments and help people understand each other.

SOURCE: Wilmot & Hocker (2007, pp. 37–38).

Let's concentrate on strength training. Did you know weight lifting does not build muscle? If done properly, a result of weight lifting is strong muscles. But the initial effect of lifting a heavy object is the depletion of muscle fiber. In fact, if exercise is overdone, muscle fiber can be seriously injured or destroyed.

Strong muscles result from three interlocking causes. First, there is the exercise that challenges the targeted muscle or muscle groups. Second, the muscles must enter into a time of rest. During the respite from extreme exercise, the fibers have the opportunity to rebuild at a greater capacity. Finally, the body must have proper nutrition to rebuild the muscle.

Conflict resolution works in the same way. First, a problem arises that challenges those involved. This initial event is necessary because it draws attention to the problem and sets in motion a rebuilding process. Second, a conflict should be *rested*. Note that *resting* and *avoiding* aren't the same things. In this context, resting refers to a conscious effort to separate people from the problem and to deal with the problem (Fisher, Ury, & Patton, 1991). In other words, we must work to attain and maintain a proper perspective. When we concentrate on people instead of the problem, we lose objectivity and our edge for problem solving. Finally, conflict requires proper nutrition—an appetite for mutual benefit and a penchant for understanding.

Just as in bodybuilding, conflict resolution requires the participant to be open to conflict (exercise), perspective (rest), and a desire to bring mutual benefit whenever possible (nutrition). Skipping any of these elements leads to disaster. Even though the conflict experience may be distasteful, an effective school leader will embrace the conflict and do everything possible to bring perspective and mutual benefit to all parties.

"Yeah, right," you're saying. "That won't work with my crowd."

No, it doesn't work out that easily all the time. Sometimes you just have to be the boss and make hard decisions. It comes with the territory. Yet, if that's the only way you deal with conflict, you won't be viewed as an effective leader. Dictators can be extremely efficient, but in the long term, they are rarely effective. Nowhere is this more apparent than in the school. You're an educator. Just because the sign on your door says *Principal* doesn't mean you've been stripped of your teaching credentials.

Problems are opportunities for teaching. If you really want to have a lasting impact on your students, your faculty, and your community, handle conflict in a way that builds understanding and teaches others to do the same.

The Principal's Peace Primer

Remember, peace can always be present—even in the presence of conflict. Eight platforms will assist in bringing peace to your campus. While these are presented in sequential order, remember that peace is an environment in which conflict surfaces and stirs constantly. You'll need to develop an ability to flow toward conflict from any of these platforms, a concept personal management guru David Allen (2001) calls "mind like water" readiness (pp. 10–110). The key is an appropriate response to what is happening around you.

Here they are, eight platforms (with 16 *P*s) to guide you and your school to peace:

- Preserve Purpose
- Protect Process
- Practice Patience
- Promote People
- Prize Perceptions
- Praise Progress
- Produce a Plan
- Perfect Peace

The same platforms are used in any conflict situation. Since this book targets the role of the school leader, we will focus on dealing with teachers and other campus employees.

Case Study Application #1: Remembering Hank

The application of a case study or case studies is presented at the conclusion of each chapter to provide applicable and relevant workplace scenarios so the reader can apply, in a practical manner, the knowledge acquired through textual readings. In this chapter, an in-text case study as well as a concluding case study is included.

Henry J. "Hank" Wallace was a remarkable man. He was a fixture in the North Plains Independent School District (NPISD). Very few townspeople could remember a time when Mr. Wallace wasn't on duty at Elmwood Middle School. After almost 50 years of teaching and administration, Mr. Wallace retired to Florida. In his absence, trouble began to boil at Elmwood.

Mr. Wallace had a unique management style. He was able to turn away most problems just because of who he was. He was Mr. Wallace. And for most people in North Plains, he was "Mr. Wallace, my second-grade teacher" or "Mr. Wallace, my grade school principal."

At his retirement, the local paper, *The North Plains Picayune,* devoted a whole section to his career. Actually, that amounted to about two pages of actual stories and pictures and two more to advertising from local merchants wishing Mr. Wallace a happy retirement. In a small sidebar, the paper noted a remarkable circumstance: It seemed that every teacher and staff person working at Elmwood on Mr. Wallace's last day was a former student of his.

Mr. Wallace's retirement coincided with the last day of school. Throughout the summer, the community contemplated Labor Day and the opening of school without him. The majority of the conversation was on who his replacement might be. The most likely candidates appeared to be the two assistant principals, Lauraine Oldenburg and Garrison Passmere. In a surprise announcement at the town's Fourth of July picnic, Sam Striple, NPISD superintendent named Patsy Nunez to lead Elmwood Middle School.

Ms. Nunez had been an elementary principal in the South River School District. Her school, Greenville Elementary, had been an exemplary school noted for its strong involvement of parents and community leaders in its ongoing program. *State Teacher* magazine touted Ms. Nunez as a "school leader for the 21st century" and the "kind of principal who makes things happen." Anticipation of her arrival stirred many lively conversations in the North Plains town square.

One week before school was to open, Elmwood teachers made their way into the multipurpose room for their first official faculty meeting with Ms. Nunez. All were seated, and a hush fell over the group as their new principal burst through the door with a large box.

"Good morning! If we haven't had the opportunity to meet, I'm Patsy Nunez and I'm looking forward to being part of the North Plains community. We are going to build on the excellence Mr. Wallace and all of you have established at Elmwood. But there will be some changes."

Mrs. Oldenburg and Mr. Passmere exchanged pained expressions—an action that was not lost on the faculty or Ms. Nunez. Ignoring the reaction, Ms. Nunez dug into her box and began distributing materials—an events calendar, an article reprinted from the *Journal of Educational Administration*, and a small bound booklet titled *Guide to Professional Educators: A Handbook for the Faculty of Elmwood Middle School.*

The calendar and the article were introduced and gone over in a few moments. "I'd like to spend the rest of our time today going through the professional guide," Ms. Nunez explained. And then she did. For the next two hours, the teachers fought equal feelings of boredom and indignation as new policies and procedures were detailed and emphasized. The group broke for lunch with Ms. Nunez's promise that, in the afternoon session, an equal amount of time would be spent exploring her plan for intensive peer evaluations of every teacher.

Ms. Nunez was the first one out of the room at noon—hurrying to a luncheon with Superintendent Striple and the other school leaders from around the district. The teachers didn't move as quickly. A number of them gathered around Mrs. Oldenburg and Mr. Passmere.

"What are you two going to do about this?" Coach Swift demanded. "We're going to spend all of our time doing paperwork and in meetings. I can't—I won't be treated this way!"

"That's right!" Tina Simmons, the diminutive music teacher inserted. "This isn't the way Hank took care of things. This Nunez woman is a nuisance. Do something and do it soon. If you don't, I vote we should all call in sick for the first week of school. That'll get the attention of the administration."

Other echoed these feelings. The sentiment grew and the teachers of Elmwood Middle School coalesced into a very surly group. At 1:15 p.m., Ms. Nunez faced an angry crowd and the vocal opposition of its appointed spokespersons, Mrs. Oldenburg and Mr. Passmere. Taken aback by the reaction, Ms. Nunez's first emotion was one of anger. But taking a moment to think, she announced a short recess and asked her assistant principals to join her for a conference.

When Ms. Nunez shut the door to her office behind them, Mr. Passmere blurted, "Well, I suppose you called us in here to fire us. But I guarantee that won't be the last of it. A lot of people in this town don't want you here and you will lose the war!"

Mrs. Oldenburg blinked, her eyes watering slightly, and then nodded her agreement.

"I've not called you in here to fire you," said Ms. Nunez, "although I could, and after hearing Superintendent Striple's mandate at lunch for improving this school district, I don't think I would lose anything—not a skirmish or a major battle or even the war. No, I've called you in here because we are going to work through this problem, and we're going to walk out of here with a solution we can all live with."

"How do you suppose we're going to do that?" Mr. Passmere asked.

Ms. Nunez smiled. "We're going to do that by finding our common ground and we're going to make certain we keep our discussions centered there. So let me ask you, what are we doing here? Why have we chosen to be at Elmwood Middle School?"

"We're here for the children," Mrs. Oldenburg offered. "We're doing all of this for them, to make sure they get the best education."

"I can agree with that," Ms. Nunez said. "Mr. Passmere?"

"Agreed," he mumbled.

"So," Ms. Nunez continued, "I will make sure that, over and above everything else, our discussions preserve this overall purpose."

By setting a standard for the discussion, Ms. Nunez has provided a touch point she and the others can use to keep the conversation on task. If conversation breaks down, becomes heated, or loses focus, any one participant can call the group back to the purpose.

Preserving purpose is important as an internal guide for school leaders as well. Keeping your purpose in the forefront assists you in judging your own motives and assessing your own behavior. Words chosen with a purpose in mind are rarely words regretted.

Platform 1: Preserve Purpose

When dealing with conflict, the effective school leader must keep purpose as the center of all actions and conversations. "What are we trying to accomplish? Is it important? Is my idea of our purpose unique or does the other side share my ideals?"

Conflict resolution professionals, the people who deal with the problems of others on a daily basis, know that the most intense conflict happens between and among individuals who share, to some extent, common purposes and values. Think about it. Why would you argue and fight over something you didn't care about?

Preserving purpose allows the effective school leader to sidestep petty behavior and to call all parties back to a solid place.

Platform 2: Protect Process

The effective school leader manages conflict by drawing others into a process that ensures fairness. We often think about process as a mechanical function—a checklist of things to do. That's what it is. Yet, it is much, much more.

Process enables trust. It accomplishes this by assuring the participants that, as long as they act within the boundaries of process, they will be protected from arbitrary actions and judgments.

"With our purpose agreed on, I want to talk about the problem that surfaced in the faculty meeting a little while ago." Ms. Nunez looked from Mrs. Oldenburg to Mr. Passmere. "I saw the way the two of you reacted this morning when I mentioned we would be making some changes, and I think you need to tell me what caused your behavior."

"Here we go!" said Mr. Passmere, "I can see where this is headed."

"And where is that, Mr. Passmere?"

"You're setting us up," he answered. "You're going to trick us into saying things you don't want to hear, and then you're going to fire us."

The only sound for a few seconds was the ticking of the apple-shaped clock on the principal's desk. Mrs. Oldenburg looked down. Mr. Passmere glared directly at Ms. Nunez.

"Okay, that a legitimate concern," Ms. Nunez agreed. "Let me start by saying I will not use this conversation as a basis for dismissing you. I really need to know what you think. You've been here longer than I have. I have much to learn. The only way I can do that is to listen and observe.

"So, here's a rule I will follow. I pledge to listen to you—even if I disagree with your position. Further, I agree to make no decisions regarding your employment based on what is said in here. Please note that these are internal rules that apply to the handling of our conflict. Insubordinate behavior outside this room may require other consequences."

"What does that mean?" Mrs. Oldenburg said softly.

Ms. Nunez settled back in her chair. "That means either of you or both of you or anyone who works at Elmwood Middle School can come to me and talk about anything. I promise to listen, to try to understand, and, if I can, to come to agreement. If I can't agree, I will do my best to explain why. And I will never use the conversation to punish you."

"But you said something about consequences," Mr. Passmere stated. "What's that about?"

"I am suggesting a process that allows you or anyone else to talk to me about anything without fear of reprisal. That goes for conversations in this office and will, most often, extend to appropriate public meetings, like our faculty meetings. My hope is that those discussions will allow us to collaborate on solutions to problems. Yet there will be times when consensus cannot be reached and someone will have to make a decision. When that decision is mine to make, I must have your cooperation."

"That's certainly understandable," said Mrs. Oldenburg. "But how can we be sure you're going to honor your promise not to fire us for what we say to you?

"I hope to earn your trust in that regard. And if I violate my agreement to honor the process, I feel certain you will tell the rest of the faculty—and probably Superintendent Striple, the school board, and the newspaper." Ms. Nunez caught Mr. Passmere nodding with a sideways glance. "You see, if I really want to honor our purpose—to provide a great education for our students—I must protect this process. I must earn the trust of everybody."

Platform 3: Practice Patience

One of the most difficult principles in conflict resolution is that of persevering in patience. The effective school leader must, in order to preserve purpose and protect process, exercise considerable restraint in dealing with people. Remember, most individuals aren't accustomed to dealing with conflict in a healthy way. As a result, their anxiety or other emotions may cause them to act out in frustration. Patience requires the effective leader, whenever possible, to pause and to forgive another party's indiscretion. Karl Slaikeu (1996) notes that there is more to forgiveness than theological aspirations. Whenever people are working together and one offends another, forgiveness is a way of saying "I agree to stop holding this conflict over our heads as we work together toward the future" (p. 37).

When you are in conflict or you are working with those who are, patience is the key to the future. By allowing someone a little room to err, we have created significant territory for trust building and the nurture of relationships. But remember, patience isn't blind acquiescence. Patience demands accountability.

"I still think you're going to use what we say against us," Mr. Passmere injected.

"I understand," Ms. Nunez said smoothly. "I only ask you to trust me to whatever extent you can. I promise to do my best to earn that trust."

Another benefit of patience is that those to whom patience is extended will often return the favor. Effective school leaders have a lot of wonderful traits going for them. Being absolutely perfect, unfortunately, isn't one of them.

Platform 4: Promote People

Whenever individuals become embroiled in conflict, their most common response is one of defensiveness and caution. They believe they are personally under attack and their very survival is dependent on winning. As a result, conflicted people begin to lose sight of the problem and its underlying causes and assign the whole package (issues, interests, symptoms of the problem, anxiety, anger, fear, frustration, etc.) to the person who is at the focal point. This transference of problem to a person is unhealthy and at the root of most unresolved conflict.

We really have only two choices in how to deal with someone in conflict. We can exclude the other person or we can embrace him or her. When we exclude the other, we attempt to differentiate ourselves from them. Further, because that person is different and thus an enemy, everything that is wrong in this situation is personified in our opponent. On the other hand, if we embrace our opponent, we begin to see how he or she is like us (Dunn, 1999, pp. 42–43). That recognition leads to better understanding and an increased capacity for patience. After all, if the one we excluded (our enemy) is now embraced, we begin to see and understand how someone could disagree with us (p. 44).

"So, you're not angry with us?" asked Mrs. Oldenburg.

"No, I value your experience and your support. I would hope we could be friends and colleagues for years to come. My job is not to control you. I'm in a supervisory role, but I really want you to excel," Ms. Nunez explained. "I don't believe you are trying to cause trouble. I think all three of us are trying to get back to our common reason for being here—the students."

"You're saying you are glad things flared up in the faculty meeting?" Mr. Passmere questioned.

"Absolutely," Ms. Nunez replied. "I value the professional judgment of you and of all of my teachers. What I really need is for you to tell me what your perceptions are."

Platform 5: Prize Perceptions

Have you ever noticed that two people can witness the same event from the same location and then tell two distinct stories? If you've ever been a juror in a court trial, you also would note those two versions, even where many facts agree, could assign blame to totally different parties.

What's going on? Are the witnesses lying?

Maybe. Some people have a pathological or moral problem with being truthful. However, most people are honest. They report their perceptions of what happened, because that is all they have to work with. Perception really is reality—until you challenge it. And before you start challenging someone else's perception, begin to test your own.

Patterson, Grenny, McMillan, and Switzler (2002) have asserted that testing perception is really an exercise in developing a "pool of shared meaning" (p. 21). When we attempt to understand the perceptions of others (and the accompanying judgments and assumptions they carry), we build on our ability to understand the concerns they have. Thus, we are able to better communicate our positions and perceptions. The first step in deepening the pool of shared meanings is to prize the perceptions of others.

Develop the ability to welcome and explore the perceptions of others.

Ms. Nunez sat and looked expectantly, first at Mrs. Oldenburg and then at Mr. Passmere. Finally, Mr. Passmere broke the silence.

"Look, I'm not sure what you want, Ms. Nunez. You've talked about talking. What do you want me to talk about?"

Ms. Nunez smiled. "I'll tell you what I want, Mr. Passmere. I want you to call me Patsy. I want you to tell me, face-to-face, what is going on here at Elmwood Middle School and with you. And if you feel qualified, I want you to tell me what the other teachers are feeling." She drummed on the desk with her fingers. "That's what I want."

His mouth opened, just slightly. Then closed again.

"And that's what I want from you, too." Patsy was looking at Mrs. Oldenburg.

"You can call me Lauraine—no, make that Laurie," Mrs. Oldenburg said. "How about it, Gary?"

"You go first, Laurie," Mr. Passmere said and then whispered toward Laurie, "I want to see how this goes for a while."

For the next half hour, Laurie began to tell Patsy how things had been done at Elmwood, how Hank—Mr. Wallace—had run his operation. He

(Continued)

(Continued)

was never questioned. After all, he had been the teacher or the principal for every employee in the building. And he didn't change anything. Each new school year brought only new children. Teachers received the same classroom assignments. Hank wasn't interested in new curriculum, and the school administration didn't dare ask him to do anything differently.

By that time, Gary was feeling more confident. He told Patsy how the faculty at Elmwood felt really comfortable with the way Hank did things. "We didn't have any conflict because he didn't expect us to do anything different. Things were very settled here. And Hank protected us. No one ever poked their nose in our business."

"I'm beginning to hear that my introduction of new things and new ideas is bothersome to you—to all of the teachers here," Patsy said.

"It's not just the new ideas," Laurie inserted. "You just waltzed in and told us things were going to change. You're acting like a lot of things need to be fixed around here. I can't speak for everyone, but I don't think much of anything is broken."

"You're new, too," said Gary, almost imperceptibly.

"Excuse me?" Patsy said.

Gary cleared his throat. "Well, some of us just haven't really gotten used to the idea that an outsider would be running Elmwood." He shifted uneasily in his chair. "I don't mean any offense by that."

"And there's none taken," Patsy assured him. "I think I'm beginning to understand your perspective on all of this. That's very helpful. Why don't we go back to the faculty meeting? I'm sure everyone is wondering what has happened to us."

"I'm kind of wondering that myself," Gary whispered to Laurie as they followed Patsy back down the hall.

Platform 6: Praise Progress

Conflict resolution professionals often talk about their success. Accomplishment is measured by some as how many deals were made or agreements reached. Yet, if you looked at what conflict really is, you would apply a different standard.

Conflict occurs when two or more people get stuck. They take positions, and they spend their energy trying to get the other party to move. By concentrating on moving someone else, they lose sight of their real purpose. And they grow weary of the struggle.

The effective school leader measures success by whether the parties to conflict move. While movement isn't always in a positive direction, a leader who listens and tries to understand can usually make the most of even the slightest leaning. And once movement is detected, praise should be poured out to fuel the momentum change.

"Ladies and gentlemen, please take your seats. I apologize for the delay. Laurie, Gary, and I needed to discuss a few things I believe will be very important to all of us. I regret I had not talked with them before now." Patsy's voice was firm and unwavering.

The faculty looked anxiously at Laurie and Gary. What had this woman done or said to them? Were they okay? What is going on?

"I want to commend the two of them. In our meeting this morning, I made some assumptions and I wasn't thinking of you. They confronted me in a professional and courteous way. I'm not sure they were comfortable in doing that. However, their willingness to talk with me should be an example to you and to me."

Laurie and Gary nodded reassuringly to their colleagues. Gary even managed a thumbs-up to Coach Swift.

"I have some very specific things I want us to accomplish here at Elmwood in the next year. I don't apologize for that." Patsy paused, looking around the room. "I do apologize for failing to talk to each of you to learn of your dreams and your visions. We are—or at least we will be—a team. I pledge to you my loyalty. And I promise to honor your investment in our students.

"Thanks again to Gary and Laurie. Their leadership has moved us a long way down the road to success."

Platform 7: Produce a Plan

Conversation is essential in dealing with conflict. But if you simply talk the talk and you don't walk the walk, conflict will continue to surface. It will escalate.

An effective school leader will make the construction of a plan an important part of the conflict resolution process. Building a plan furnishes a number of opportunities to build peace.

First, building a plan helps ensure that the parties understand both the positions and perceptions of all involved. A plan is a road map to some positions and includes the perceptions of all involved. It is a road map to some desired location, and it always begins with an honest look at where you are.

Second, planning is a work in progress. While all parties to a conflict are concerned with substantive issues to some extent, each shares a common and intense interest in the process that will be used to move past the problem. Let's rewind and play it at a different speed. While we all care about how things work out, a deeper concern is that the process that was used was fair. With few exceptions, people within an organization will rally if they believe that their voices were heard and that the decisions that were made were delivered with respect to the opinions and feelings of all, even if they didn't turn out exactly as they wanted.

Third, a plan provides a way to measure future progress. Once again, because of the importance of process, it is important that progress be compared to an agreed standard. The well-considered plan provides that standard.

Finally, accomplishing a plan—or even accomplishing pieces of a plan—brings a feeling of satisfaction and fulfillment to a group.

Effective leaders are planners. But more importantly, they are planners who are willing to involve others—particularly those who have a different perspective—in the process.

Patsy began to move around the room, picking up the *Guide to Professional Educators*. The teachers fell silent as she took the booklets and placed them back in the box.

"This guide should be a joint effort. I would benefit from your input. In reflecting on my conversations with Laurie and Gary, I'm thinking we should spend a little time this afternoon putting together a committee to write *our* guide. Gary, why don't you lead the discussion?"

Gary took the marker Patsy offered and made his way to the whiteboard. "Okay, let's start with an understanding of what our purpose is. . . ."

Platform 8: Perfect Peace

Peace exists in the face of conflict. It balances on a thin edge between justice and mercy. It feeds on understanding and conversation. While conflict rages, peace can be perfected. Perfecting peace requires preserving common purpose, protecting the process, practicing patience, promoting people (over personal gain), prizing the perceptions of all involved, praising the progress made, and producing (and reproducing) plans that bring people together—and back to the common purpose.

Effective school leaders will constantly hone their peace skills. Conversation will be encouraged. Understanding will be insisted upon. And patience will bring all to a sense of community.

Application Questions

1. When confronted by her faculty, Ms. Nunez immediately called a conference with Mrs. Oldenburg and Mr. Passmere. What would be the advantages of meeting with the entire faculty to talk through the issues and interests? What would be the disadvantages?

2. Because of the importance of process, committing the details of a conflict resolution process to writing can add credibility. What do you think the three most important principles for such a process would be?

3. Capturing the perceptions of others can be difficult. What standard questions could you ask to help others share their perceptions and provide insight to a deeper understanding?

4. Conflict exists in many forms and intensity levels. Some conflicts emerge as common, everyday issues. What platforms from the Principal's Peace Primer could you use in solving simple problems?

Celebrating Success

School leaders must not underestimate their impact on the school's culture. The leader establishes the tone for the school. In an era of increased outside accountability systems along with fiscal constraints, stakeholders in schools are experiencing tremendous stress. Teacher attrition is the largest single factor in determining the shortage of qualified teachers in the United States (Dove, 2004). Stress manifests itself with employees taking mental health days in order to flee the many sources of stress in their lives. Leaders must be cognizant of this underlying current in their schools.

Complainers abound in today's society. At times, complainers revel in their venting and, in some instances, in the intimidation of school employees. Educators often receive exponentially more complaints than they do compliments. Yet a major motivation for people entering this field is an intrinsic one—one of personal satisfaction for helping others (Ryan & Cooper, 2004). Everyone holds precious memories of those notes and conversations in which appreciation was given for efforts. There are times when every educator mentally recalls these celebrations of success to help cope with a current stress-filled situation.

Ubben and Hughes (2016) caution leaders not to underestimate the efficacy of public achievement awards. Effective organizations celebrate success. There are many terms of endearment for celebrating success; among them are *fradela, hullabaloo, hoopla, tadoo, wingding,* and *heehaw.* The school leader must be the Director of Hullabaloo. Leaders must set the tone of the school. Leaders cannot shuffle this obligation to anyone else. They must lead in the establishment of a culture that appreciates success.

Leadership in celebrating success manifests itself in any number of ways. It is only limited by one's imagination. Leaders lead celebrations at their schools for achieving goals by performing out-of-character acts such as kissing a pig, shaving their heads, sitting on the roof, dancing in a pink tutu, doing an Elvis impersonation, and even riding a Harley-Davidson through the gym. These manifestations of success celebration often bring with them the side benefit of positive local media attention to schools. Sometimes leaders must let stakeholders have a little fun at the leader's expense. Leaders do this because they know a school culture with an atmosphere of love and support for stakeholders will accomplish miraculous transformations in student performance.

Celebrating success is not limited to attention-getting public stunts. Celebrating success can also be private. A handwritten note of thanks is worth a million dollars to the recipient. Who doesn't treasure personal notes of gratitude? These notes are often tucked away and read again in moments of frustration or times of reminiscing. A face-to-face verbal compliment reaps a positive benefit to the recipient as well as to the giver. Compliments need not be lengthy; they only need to be sincere. As a sidebar, leaders must know how to model accepting a compliment. School leaders should not try to brush away a compliment by saying things like, "It was nothing." Instead, we must honor the compliment giver: "Thank you so much. I appreciate you recognizing my work and the work of my colleagues."

Celebrating success manifests itself in many other ways: awards assemblies, bulletin boards, newsletter references, marquees, parking privileges, covering a class so a teacher can have a longer lunch, T-shirts, and any other positive ideas you possess.

The Success Zone

Opportunities to celebrate success increase when the budget is aligned with the school's vision and planning. Figure 2.1 illustrates the alignment of these three factors—vision, planning, and budgeting. Overlapping circles represents these factors. The overlapping represents alignment of the processes. For example, the

Figure 2.1   Integrated Vision, Planning, and Budgeting

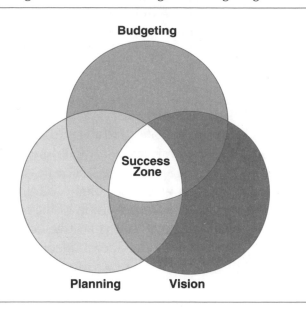

area where the budgeting circle and vision circle overlap is where the budgeting and vision processes are aligned. The areas where they do not overlap are opportunities for improving the alignment process.

The area labeled *Success Zone* is where all three processes are aligned. The success zone is where leaders need to lead their schools. This is where the budget–vision–planning processes are fully aligned and integrated. The greater the alignment, the more the circles migrate toward the center of the figure and the larger the success zone becomes. Perfect alignment would manifest itself with all three circles stacked on top of each other with the success zone itself becoming a perfect circle.

When leaders lead their schools using the collaborative planning process to implement the integrated budget model, the size of the success zone will increase. This in turn leads schools to greater opportunities for success. Bathing schools in the celebration of success encourages the integration of budgeting, visioning, and planning. Schools just might reach Nirvana; that is, when their circles are completely stacked.

Celebration should be an all-inclusive process. Do not limit it to teachers and students. Include everyone—the custodians, bus drivers, cafeteria help, parent volunteers, and community members. A positive, optimistic, and supportive school culture increases energy and motivation, and this is contagious to all stakeholders (Deal & Peterson, 2009). School leaders encourage teachers to help their students celebrate success. Be the head cheerleader for your school—you might even get to wear the uniform! School leaders who fail to celebrate success may find their goose cooked.

Final Thoughts

Cultures can change. School leaders must (1) act purposely in growing a healthy culture, (2) be results oriented and data driven, (3) resolve conflicts on their campus, (4) celebrate success, (5) ensure efforts are ongoing, and (6) see the value of all stakeholders. Schools are more likely to fulfill their vision and mission when they align vision, budgeting, and planning. Fostering a culture of shared vision of the school's purpose and future as they take deliberate and collective action to put their money where their mouth is and align their budgets and commit their resources to the school's vision. The best way to make a school successful is to foster a culture in which the stakeholders have a shared vision of the school's purpose and future and "take deliberate and collective action with them in mind" (Shaw, 2012, p. 184).

Discussion Questions

1. Consider three values you share with your school. How have these shared values impacted your school's culture?

2. How do the beliefs and attitudes of the various stakeholders impact your school's culture? Provide positive and negative examples.

3. How do the school leaders affect school culture positively and negatively?

4. List your top ten data sources for building your campus budget. Why did these sources make the top ten list?

5. How can the effective use of data impact your school's culture?

6. How does the effective use of data impact your school's budgeting process?

7. How can the data types in Table 2.1 impact your campus in a constructive way?

8. How have you witnessed data being used in the decision-making process at your school? Was it used effectively? Defend your response.

9. How do the beliefs and attitudes of the various campus stakeholders impact your school's culture? Provide positive and negative examples.

10. What would happen if the Principal's Peace Primer became inculcated on your campus?

11. How does the success zone in Figure 2.1 manifest itself on your campus?

12. Use your campus to answer questions associated with Figure 2.1. Provide an integrated budget example of the following intersections in Figure 2.1:

    • planning and budgeting
    • budgeting and vision
    • planning and vision
    • planning, vision, and budgeting

Case Study Application #2: LBJ Middle School

The application of a case study or case studies is presented at the conclusion of each chapter to provide applicable and relevant workplace scenarios so the reader can apply, in a practical manner, the knowledge acquired through textual readings.

LBJ Middle School, a school of 540 students in Grades 6 through 8, is located in a southern border state less than 200 miles from the U.S.–Mexico border. It is 62% Hispanic and 38% Anglo. It is one of six middle schools in Kilnwood City. Juan Quervo is the principal. Although LBJ Middle School has always been predominantly Hispanic, Dr. Quervo is the first Hispanic to be named as the principal of LBJ in its 42 years of existence. Dr. Quervo has been enthusiastically accepted by all of the school's stakeholders. He is using this acceptance capital to make needed instructional changes to ensure that all children meet with academic success.

Table 2.2 contains two years accumulation of achievement data for LBJ. Table 2.3 contains a partial report on the responses to the parent survey for the last two school years. Use these data to respond to the following questions.

Application Questions

1. Using the data provided, identify at least two instructional concerns at LBJ Middle School. What types of data did you use to identify the concerns?

2. Using the data provided, what would you recommend to Dr. Quervo as the top instructional priority? Support your recommendation with data.

3. There was a noted increase in the positive perception of LBJ Middle School by the parents between the first year and the second year. Is there anything in the given data that might explain the recent upward swing in the campus's public perception? Support your response.

4. What data are not provided that you would like to have to be better informed about the needs and strengths of understanding LBJ Middle School?

5. Make a connection between a PSEL standard and the LBJ Middle School case study. Is there more than one?

3

A Model for Integrating Vision, Planning, and Budgeting

Alice: *Would you please tell me which way I ought to go from here?*
The Cat: *That depends a great deal on where you want to get to.*
Alice: *I don't much care where—*
The Cat: *Then it doesn't matter which way you go.*
Alice: *—so long as I get somewhere.*
The Cat: *Oh, you're sure to do that…if you only walk long enough.*

—Carroll (1993/1865, p. 73)

Are We Somewhere in the Nowhere?

Alice and the Cat in Lewis Carroll's *Alice's Adventures in Wonderland* had a provocative conversation on visioning and planning. Alice is seeking direction on where she needs to go. The Cat replies he cannot help here unless she knows where she wants to go. Sadly, Alice doesn't know or even care where she goes. Alice's attitude allows the Cat to tell her it makes no difference since she just wants to go somewhere. The Cat concludes the conversation by telling Alice to keep walking and she'll get somewhere.

Unfortunately, many schools are like Alice. They are going somewhere—anywhere. These schools appear not to care much where they go just as long as they go somewhere. In this chapter, a case is made that it *does* matter where a school goes and how it gets there. The Sorenson-Goldsmith Integrated Budget Model provides a purposeful map for a successful, meaningful school journey. Walking aimlessly, somewhere in the nowhere, might be acceptable to Alice, but it is not acceptable for our schools and our students.

In an earlier examination of the integration of the vision, budgeting, and planning processes, a school leader made the important delineation between school finance and school budgeting. Next, the budget relationship to Professional Standards for Educational Leaders (PSEL) standards was completed. Finally, a closer examination of the budgeting and vision relationship with an emphasis on culture, climate, and data-driven decision making took place. Now it is time to allow these underlying principles to manifest themselves into a practical and workable budget model.

Figure 3.1 provides an illustration of such a model. It is necessary to consider each component of the Sorenson-Goldsmith Integrated Budget Model individually to ensure a thorough understanding of this model's integrative nature. The Sorenson-Goldsmith Integrated Budget Model employs many principles associated with the site-based decision-making (SBDM) process. The SBDM process, a decentralized collaborative process, involves the various campus stakeholders. Stakeholders include parents, faculty, paraprofessionals, community members, and students. Typically, the campus faculty and staff elect the SBDM members. This process is required in numerous states and school districts throughout the United States (Clover, Jones, Bailey, & Griffin, 2004).

The SBDM process functions at either the campus or district level but it functions best when applied at both levels. The term *school* in the remainder of this chapter refers to either a campus or a district. The level of planning in which the Sorenson-Goldsmith Integrated Budget Model is utilized determines which definition of *school* is employed. Campuses who employ the SBDM process expect improved student performance as a result of

- effective campus and school district planning for the purpose of improved student performance,
- improved community involvement in the school improvement process,

Figure 3.1   Sorenson-Goldsmith Integrated Budget Model

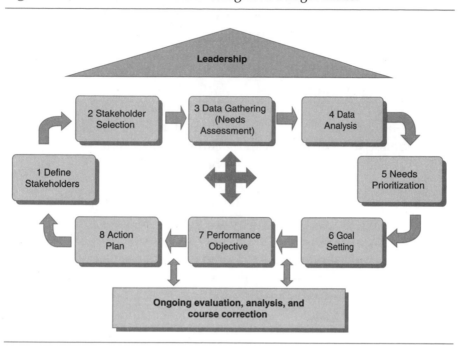

- clearly established accountability parameters for student performance,
- increased staff productivity and satisfaction,
- improved communication and information flow,
- consensus-based decision making,
- pervasive and long-range commitment to implantation,
- increased flexibility at the campus level in the allocation and use of both human and fiscal resources, and
- coordination of "regular" and special programs or service components. (Texas Education Agency [TEA], 2017a)

Sorenson-Goldsmith Integrated Budget Model

Leadership

Leadership is located at the top of the model not to symbolize top-down leadership but rather to represent the relational leadership exhibited between a shepherd and the sheep. For centuries, shepherds have tended flocks in isolated areas. Shepherds assist in meeting a host of needs of the sheep through service and openness, producing a trusting relationship. Shepherds feed their sheep, find water for them, and protect them from predators. If a sheep is lost, shepherds search for it. Shepherds know each lamb in their flock by name. Shepherds do not walk behind their sheep; they lead them. Likewise, the sheep recognizes the shepherd's voice and touch (Anderson, 1997). School leaders must provide this same relationship and communication as they assist and nurture their flocks using a collaborative planning process.

Rigid top-down leadership might initially produce positive results—but at a cost to the collaborative planning process. Decisions may be made in an orderly meeting run with firm control, but apathy and resentment may be the price to be paid (Yukl, 2012).

Communication is an essential leadership skill in working with the school planning committee. The school leader must communicate passion for the school's mission. The leader must kindle the imagination of all the stakeholders about what can be done to help the school achieve its vision and mission. A leader cannot be a visionary without being persuasive. The school planning committee must witness the leader's passion for the school.

Leaders must foster the crafting of a clear school vision, one resonating with all stakeholders. Leaders must inspire committee members to fulfill the school's vision. It is incumbent on leaders to provide stakeholders with opportunities to envision, understand, and experience the school's vision as they develop the school's action plan and budget using this model. Vision is not free. It costs time, money, and energy. The components of this model will be individually examined in an effort to make the vision a reality.

Component 1: Defining Stakeholders

If the entire learning community is to share ownership of the SBDM process, then it must commence by involving all stakeholders. Expected stakeholders include

- teachers,
- staff members,
- other professionals,
- administrators,
- parents,
- community members, and
- students.

Every stakeholder is valuable to the collaborative or SBDM and planning process as each stakeholder brings a unique perspective to these processes. The process of site-based decision making and why it is essential to effective leadership and followership, along with the defining of stakeholders and their role in building the school budget, is examined in greater detail in Chapter 6.

Teachers are the stakeholders who have the most contact with students on a daily basis. *Staff members* refer to those who are noncertified employees. They include but are not limited to paraprofessionals, cafeteria workers, bus drivers, and custodians. *Other professionals* are degreed individuals such as counselors, nurses, and educational diagnosticians. *Administrators* include both campus and district administrators. *Parents* are those adults who have guardianship over the children who attend the public schools. Finally, *community members* are people who live in the community but have no child in the public school system.

It is important to note the majority of households in this country do not have children in the public schools, yet schools must seek and gain the support of these households if school funding and bonds are to be enacted into law. It is imperative this group of stakeholders be represented in the campus planning process.

Component 2: Stakeholder Selection

An examination of state and local policies is appropriate to ensure compliance with any state laws or regulations in selecting stakeholders.

Local policies and administrative procedures must be put into place to determine the structure and authority of the school collaborative planning committee. Procedures should also be established defining the roles and responsibilities of the committee.

Committee Size and Structure

The size and structure of the collaborative planning committee must be considered. The authors believe teachers should comprise somewhere between a majority to a supermajority of the committee positions. The election and selection of committee members should be as simple as possible. While it might serve well to elect faculty and staff committee positions, it would be more efficient if other positions, such as parents and community members, were appointed. Once again, clear procedures must be in place.

Diversity

Careful consideration should be given to creating diversity on the committee in the selection of appointed committee members.

Appointments should represent the community's diversity. Besides ethnic diversity, other populations should be represented. Parent representatives must also reflect the diversity of the student population. Among those populations to be considered are parents of children who

- speak English as a second language,
- have special needs,
- have special gifts and talents, or
- come from a variety of socioeconomic situations.

There are several actions administrators should take to increase the diversity of the SBDM committee. Chief among those actions are

- posting on the school's or district's websites,
- advertising in the local newspaper,
- securing public service announcements on local television and radio stations,
- seeking nominations from parent–teacher associations (PTAs) or parent–teacher organizations (PTOs),
- seeking nominations from local businesses, and
- seeking nominations from community organizations (such as the Chamber of Commerce) or service organizations (such as the Kiwanis Club).

Members who are nominated must be willing to serve and invest time in the school's planning process. This is not the time for arm-twisting. An unwilling volunteer will likely lead to an empty seat and a missed opportunity for diverse representation.

The administrator or selection committee that finalizes the selection of the school planning committee members must deliberate conscientiously over the nominations. Some questions to consider include the following:

- Does this individual have the time to attend committee meetings?
- Will this individual be willing to attend site-based training on the committee?
- Does this individual demonstrate the capacity to consider all sides of an issue?

Committee Member Training

Committee members need training to understand their role in the collaborative decision-making process. McCloskey, Mikow-Porto, and Bingham (1998) reveal that frequently, principals and faculty members have not been trained adequately to meet with success in the collaborative planning process. The committee needs designated areas to examine budgeting, curriculum, staffing patterns, staff development, and school organization if it is to improve school performance (Odden & Wohlstetter, 1995). These areas must be clearly defined in the training process. Training prevents misunderstandings about the committee's function and authority.

Committee members benefit from training in team-building skills. Committee members must develop their listening skills, understand other cultures, and know how to use conflict resolution skills. Finally, training must be provided in the collection and interpretation of data. The committee must be convinced of the merits of using data as the basis for creating change in the school (Earl & Katz, 2005).

Staggering the Terms

Consideration must be given to staggering committee members' terms. This technique ensures stability and experience over time. If members serve two-year terms, then at least 50% of the school planning committee would be experienced members at any given time. Three-year staggered terms allow for two-thirds of the committee to be experienced members with institutional memory. This strengthens the process as well as assists the one-third that is starting to serve on the committee.

Component 3: Data Gathering (Needs Assessment)

Like businesses, schools are expected to verify their performance with solid data. Previous federal law added new responsibilities for schools to gather, collect, and analyze data from a wide range of sources, requiring state education agencies to report student performance by income, English fluency, migrant status, race, gender, and disability. The increased pressure for external accountability heightened the need for schools to be data driven (Creighton, 2006; Harris, 2004; Laffee, 2002; Mandinach & Jackson, 2012). A school's program success is dependent on how efficiently data measuring the change being implemented in the school are collected (Fullan & Stiegelbauer, 1991; Learning Point Associates, 2004).

Needs assessment requires the school planning committee to ponder, "How well is our school doing in meeting our school improvement plan goals?" The answer to this question goes beyond the hunches and feelings of committee members. No longer can schools simply proclaim, "We had a great year. Our students made tremendous progress." The answer to this question requires the committee to gather data from an array of sources in order to complete a comprehensive needs assessment of the school (see "Conducting a Needs Assessment" in Chapter 5 for a more in-depth examination of how to effectively direct the needs assessment process). The more data collected from a broad range of sources, the greater the likelihood the committee will accurately respond to the posed question.

Philip Streifer, a superintendent, accurately described data collection when he said,

> Data collection is a messy, messy business. It is done in different formats, some electronically, sometimes on cards or paper; often it's incomplete. Teachers collect it differently and not everybody has the same access to it, which means not everybody is going to be on the same page. (Laffee, 2002, p. 7)

Data originate from a wide array of sources. A partial list for collecting school data includes the following:

- Student achievement test results
- Campus and district websites
- State education agencies' websites
- Attendance data (student and faculty)
- Dropout data
- School budget reports
- Parent surveys
- Student surveys
- Faculty surveys
- Focus groups
- Volunteer logs
- Transfer requests (student and faculty)
- Retention data
- Failure reports
- Discipline data
- Facilities reports
- Organizational description (mission, vision, values)
- Staff development needs
- Staffing patterns
- Accident reports
- Extracurricular data
- Special populations data
- Mobility rate

- Unusual events on the campus (i.e., death of a student, fire, shooting, etc.)
- Any other information useful in measuring the school's performance

As data are gathered in an ongoing process, a school profile emerges. This profile reflects the school's operating environment, key educational programs, resource allocation, and other facets of the school. Once data are gathered, the committee must sift through them to derive meaning from the sea of numbers and reports. Needs assessment never ends. Schools constantly gather data. Data gathered must go to the next step—data analysis. After all, what good does it do to gather data and not analyze it?

Component 4: Data Analysis

A discussion of measurement, analysis, and data management as keys to improving student performance began in Chapter 2 and continues in Chapter 5 (see "Performing an Information Analysis," p. 163). Data analysis takes needs assessment or data gathering one step further. Data analysis provides the crucial linkage between data examination and the development of effective strategies. In this process, the school planning committee interprets probable causal factors. These factors can be anything from a high dropout rate to a low attendance rate to low academic performance in specific curriculum areas.

In the simplest terms, the Sorenson-Goldsmith Integrated Budget Model component is the "brain center" for aligning the school's delivery of instruction and related services to meet individual student needs. This component addresses knowledge management and the basic performance-related data and comparative data, as well as how such data are analyzed and used to optimize the school's performance.

Individual facts and isolated data do not typically provide an effective basis for establishing organizational priorities. The model's data analysis component emphasizes the need for an alignment between analysis and school performance. This alignment ensures relevancy in decision making, thus precluding decisions made using irrelevant data, statistical outliers, or personal prejudices.

Collecting data without analyzing them is an exercise in futility. Data analysis can be a daunting task for the school planning committee, particularly for the nonschool employee members as they face the infamous "stack of stuff." This is where the school leader provides much-needed assistance and assurance, particularly to the nonschool committee members. The leader ensures that committee educator members do not freely throw around acronyms and educational jargon at the expense of the noneducator members' comprehension of the data. Educators may inadvertently speak in shorthand by using phrases like *ELL* (English language learner), *IDEA* (Individuals with Disabilities Education Act), *Title I*, or *two deviations below the norm.* Remember, this lingo is foreign to most nonschool committee members. The school leader must be sensitive to this issue and be certain the dialogue remains inclusive to all committee members; not doing so is a lapse in professionalism.

Data must be disaggregated to obtain the level of specificity required to ensure that all students meet with success. Data disaggregation requires data differentiation by subpopulations. Examples of subpopulations include race, gender, and economic status.

One example of data disaggregation is found in student achievement data. To better illustrate disaggregation of student data, we will examine an abridged report on student achievement in fifth-grade mathematics at the fictitious Fort Chadbourne Elementary School (FCES) identified in Table 3.1.

In reviewing these data, several observations can be made about the mathematics achievement of students at FCES. The *Low SES* score refers to students who are of low socioeconomic status. Low SES is typically defined as being eligible to participate in the federal free or reduced-price lunch program.

Before reading the following list of the authors' observations about FCES, stop and construct a mental or physical list of observations based on a data analysis of the FCES performance report

Table 3.1   Fort Chadbourne Elementary School State Academic Performance Report

Fifth-Grade Mathematics

5th Math	Percentage Passing							
State	*Campus*	*Anglo*	*Hispanic*	*African American*	*Low socioeconomic status (SES)*	*Male*	*Female*	
Second year	88	87	94	81	78	68	91	85
First year	84	86	94	77	69	57	87	81

in Table 3.1. Compare the findings of the data analysis with the authors' observations.

- The campus performed above state average last year and below state average this year.
- The Anglo subpopulation performed the highest in both years.
- The Hispanic subpopulation performed second highest in both years.
- The Hispanic subpopulation increased its performance by four points in the current year.
- The African American subpopulation performed the lowest of the three subpopulations both years.
- The African American population had the greatest increase in performance (nine points) of the three ethnic groups.
- The gap in achievement between the three ethnic groups is narrowing.
- The lowest-performing subpopulation of any is the low SES group.
- Students who were in the low SES group made the greatest gains of any subpopulation.
- Males outperformed females each year.
- Males and females each improved their performance by six points.
- The profile of the most at-risk student at FCES based on these data is an African American female student who is on free or reduced-price lunch.

Hopefully after this brief analysis of abridged data, other questions are forming about FCES—questions requiring additional data gathering by the collaborative planning committee.

What additional questions would provide a better understanding of the issues at FCES based on the data? Stop and develop a list of questions about FCES based on these limited data. Considering the following, a partial list of questions that might come to a committee member's mind based on data presented in Table 3.1 includes

- What, if any, intervention was initiated that improved the performance of the Hispanic, African American, and low SES subpopulations?
- What was the performance of these same groups of students on the tested mathematics objectives?
- Did students perform poorly on the same math objectives each year?

- How did students at the lower grades perform on mathematics in comparison to the fifth-grade students?
- Are there problems on the same type of objectives between grade levels?
- How did this same group of students perform on the mathematics exam last year?
- Is the FCES mathematics curriculum aligned with the concepts assessed on the state exam?
- Do the same subpopulations have the lowest scores in other areas of the exam?
- What interventions were in last year's FCES school improvement plan? How effective were they?

This initial examination of the snippet of gathered data in Table 3.1 led to some obvious observations, which in turn led to a greater depth of questioning and a need for assimilating additional data. (This requires the committee to revisit *Component 3: Data Gathering*.) The analysis also led to the previous year's school plan and into the arena of school plans evaluation. Hopefully, a need for additional data was raised.

Had it been feasible to make the FCES example include more data than the student performance on mathematics at one grade level over a two-year period, more questions would have been generated. These questions would likely be more specific and of greater instructional depth. With a broader array of data, a broader field of needs would be identified. Earl and Katz (2005) call to our attention, "Data do not provide right answers or quick fixes, but data offer decision-makers an opportunity to view a phenomenon through a number of different lenses to put forward hypotheses to challenge beliefs, and to pose more questions" (p. 19). This leads to needs prioritization, the fifth component of the Sorenson-Goldsmith Integrated Budget Model.

Component 5: Needs Prioritization

After completing the data-driven process of identifying the school's needs, the school planning committee is frequently confronted with more needs than can be realistically addressed within the confines of both human and fiscal resources. At this point, the committee must determine which needs receive priority. Hopkins and West (1994) note that successful schools prioritize their needs and address a few at a time.

Data review is an integral part in prioritizing needs. Failure to use data knowledge effectively is costly to schools (Creighton, 2006;

Yeagley, 2002). Loeb and Plank (2007) recommended training in data analysis at all levels in the education system. Educators must learn to use data to inform academic progress (Data Quality Campaign, 2009). Committee members must review the data at hand and reach consensus on what needs should receive top priority in order to propel the school toward the fulfilling of its mission. Fullan and Miles (1992) report a cross-role group (i.e., school planning committee), a term they use to define a group with a variety of stakeholders, can assist in change. They observed, "different worlds collide, more learning occurs, and change is realistically managed" (Fullan & Miles, 1992, p. 752).

Conflict can arise while planners are attempting to reallocate resources. When needs are identified using a data-driven process, the identified needs immediately possess a stronger status than those identified from a purely partisan process.

Prioritizing limited resources for data-driven needs is no doubt a challenge for all involved. The school leader must approach the situation in a nonpartisan manner. This is a situation in which those skills and attributes embedded in PSEL 5 are so important.

In the discussion of this standard in Chapter 1, fairness was examined. Fairness—to be free from bias, dishonesty, or injustice. Fairness necessitates that principals model to the planning team how to put the interests and needs of others above their own interests and needs. It also requires that leaders and their teams remember that best meeting the needs of students does not necessarily translate into equal distribution of the resources. Leaders need to allocate ample time for all to be heard and try to reach consensus. If the planning team approaches the situation with this mindset, then the chances dramatically increase for a successful resolution that can be supported by the majority.

Cope, in Sorenson and Goldsmith's *The Principal's Guide to Managing School Personnel* (2009) writes, "Peace can always be present—even in the presence of conflict" (p. 89). As previously noted in Chapter 2, Cope offers what he calls *The Principal's Peace Primer* with eight platforms to assist principals in guiding the campus collaborative planning committee.

But what if resolution cannot be achieved? Then the leader must make a decision. This should be done with great caution, for it has the potential to cause stakeholders to feel they really have no voice in the process and to become disenfranchised. If the situation is particularly sensitive, the planning committee should consider bringing in a knowledgeable neutral party who possesses conflict resolution skills to help them overcome their impasse. In the end, the process could draw the planning team closer together emotionally as well as missionally. Once the needs have been prioritized, the SBDM committee is ready to start setting goals.

Component 6: Goal Setting

Goal setting is a crucial component in the integrated budget model. Goals unify stakeholders by providing meaning and purpose. Goals are broad statements of expected outcomes consistent with the mission, vision, and philosophy of the school. Goals must be driven by student performance-based needs and must be consistent with the school's vision and mission statements (Oliva, 2005).

A school leader must be sensitive when beginning in earnest to develop data-driven goals. Data will reveal differences in performance. They point their digital fingers to strengths and weaknesses in the school. This makes some stakeholders uneasy. The collaborative committee process must not ignore where data are pointing, nor can it bury the facts. Academic integrity demands that the committee examine the actions dictated by the data and develop the appropriate goals.

The school planning committee must be involved in the goal-setting process because goals reflect the essence of the school's culture. When goals are assimilated into the school's culture, stakeholders are more motivated to achieve them and more likely to punish members who abandon them. In fact, goals can become so incorporated into the school's culture that they continue to exist through changes of administration (Gorton, Schneider, & Fisher, 1988). Maeroff (1994) asserted that results-driven goals motivate and engage effective teams. It is imperative that the collaborative planning committee assist stakeholders in making the connection between goals and improvement if there is to be a significant chance for improving the school.

The planning committee has gathered data, analyzed data, and prioritized needs. By this time in the planning process, each committee member should have a greater understanding of why things are the way they are at the school. Ubben and Hughes (2016) provide four assumptions to guide a principal in working with the school planning committee on goal setting:

1. People at the working level tend to know the problems best.

2. The face-to-face work group is the best unit for diagnosis and change.

3. People will work hard to achieve objectives and goals they have helped develop.

4. Initiative and creativity are widely distributed in the population.

It is the leader's responsibility to keep the goals in front of the stakeholders. Goals must be distributed and displayed in a variety of forums such as PTA/PTO meetings and community service organization meetings. Goals must be reviewed at every faculty meeting, every grade level, or every department meeting. They must appear in faculty newsletters or e-mails; they must be posted on the school's website. They must be embedded in parent communications. In other words, they must be constantly kept in front of the stakeholders. Leithwood (1990), in describing goals, cleverly wrote,

> The glue that holds together the myriad actions and decisions of highly effective principals . . . [is made up of] the goals that they and their staff [school planning committee] have developed for the school and a sense of what their schools need to look like and to do in order to accomplish those goals. (p. 85)

Component 7: Performance Objectives

Once goals congruent with the school's vision and mission are established through the collaborative planning process, performance-based objectives must be developed to provide increased definition to the course of action. Performance objectives identify specific, measurable, and expected outcomes for all student populations served. Performance objectives must be driven by student performance-based needs-assessment data. Table 3.2 contains two objectives. The first objective is not a performance objective. The second objective is a performance objective.

Table 3.2   A Comparison of a Nonperformance Objective to a Performance Objective

Nonperformance Objective	Students will do well in mathematics this school year.
Performance Objective	Student scores in the state assessment exam on mathematics will increase by 5% in each of the ethnic subpopulations with an $N > 30$.

The first objective is not measurable because the students are asked to do "well" in mathematics this year. *Well* is a subjective term and can vary from individual to individual in definition. This objective is also vague in that it not only lacks specificity, it does not prescribe a method for completing the measurement.

The second objective is a performance objective for three reasons: (1) A data source for the assessment is identified—the state assessment exam; (2) a specific improvement of 5% is expected in each of the ethnic subpopulations; and (3) it adds specific accountability to subpopulations.

It is essential that all objectives in the school action plan be measurable if the school is to be data driven in its planning. When objectives are not measurable, it is left up to each individual to employ personal feelings on whether the objective has been achieved. Ten different individuals could evaluate the objective 10 different ways.

Component 8: Action Plan

The action plan is the *living* document that serves as a guide for all stakeholders. Emphasis was added to the adjective *living* to call attention to the fact the action plan is not static. (If it's static, it's likely to be dead.) The action plan is a living, breathing document. This point cannot be overemphasized. A quick review of the Sorenson-Goldsmith Integrated Budget Model in Figure 3.1 reminds the principal and team that much effort is required to produce this meaningful document. The process began by defining and selecting the stakeholders to create the school planning committee. Gathering and analyzing data from a plethora of sources followed the creation of this committee. Next, needs prioritization allowed for the identification of the actions essential for the school to fulfill its mission. Goals and objectives were then put in place to create a step-by-step blueprint to turn the prioritized needs into prioritized fulfillments.

This entire process is chronicled in the action plan, where greater detail is added by including strategies and actions. But the process does not stop when the plan is put in writing and posted online. This is just the beginning of the action plan's function. At the base of the model in Figure 3.1 is a box with three terms—*ongoing evaluation, analysis,* and *course correction.* This foundational concept of the model demands that the action plan be a breathing document. *Ongoing* means the process never ceases. Ongoing evaluation and analysis require continuous monitoring. This action manifests itself in ongoing course correction that results in editing marks appearing throughout the action plan.

A Planning Metaphor

Prior to boarding a flight in New York City to Los Angeles, the pilot has already filed a flight plan with the proper authorities. Once the plane departs New York, the pilot, copilot, and navigator continually reference the flight plan to ensure that the plane and its passengers meet the goal of the flight—to arrive in Los Angeles with all the passengers and the plane in safe condition. Despite the flight crew's effort in submitting a viable flight plan that, when implemented under static conditions, would allow the flight crew, passengers, and plane to meet its goal, events will occur during the flight that will require the crew to make course corrections in the flight plan.

KILLING TREES

Lost Pines Elementary School's campus action plan is posted somewhere on its website. The teachers were provided a hard copy of it. The principal and some other "district types" wrote it and asked the faculty to sign off on the plan. Plans were printed, distributed to all stakeholders, and placed somewhere. The action plan was required of all schools. But it didn't seem to be the effective tool it was touted to be.

Pause and Consider

- Faculty and staff see no purpose in the campus action plan. Why do you think they fail to see the purpose in the campus action plan?
- Have you had a similar experience? If so, what were your thoughts about the campus action plan?
- Why is the campus action plan being ignored? What could be done to transform it into a living, breathing document?
- How does this scenario connect with the Lewis Carroll quote in this chapter's opening?

As the plane approaches Missouri, it encounters severe thunderstorms. The pilot and crew consult and agree upon modifications to the plan so as to circumvent this unexpected weather event. Later, as the plane is approaching Nevada, a passenger becomes seriously ill. After a quick needs assessment of the situation, the crew decides to make an emergency landing in Las Vegas to secure the appropriate medical treatment for this passenger.

The plane leaves Las Vegas to finish the flight to LAX. Unfortunately, air traffic is stacked up and the plane is diverted to a holding pattern until space was available. After 45 minutes of circling Los Angeles, the plane makes a safe landing. The flight plan, along with the course corrections initiated by the flight crew, allowed everyone to celebrate the success of the plan by experiencing a safe arrival. But what about the passenger who was left in Las Vegas? This passenger received the appropriate medical treatment. The airline provided the passenger a ticket from Las Vegas to Los Angeles so he could reach his final destination. Granted, he did not reach it at the same time as the others. But through the appropriate accommodations, he achieved the goal of the original flight plan.

Several similarities exist between this flight and a school year. Like the flight crew, the school planning committee creates and files a flight plan, but it is called a *school action plan*. The plane's flight is representative of the implementation of the flight plan. Likewise, the school's activities during the school year represent the implementation of the school action plan. Both the plane and the school will encounter unanticipated events that require its crews to revisit the original plan and incorporate the necessary changes to keep the plane or school on course to meet its goals. Failure to understand that no action plan is ever developed that does not require constant monitoring and adjustments dooms the flight or the school to failure.

This constant monitoring and implementation of change is represented two ways on the integrated budget model in Figure 3.1. First, it is represented by a pair of double-pointed arrows above the ongoing evaluation, analysis, and course correction box at the model's base. These arrows illustrate the need for constant monitoring of the action plan. Likewise, the quad arrow at the center of the model symbolizes constant monitoring. Constant monitoring and adjusting is at the center of the model's effectiveness. Visualize the quad arrow rotating while moving along a horizontal axis between the eight components. This visualization reminds everyone that the planning process must not only be constantly monitored, but it is also not a linear process.

Planning may progress from Component 1 through Component 8, but in the monitoring process, the committee can return to whatever component is necessary to make the appropriate course correction. For example, new data might be gathered (Component 3), which will be analyzed (Component 4), which will then necessitate action in Components 7 and 8.

This is exactly what happened in the New York-to-Los Angeles flight. The flight crew analyzed new data—a weather report. This analysis caused the crew to modify the flight plan to meet the goal of a safe flight. School leaders must ensure that action plans (which, in reality, are flight plans) are constantly monitored and appropriately adjusted.

The Elements of an Action Plan

It is time to construct a flight plan—that is, an action plan. The process begins with an overview of the elements of a school action plan:

- Coversheet
- List of SBDM committee members
- School vision and mission statements
- School goals (if a campus plan, district goals should also be in place and cross-referenced where applicable)
- One action plan strategy page for each strategy

The coversheet design is an individual school's choice, as is the design of the listing of the school planning committee members and the vision and mission statements. It is important to include the vision and mission statements to keep them in front of all of the school's stakeholders, since they are at the core of the school's culture and climate. People are busy and are bombarded with information. Including these statements makes it convenient for the stakeholders to refresh their memories on these important statements.

The GOSA Relationship

Goals, objectives, strategies, and actions bring structure and detail to the planning process. These facets of planning are integrated on the action strategy pages in the school action plan. Understanding the relationship between these four planning facets is essential to understanding the school action plan. This relationship is illustrated in Figure 3.2.

Goals (the G in GOSA) were examined earlier in Component 6 of the Sorenson-Goldsmith Integrated Budget Model. Measurable objectives (the O in GOSA) were explained in the discussion of Component 7 of the model.

Figure 3.2   The GOSA Relationship

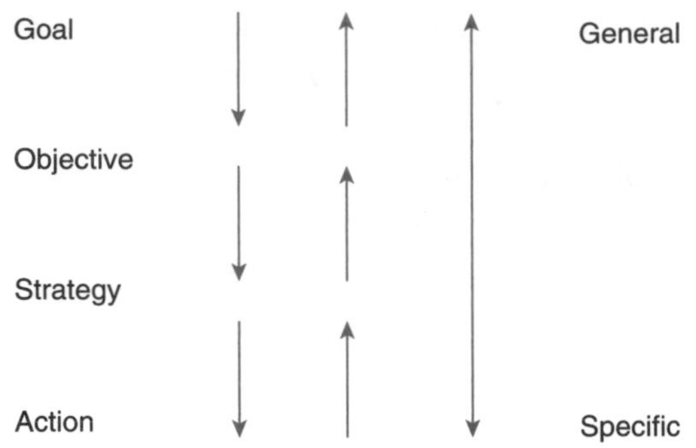

Goal   General

Objective

Strategy

Action   Specific

The *S* in GOSA is strategy. A strategy is a statement that assigns resources to accomplish the goal and the objective that it supports. Examples of resources include but are not limited to fiscal, information, employee, material, spatial, and technology. Strategies can also be broad initiatives that cover the breadth of a school. Examples include a math-manipulative program, a new tutorial design, or a dropout prevention intervention. The strategy should be expected to significantly impact the performance of the targeted populations. An example of a strategy statement is "Implement a computerized reading lab targeting students who are reading one or more grade levels below their grade placement."

The *A* in GOSA is activity—a particular action that is required to implement a strategy. An example of an activity to be used in the strategy is "The director of technology will order 20 computers according to bid specifications."

Reading the GOSA elements in Figure 3.2 from the top to the bottom increases the specificity. The opposite occurs when they are read from the bottom to the top. The elements become increasingly general. This unique relationship allows the document to be examined on four different levels of detail. Reading only the goals and objectives provides the reader with a quick general understanding of the school action plan. Reading all four levels provides the reader with the detail required for implementation of the goals and objectives.

An Example

Figure 3.3 is a completed strategy page from a school action plan. There is one goal on the page—all students will master the objectives of the mathematics curriculum. The goal is a broad statement supporting the school's mission of academic success for all students. It is also linked to student performance-based needs.

The objective is specific and measurable. It focuses on the mathematics goal and uses the results of the state assessment examination as its measure of mastery. Greater accountability is further achieved in that the objective is calling for a 5% increase in the performance of all identified student subpopulations.

The strategy—using the *Math Ace It* software program—assigns resources to support the goal and objective. Greater specificity of who, what, when, and where is provided with the inclusion of six specific action statements. For example, responsibilities are assigned to the principal, counselor, lab supervisor, and lead teacher. An accountability system is also in place for both formative and summative evaluation. The location of the evaluation data is even specified.

Finally, on this strategy page from a campus action plan, the integration of the budget with the vision and planning process is clearly in evidence (see Table 3.3). Fiscal resources were budgeted, as evidenced by $18,500 in funds being assigned to this strategy as well as personnel resources and facility resources. The allocated resources supported the school's vision of having all students master the mathematics curriculum. Planning is evidenced in the campus action plan through the strategy pages and minutes of the planning committee.

GOSA Mapping

The school action plan is actually the integration and coordination of multiple GOSA relationships that are designed to fulfill the school planning committee's identified and prioritized school needs. A truncated illustration of this integrated GOSA design embedded in the school action plan is provided in Figure 3.4. Notice

Table 3.3   Integration of Vision, Planning, and Budgeting in the Fort Chadbourne Elementary School

Strategy Page	
Budget	$18,500, personnel assigned, facility space assigned
Vision	Seeking mastery of mathematics by all students
Planning	Use of a planning team, page from the campus action plan

Figure 3.3   Strategy Page From the Fort Chadbourne Elementary School Campus Action Plan

Goal 1: All students will master the objectives of the mathematics curriculum.

Objective 1: Student mastery of the mathematics curriculum as measured by the state assessment exam will increase by 5% or more in each identified subpopulation.

Strategy 1: Students will use a diagnostic and instructionally managed *Math Ace It* software program to remediate specific mathematics objectives they are having difficulty in mastering.

Actions	Responsibility	Timeline (Start/End)	Resources (Human Material Fiscal)	Audit (Formative)	Reported/ Documented
1. Purchase *Math Ace It* software.	Principal	May 05/ July 05	$ 7,000	Purchase order	Principal's office
2. Provide faculty training on *Math Ace It* software.	Principal	August 05	Consultant, $ 1,500	Purchase order agenda	Principal's office
3. Provide math teachers with a list of identified students based on state assessment scores.	Counselor	August 05	Counselor	Student lists	Counselor's office
4. Assign students to three 30-minute sessions per week in the computer lab.	Lab supervisor	August 05/ Ongoing	Lab supervisor	Student lists	Computer lab
5. Provide teachers with progress reports on students.	Lab supervisor	2nd & 4th Fridays	Lab supervisor	Progress reports	Teacher files
6. Schedule monthly planning meetings with the principal.	Lead teacher	4th Friday	Teachers	Agenda/ minutes	Lead Teacher

Evaluation (Summative): State Assessment reports, *Math Ace It* Reports

Figure 3.4   GOSA Relationships Map

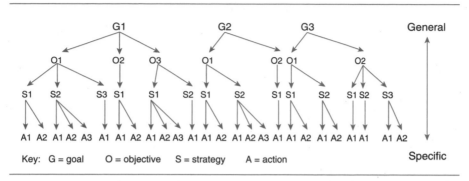

Key: G = goal   O = objective   S = strategy   A = action

how specificity increases in Figure 3.4. Reading upward, generality increases. This is, in essence, a graphic depiction of the school action plan. How many action plan strategy pages would be used in the plan in Figure 3.4? Fourteen is the correct answer. The incorporation of the action plan process into the building of a school budget moves from discussion into the reality of practice in "Case Study Application #3: The Budget Development Project" in Chapter 6.

Final Thoughts

Implementing an integrated vision, planning, and budget model does not happen overnight. It requires a significant amount of commitment and labor from all stakeholders, but students as well as all other stakeholders will reap benefits in the long run. The transition to an integrated budget–vision–planning process evolves through four stages (see Figure 3.5). The first stage, the Reactive Stage, is characterized by poorly defined goals and random strategies and activities designed to meet immediate needs. There is no coordination between the three factors, since they are headed in completely different directions. The second stage is the Transitive Stage. In this stage, there is evidence of a beginning of the alignment of goals, objectives, and strategies. Vision, planning, and budget are pointed in the same general directions. There are still deficiencies in planning and coordinating between the three elements. In the third stage, the Aligned Stage, alignment has been achieved between the budget, planning, and vision processes, but there is not integration among all elements. The final stage is the Integrated Stage. By this time, an amalgam has been created using vision, planning, and budget. Collaboration and communication are now valued. Continuous evaluation and course correction are in place. The three elements are now one. They are all aiming toward the center, pointing

Figure 3.5   The Four Stages of the Implementation of the Sorenson-
              Goldsmith Integrated Budget Model

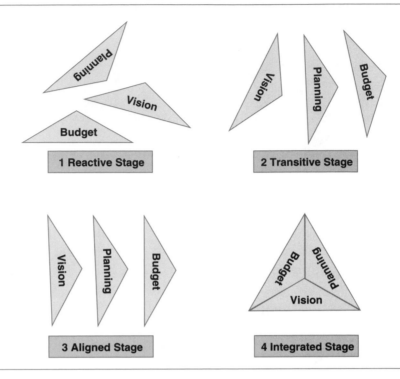

toward success. Be patient with each other as you move through these four stages.

Schools need all stakeholders working together to ensure academic success for everyone. Barth (2001) reminds educators, "I learned over and over again that the relationship among the adults in the schoolhouse has more impact on the quality and the character of the school—and on the accomplishments of youngsters—than any other factor" (p. 105). No family wants their child to be the student who does not meet with academic success. The construction of a school action integrating the school's vision with its budget greatly increases the likelihood of achieving the school's vision and mission.

It is up to the school leaders to keep the vision and the plan in front of the stakeholders. Remember, like the flight from New York to Los Angeles, a school year will have situations requiring the school planning team to revisit the school action plan and make the necessary course adjustments throughout the school year. In the end, if everyone works collaboratively and commits to a well-constructed and managed plan, success happens.

P.S.

Odden and Archibald (2001) make an interesting point: "A reform goal is rarely accompanied by a 'fiscal note' which is legislative lingo for identifying the cost of achieving such a goal" (p. 2). Schools will never have enough resources to do everything for their students. The integrated budget model provides leaders with an opportunity to rearrange resources and use them in a more efficient manner. Stop and think about it: This is, in reality, an *increase* in revenue without asking more from the taxpayers.

Discussion Questions

1. What are the advantages of having procedures and policies in place to define the roles and responsibilities of the school planning committee?

2. What are the advantages of providing training to school planning committee members?

3. Describe four attributes of a data-driven school. Describe how those attributes manifest themselves on your campus. If they are not manifested, what would need to happen for them to be manifested on your campus?

4. Data analysis, the fourth component of the Sorenson-Goldsmith Integrated Budget Model was referenced as the "brain center" of this model. What is the significance of this nickname for the fourth component of this model?

5. Why is the quote at the beginning of the chapter relevant to this chapter?

6. Rewrite this nonmeasurable objective into a measurable objective: "More students will take advanced placement (AP) courses next year." Defend your revision.

7. Why does the Fullan and Miles quote, "Different worlds collide, more learning occurs, and change is realistically managed" (1992, p. 752) manifest itself in the needs prioritization step of the process?

(Continued)

(Continued)

8. How would the flight metaphor play out at your school?

9. Using Figure 3.5, which stage is your campus at in the implementation of the Sorenson-Goldsmith Integrated Budget Model? Defend your choice.

10. Using your response to Question 9, provide three recommendations to bring your use of the budget model to the next stage. If your campus is at Stage 4, describe three actions you took to get to Stage 4 from Stage 3.

11. In "Final Thoughts," the authors ask the readers to "be patient with each other." Why do you think they gave this advice? What does "be patient with each other" look like?

Case Study Application #1: Shifting Paradigms With Changing Times

The application of a case study or case studies is presented at the conclusion of each chapter to provide applicable and relevant workplace scenarios so the reader can apply, in a practical manner, the knowledge acquired through textual readings.

Note: This case study is designed to lead the reader through the Sorenson-Goldsmith Integrated Budget Model. In order to assist the reader in obtaining a global view of how this model functions, parts of the process are provided. The budget amounts are unrealistic but were kept small so the reader does not become bogged down in mathematics. Frequent references to Figure 3.1 can assist in observing the flow of the model through this case study. A continuation of this case study is found in Chapter 6.

Part 1: The Deal—Components 1 and 2 of the Integrated Budget Model

The Situation

Waterview is a prosperous suburb on Pecan Bay, just south of the thriving seaport of Indianola. With a population of 25,000, Waterview has grown in the last 25 years from a sleepy coastal village to a thriving community where new industries and businesses continue to locate. Waterview is the county seat of Fannin County. Fannin Consolidated School District (FCSD) has two high schools, four middle schools, and 10 elementary schools. While the county's population has continued to decline for the past 20 years, Waterview is an exception. As a result of the population growth, two new middle schools and four new elementary schools have been built in Waterview in the past decade.

Two years ago, Dr. Ronald Scotts was named superintendent of FCSD. Dr. Scotts, a 48-year-old father of 13-year-old twin girls, moved with his wife, Juanita, from the upstate town of River City. While serving as the associate superintendent for finance, Dr. Scotts earned a reputation in River City as a strong and competent leader. The FCSD board hired Dr. Scotts to bring about change to the school system. Academic performance for the last 10 years was consistently mediocre. Routines had become the norm. The last innovation in the district was 10 years ago, and it was an automated substitute teacher assignment system. The board with its three newly elected members wants FCSD to move from an attitude of mediocrity to one of excellence.

During his first year as superintendent, Dr. Scotts started a dialogue with the administrators about a decentralization plan for the school district. At the end of this year, before the principals started taking their vacations, Dr. Scotts announced that in the fall, he would provide an allocation of $25,000 to schools that wanted to receive training in a collaborative planning process. Principals would need to submit a plan outlining how the funding would be spent to train the faculty in the collaborative planning process. Dr. Scotts further told the principals that campuses with an operational campus planning committee would assume responsibility for the development, spending, and monitoring of the campus budget with the exception of salaries and maintenance and operations. With this newfound autonomy came accountability for the effective use of the budgeted funds.

Dr. Hector Avila and Ms. Abigail Grayson are in their second year at Pecan Bay High School (PBHS). Dr. Avila had previously been a middle school principal in an urban district before being named principal at PBHS. He is the first Hispanic principal in the district. He has been well received by the community. Dr. Avila was hired to be a change agent at PBHS. Dr. Avila has the gift of being able to unite people behind a shared vision. Ms. Grayson had taught mathematics and served as the girls' basketball and softball coach at PBHS for the past five years. Ms. Grayson has a much-deserved reputation as an innovative classroom teacher who is willing to try new teaching strategies. Ms. Grayson attended mathematics training at a local university through a Teacher Quality Grant during the past two summers. Hector and Abigail like each other, and each one's talents complement the others.

After Dr. Scotts concluded his $25,000 challenge, Hector and Abigail immediately and aggressively spent two weeks on campus writing a proposal that was well documented by research and contained a detailed implementation plan based on the Sorenson-Goldsmith Integrated Budget Model. The two delivered the plan in person to Dr. Scotts, demonstrating their enthusiasm for the project. Dr. Scotts inwardly smiled and thanked the two for the proposal. Two weeks later, PBHS became the first campus in FCSD to have its collaborative planning proposal approved.

During the first day of staff development in late summer, Abigail and Hector excitedly explained to the faculty their proposal using a PowerPoint presentation with coordinated handouts. The faculty was quiet. The principals were picking up on the body language that they were bombing. Finally,

Ed Feeney, a veteran teacher of 27 years at PBHS, broke the passive silence and asked, "Whose idea was this? Sounds like the superintendent wants us to do his work. I'm busy enough as it is." There was some applause. Latasha Jackson, a fourth-year drama teacher, asked, "Is this another one of those fads that goes through schools? I bet the state is up to this." Kelly Tyres, a paraprofessional, commented, "No one ever asks us what we want. They just keep shoving stuff down our throat like the 'highly qualified' stuff from No Child Left Behind."

The two principals let the teachers go to lunch 30 minutes early (very popular) and went back to their offices, surprised and beaten. They kept repeatedly saying things to each other like, "Where did we go wrong?" and "I can't believe they are so negative" and "Where do we go from here?"

Thinking It Through

Hector and Abigail desperately need your assistance. Where did they go wrong? Where do they go from here? Hector and Abigail have a great proposal and are very capable administrators; yet they encountered strong resistance from the faculty. As that other set of eyes, you need to stop at this point in the case study and write a step-by-step plan for these principals to win over the faculty. Some Handy Hints have been included to help you with this process.

You will discover if you do this activity with several colleagues that your intervention plan will be stronger than if you complete it by yourself.

Handy Hints

• Involve all stakeholders
• Talk mission and vision
• Communication
• Shared decision making
• Identify challenges
• Identify strengths
• Identify outside resources

Part II: The Needs—Components 3 Through 5 of the Sorenson-Goldsmith Integrated Budget Model

Checking It Out

Thank you for your assistance in developing a step-by-step plan for assisting the PBHS faculty to reconsider and adopt the collaborative planning process! Your work is not done. Learning to use the collaborative process requires time and effort by all the school stakeholders. Read on and be prepared to provide assistance again as the process continues to unfold.

With the arrival of spring, the campus planning committee was established and the training completed. It is time to begin constructing PBHS's first-ever campus-based action plan with an integrated budget. The campus planning committee has been provided with a data packet courtesy of Dr. Avila and Ms. Grayson. Data were gathered from a variety of sources. The principals spent countless hours gathering these data but only did so as a way to assist and encourage the committee in its inaugural year. The committee is free to gather any other data as it deems necessary. The two principals volunteered to assist the committee in data gathering. Dr. Scotts was pleased to inform the campus planning committee that PBHS would receive an additional allotment of $200,000 for the next school year. Nelson Clampett, the assistant superintendent of finance, trained the appropriate individuals on the district's budgeting software. Nelson is anxious to see his old alma mater meet with success. In fact, it was 17 years ago that he led the Fighting Squirrels baseball team to the state championship by pitching a no-hitter in the state championship game. Since that time, the school has not received any athletic or academic awards.

In order to assist the flow of this case study, the planning committee's work of data gathering and analysis (Components 3 and 4) has been completed for you. The committee spent several meetings analyzing the box of data provided by the principals. They requested additional data and were provided with all the data they requested.

Make a list of data you would want to have if you were on the Fighting Squirrels campus planning team.

Thinking It Through

It is now time to proceed to Component 5 of the Sorenson-Goldsmith Integrated Budget Model. Take a look at Table 3.4. You must take the nonprioritized list of 10 identified needs by the PBHS planning committee and prioritize them. Remember, PBHS has an allocation of $200,000. The committee cannot exceed the budget allocation! Note that the identified needs will cost substantially more than the campus's allocation. It is time for the committee to make some tough decisions. Assign your priority numbers to the needs using the column on the far left. Provide a written rationale to share with the faculty and administration to defend your needs prioritization.

Part III: The Action Plan—Components 6 Through 8 of the Sorenson-Goldsmith Integrated Budget Model

Now that you have prioritized the needs, it is time to construct an *abridged* action plan. For the purpose of this case study, you will only use the top two prioritized needs. As you proceed through this portion of the case study, it might be helpful to review the figures in this chapter as well as the information in Components 6 through 8.

Using the number-one prioritized need, complete a strategy page to address the prioritized need. It may be necessary to use more than one strategy page due to space constraints. A clean copy of the strategy page is located in Resource A.

Repeat the process for the need you designated as the second priority. Once you have completed both priorities, review your pages. Are the goals, objectives, and strategies aligned and logical? Do the actions clearly define what was being done in order to implement the strategy? Are the resources, personnel, and evaluations in place?

Table 3.4   IPBHS Nonprioritized Identified Needs

Next Year

Your Priority	Cost	Identified Need	Committee Rationale
	$20,000	• Copier contract	• Used by all departments • Basis of many academic assignments
	$30,000	• Reading intervention plan • $12,000 for software • $3,000 for training	• Percentage of freshmen reading below grade level is twice the state rate • Percentage of Hispanics reading below grade level is three times the state rate • Teacher survey shows reading issues are the number one on teacher concerns
	$40,000	• General supplies	• Meet basic office/classroom needs of paper, staplers, tape, and so on
	$6,000	• Special Olympics	• Add this program since these students are unable to participate in other extracurricular events • Parent advocacy group has made an appeal to the SBDM committee
	$30,000	• New band uniforms	• Current uniforms are 23 years old • Uniforms were water damaged and now have a mold problem
	$12,000	• Vernier instruments, other digital equipment	• Needed in advanced science and math classes • Essential to meet state curriculum requirements • Needed in Pre-AP, AP, and dual credit courses
	$17,000	• Professional travel	• New category • Teachers need to be able to expand their knowledge by attending professional development events • Number 4 need on the teacher survey

Next Year

Your Priority	Cost	Identified Need	Committee Rationale
	$60,000	• Expanded technology in the library and computer center • $45,000 tech services • $5,000 printers • $10,000 supplies	• Students need access to internet and other technology for AP and dual-credit courses and for research • Identified by teachers of AP courses as a number-one priority
	$60,000	• 9th-grade school-within-a-school • $5,000 training • $35,000 facility upgrades • $20,000 curriculum materials	• High failure rate in freshmen classes • High referral rate to office • High absentee rate
	$7,000	• Spring athletic banquet • $5,000 honorarium for speaker • $2,000 catered meals for 200	• Boost enthusiasm for athletics • Increase school spirit

Using your strategy pages, construct a GOSA map for your abridged action plan. Use the following scaffolding items to assist you in the construction of your GOSA map.

- How many different goals did you have? _____ (Probably 1 or 2)
- How many different objectives did you have? _____ (Probably 1 or 2)
- How many strategies did you have? _____ (Probably fewer than 5)
- How many actions did you have? _____ (Probably many more than the number of strategies)
- Review your GOSA map. Does it contain the same number of the different elements you identified in the previous questions? If so, that is a strong indication that your mapping is on the right track.
- Using your strategy pages and your GOSA map, compare your actions to the strategies on the strategy pages to their counterpart on the map. Do they connect on the map as they do on the strategy pages? Repeat the process for the strategy–objective relationship and the objective–goal relationship. If they are aligned, this, along with a *yes* answer to the previous questions, indicates you have successfully completed this final portion of the case study.

Now that you've experienced, in this case study, a brief taste of the budget process, read the next three chapters and encounter the nuts and bolts of effective, efficient, and essential budgetary procedures. In these chapters, you will

1. investigate the sources of school funding,

2. learn the critical steps to budgeting success,

3. become familiar with expenditure accountability and control as well as accounting and auditing procedures,

4. examine the budgetary leadership role as related to ethical and moral behaviors, and

5. master a detailed examination and application of proper coding and how to build a school budget.

4

Understanding the Budgeting Process

A budget will not work unless you do!

—Anonymous

The Basics of School Budgeting

School leaders must devote a vast amount of time and energy to funding and budgeting issues in any era, but especially in today's era of fiscal conservatism. Leaders who fail to do so commit a terrible disservice to their schools and, more importantly, to their students. Why is budgeting so essential beyond the stated reason? First and foremost, the budgeting process enables school leaders to develop an understanding of the need for strong organizational skills, technical competence, and the collaborative process so essential to ensuring organizational trust and development. Numerous studies have documented the importance of strong organizational skills to a leader's success and effectiveness. Hughes, Ginnett, and Curphy (2015) reveal that technical competence relates to a knowledge base and the particular behaviors a leader brings to successfully completing a task. School leaders generally acquire technical competence, specifically in relation to the budgetary process, through formal education or training, but more often than not, from on-the-job experiences (Yukl, 2012). Thus, the reader immediately recognizes that one of the primary purposes of this book is to serve as a school leader's guide to appropriate and effective school-based budgeting.

Effective school leaders know how to properly develop a school budget. They also understand why budgeting and accounting procedures are integral parts of an instructional program. The best school leaders understand that goal development and instructional planning are significantly impacted by the budgeting process. Appropriation of public funds for a school is ensured by adopting a fiscal year budget that includes all estimated revenues and proposed expenditures. Budget accounts, in most states, are reported electronically by means of a Fiscal Education and Information Management System (FEIMS). The FEIMS process will be examined in greater detail in Chapter 5. Therefore, the adoption of a district budget by the local school board provides the legal authorization for school leaders to expend public funds.

School leaders, early in their careers, realize that setting goals, establishing measurable objectives, developing action or improvement plans, incorporating the entire learning community in a collaborative or participatory process, developing trust, acting with integrity, and making student enrollment projections are essential components in the development and implementation of an effective school budget. Said qualities further ensure effective and strong school leadership (Sorenson & Goldsmith, 2009; Sorenson, Goldsmith, & DeMatthews, 2016; Sorenson, Goldsmith, Méndez, & Maxwell, 2011). School leaders must recognize that it is not by mere coincidence that the budget planning and development processes coincide with the instructional or school action planning process. Both processes are essential to the overall success of any school or, for that matter, any school leader (Brimley, Verstegen, & Garfield, 2015). These two processes must be developed via an integrated approach to achieve the maximum benefits for schools and students (refer back to Chapter 3). As previously noted, a school budget must have as its foundation the action or improvement plan that details the educational programs and initiatives of a school. Such a plan must be consistent with the school's vision or mission (Sorenson & Goldsmith, 2007; Sorenson et al., 2016). Each program, initiative, and/or activity within an action or improvement plan dictates how appropriate budgetary decision making—as related to funding appropriations—will occur and how such decision making ultimately impacts student achievement.

Breaking the Budgeting Myths

Many school leaders begin their careers with several mythical notions related to the budgetary process. The reason for such thinking may simply relate to the leadership role. Numerous myths are readily associated with leading and have been documented in the research literature (Hughes et al., 2015). For example, one leadership myth, most applicable to the budgetary process, stipulates that leaders are born, not made. While certain natural talents or characteristics may provide some individuals with advantages over others, one's training and experiences play a crucial role in the development of leadership abilities, traits, and skills. This is especially true when one considers that most school leaders have limited knowledge about budgeting but quickly realize that they must build upon their minimal skills. Interestingly, several school-based budgeting myths quickly come to mind. These myths frequently serve to complicate the budgeting process and can, in fact, disengage a school leader from monitoring and managing an important, if not a critical, aspect of the education business—the school budget. Listed below are 10 myths often experienced by and associated with school leaders and school-based budgeting (Sorenson, 2010; Sorenson & Goldsmith, 2004, 2007; Sorenson et al., 2011). These myths will be dispelled throughout these final three chapters.

1. School leaders must have an analytical mindset.

2. School leaders must have an accounting background or degree.

3. Budgeting, like any fiscal accounting procedure, is difficult.

4. Educators are right brained and, as a result, would rather create than compute.

5. Budgeting is for the site-based decision-making team to figure out.

6. Physical school-site inventories have little to do with the budgeting process.

7. Instruction and curriculum are more important.

8. School leaders simply do not have the time to meet the demands and dictates associated with the school budget.

9. Central administration retains most of the money anyway.

10. District chief financial officers, business managers, or comptrollers do not care about or understand the fiscal needs of
individual schools.

Few factors pose a greater obstacle to the school leader than
untrue, unsubstantiated, and self-limiting budgetary beliefs or
myths. It must be argued that by acknowledging and then avoiding
these untruths, the school leader is provided with the basis for better
understanding, developing, and handling a school budget. The 10
myths are unfortunately, yet frequently, prevalent in the world of
school administration. However, recognition of said myths provides
school leaders—particularly novice administrators—with insights
that allow for the development of essential budgeting skills. Mastery
of such skills permits the school leader to emerge as an effective
manager of a campus budget. Being able to recognize and analyze
our own experiences in terms of the budgeting myths may be one of
the single greatest contributions this text can provide. Remember, a
budget will not work unless you do!

Delineating Between School Finance and School Budgeting

School business is big business. Many school districts across the nation
are by far the largest enterprises in their communities in terms of revenues, expenditures, employment, and capital assets. Unfortunately,
school leaders often fail to understand the basis for funding public
schools. As a result, they become victims of their own demise, failing to recognize the financial challenges that are frequently associated
with being a fiscal leader in a big business. School leaders often fail to
understand the fundamentals associated with school budgeting. In far
too many instances, school leaders possess limited background, experience, or expertise with the budgeting process. This dilemma is further
complicated by the fact that school leaders have an inadequate understanding of the basic delineation between school finance and school
budgeting.

School finance is regulated by state and federal legislation as
well as the courts. Each governmental entity has initiated, by law,
stringent policies and procedures to infuse greater accountability
through the development of financial plans and reports. Such reporting is related to a process that records, classifies, and summarizes
fiscal transactions and provides for an accounting of the monetary

operations and activities of a school district. School finance is most assuredly a concern for superintendents, district chief financial officers, comptrollers, and/or business managers. The reason? The adequacy and equity of state and federal funding is the fiscal lifeline of a school district. However, this book is not about school finance. This read is from the perspective of the school site leader who must be dedicated to better understanding and appreciating the inter-relationship of school-based budgeting and the academic planning process.

While many school leaders are focused on augmenting revenue for their schools in an era of increased mandates and state and federal funding constraints, other school leaders are focused on a much more timely and relevant question: Are schools allocating, budgeting, and spending their money strategically, notably dur-ing this time of fiscal restraint and conservative funding? A recent review by the National Conference of State Legislatures (2011, 2016) revealed that states continue to face fiscal barriers with fewer fund-ing options for public schools. While this statement sends chills up and down the spines of school officials across the nation, this truth readily relates to the fact Congress and state legislatures have, post-Great Recession, signaled a continued squeezing of federal and state pocketbooks when it comes to funding schools. A 50-year overview of K–12 public education funding reveals an almost continuous funding decrease since the mid-1960s (National Center for Education Statistics, 2016a).

Budgeting in Times of Fiscal Constraint and Conservative Funding

The funding of schools has always been a difficult prospect. Ever-increasing inflation rates from the 1970s to the present have only aggravated the funding of public schools. Great Recession (2008–2010) inflation actually became deflationary with the economy becoming terribly depressed. By mid-2009, inflation leveled, but only to a low of −2.10% (Stokes, 2011). In recent years following the Great Recession, school districts unfortunately found that drops in hous-ing prices and property valuations, lingering decreases in property tax revenues, and community job losses—frequently associated with the reduction in crude oil prices—only increased the need for drastic budgetary measures. Additionally, school districts found the politi-cizing of public school education to be a detriment to securing neces-sary federal and state funds.

Today, most states continue to cut school funding. The Center on Budget and Policy Priorities (Leachman, Albares, Masterson, & Wallace, 2016) reports that, as of the 2016–2017 school year, some states project additional funding cuts to schools. The United States Census Bureau, in their annual report, *Public Education Finances: 2014* (2016), reveals that the average per pupil spending in the United States is $10,700. States spending the most, per pupil, are New York (the very most), Alaska, the District of Columbia, New Jersey, and Connecticut. States spending the least per pupil, are in this order: Texas, Tennessee, Mississippi, Oklahoma, Arizona, Idaho, and Utah (being the very least). In Texas, for example, the per-pupil expenditure is $8,681, with 44.5% being allocated for salaries (instructional employees); 14.3% for pupil support services; 10.6% for school administration, and 30.5% for other, which would include but not be limited to general administration, instruction, instructional staff support, instructional employee benefits, capital assets, debt services, and noninstructional employee payroll.

Interestingly, most states provide even less support per student for elementary and secondary schools than before the Great Recession. In some states, funding is actually *significantly less* than before the Great Recession. The budgetary facts are as follows:

- Thirty-one states provide less state funding per student than during the 2008–2009 school year. Some have school funding cuts as high as 10%.
- In 18 states, local funding per student has decreased since 2008. In 27 states, local funding did increase but frequently failed to make up for state funding cuts.
- Twenty-five states are currently providing less general or "formula" per-pupil funding (the primary source of funding for schools) than before the Great Recession.
- Twelve states in 2016 imposed new funding cuts even as the national economy improved. Some states, including Oklahoma, Arizona, and Wisconsin, made the deepest cuts in education funding. The reader might ask, why? The authors of the text would note that politics far too often play a significant role in budgetary cuts for education. Underfunding public schools is but one means of inflicting the soft bigotry of decreased instructional endeavors along with low academic expectations upon economically disadvantaged kids and minority students.

- Four states with the deepest K–12 cuts decided to slash corporate taxes (Leachman et al., 2016; National Center for Education Statistics, 2016b).

Finally, as most states provide nearly half of school funding, local schools are becoming hard-pressed to replace lost state revenue. Restoring school funding at the state level must be an urgent priority. Funding cuts have serious consequences to include, but not limited to, the following:

- Inadequate educational services
- Local school districts, especially property-poor districts and districts of a disproportionate percentage of students of color, find it particularly difficult to raise additional revenue through taxation increases—which are politically challenging even in times of economic upswings.
- More than 300,000 teaching positions were cut by 2013, long after the Great Recession. These job losses reduced the purchasing power of families, weakened overall economic consumption, and resulted in a continued slow economic recovery to date.
- According to the American Society of Civil Engineers' 2017 Infrastructure Report Card, published every four years, schools received a grade of D+ as districts are not receiving the necessary funding to maintain campus buildings. At least one-fourth of our school facilities are in poor condition. The United States continues to underinvest in school facilities, leaving more than a $40 billion annual funding gap.
- Funding cuts to schools impede priority educational reforms such as improving teacher quality, reducing class sizes, and increasing student academic achievement (American Society of Civil Engineers, 2017; Leachman et al., 2016).

These trends reveal a poignant fact: As state funding sharply decreases and local funding fails to bridge the gap, the economic health of schools, let alone the nation, is at risk. If schools are neglected fiscally, the creativity and intellectual capacity of our society diminishes and democracy weakens. Consider the following scenario.

LEADING AND BUDGETING IN TIMES OF FISCAL CONSTRAINT AND CONSERVATIVE FUNDING

Galen Adams sat in his office early one morning, prior to the start of the school day. Dr. Adams had been principal at Waldo Binny School for seven years and during his tenure, he had witnessed continued fiscal constraint in school funding. He recognized that he was serving as an instructional leader and budgetary manager during a period of conservative school funding.

This particular morning, he was attentive to an account he had read in the *Morning Times* newspaper. The journalistic piece echoed a political outcry for redirecting federal school funds. He was not a political animal. At the same time, he was not oblivious to national, state, and local news and politics he deemed noteworthy, especially when it came to education.

Dr. Adams was logging off his favorite news website and finishing his last drop of coffee when his assistant principal, Kitty Russell, walked into his office with a cheerful "Good morning, Doc. How are you today?"

Galen responded, "Fine, Kitty; have you read this morning's front page of the newspaper?"

"No, sir, I haven't opened my e-tablet yet," said Kitty, "Why do you ask?"

Dr. Adams went on to describe the news article that had captured his attention. Ms. Russell took a seat in front of Galen's desk and listened quietly. The following conversation ensued:

Dr. Galen Adams: Here's the gist of the article, Kitty. Seems Congress wishes to redirect federal funds, already limited to schools, to a tune of about $20 billion toward a school voucher plan. It seems the proposal would redirect huge funds from the federal education budget away from school districts and toward lower-income parents, permitting them to spend a voucher at a public or private school of their choice, potentially including for-profit, virtual, and religious schools.

Kitty Russell: Sounds interesting. Tell me more.

Dr. Galen Adams: Did you see the recent public survey in the *Education Journal of Schools* detailing how families like having school choices, especially where school choice has driven academic gains for students, producing mild reductions in racial and socioeconomic segregation of poor students of color?

Kitty Russell: Yes, I did read the journal article a couple of weeks ago. I thought at the time how it related to our situation here at Waldo Binny School.

Dr. Galen Adams: Yes, me too! Well, there are also potential downsides that could be significant. Think for a minute: In some states, recent studies found that students who use vouchers actually score lower on state accountability exams, losing as much as 13 points of learning in mathematics; and in some states, the most exclusive schools are not accepting of a more instructionally challenging student population.

Kitty Russell: Yes, I understand. I'm very familiar with how such a plan could lead to a redistribution of Title I funds away from public schools like ours that serve large percentages of poor children of color and thus provide individual families with voucher funding.

Dr. Galen Adams: Exactly, Kitty. Here's a point worthy of consideration during this time of fiscal constraint and conservative school funding: With 11 million school-aged students living in poverty, $20 billion in federal funding equals to an $1,800 voucher per student. That seems way too small of an amount to pay for a year of education in any school—especially a for-profit school! On top of that, such a process of funding schools could lead to serious reductions in funding for public schools—especially those, like our school, which serves the poorest of students.

(Continued)

(Continued)

> **Kitty Russell:**   Well, sir, I'm not certain I have any answers to your points. Do you? Also, how do you think such changes in funding might affect our school budget?

Pause and Consider

- Assistant Principal Kitty Russell, in the scenario above, stated to Principal Adams, "I'm not certain I have any answers to your points. Do you?" Reflect upon the scenario and respond to Ms. Russell's query.
- How do you think the noted changes in funding could affect school budgets?
- Utilize an internet search engine to determine the yearly cost of tuition at a parochial or for-profit school in your area. Would the proposed voucher funding amount of $1,800 equate to the tuition rate? Compare the per-pupil public school allocation in your state to the voucher allotment and the noted tuition rate. Your thoughts?
- Should a school leader have a vested interest in educational politics? Why or why not? How might the political process impact school-based budgeting?

Politicizing Education and the Funding Impact

Recent testimony before Congress reflects deeply drawn criticism from both ends of the political spectrum regarding federal education spending and, most notably, spending cuts into the billions of dollars. The push to provide more educational choice to parents and thus to privatize education may sound alarming. Partisans on both sides of the aisle have described the privatization agenda and the slashing of public school funding as being more than alarming, using terms such as *difficult to defend*, *all but impossible*, *abysmal*, and *discriminatory*. Many educators see the strong impetus for recently proposed educational initiatives as anything but reforming. Simply put, these initiatives have been described as nothing more than a means of slashing funding for public schools and placing federal education dollars in the pockets of those business interests who advocate and lobby for an extreme privatization agenda. School leaders must serve not only as student advocates on the school grounds, they must also advocate publicly and politically promote a critical realization: Our democracy is built upon a free and public education for each student—no matter of race, color, national origin, religion, sex, disability, or economic advantage or disadvantage.

PUBLIC SCHOOL FUNDING AND PRIVATIZATION: NEW AND IMPROVED AT WHAT COST, OR DOES IT REALLY MATTER?

School leaders must be aware of this era of contention in which we are living and working. An era where issues and ideas of expanding alternatives to traditional public school funding are a top priority at both federal and state houses. An era of new and improved—but at what cost, or does it really matter? The authors recently came across a product that read on the front of the package, *new and improved*. Wondering how the product was new and improved, the authors read more carefully and determined the product was *new* simply because it had a revamped package design. The *improved* aspect of the product was more fruit colors but fewer ounces per package, at an increased cost to the consumer.

School leaders recognize that educational change is inevitable and can be very good in some instances. However, change must be meaningful and beneficial—most notably to students and stakeholders. Is the potential change to public school funding new and improved and at what cost? Or does it really matter? Listed are four critical considerations, subject to study and debate, as related to school funding, public and private education, and related change.

1. **Publicly funded vouchers and privatization**. Proponents of privatization acknowledged that private schools of choice accept students, in some states, with publicly funded vouchers and said schools should be able to discriminate against students for reasons such as race, color, creed, religion, sexual orientation, and/or disabilities—to the point of voucher recipients giving up their Individuals with Disabilities Education Act (IDEA) rights.

2. **Title I dollars and privatization**. Proponents of privatization recommend using at least $1 billion in Title I funding for a school of choice portability program—in other words, less money for traditional public schools. Congress rejected this funding procedure in 2015. However, the plan remains highly publicized and politically pressed.

(Continued)

(Continued)

3. **Accreditation, accountability, and privatization**. Proponents of privatization hedge on whether the traditional public school concepts of accreditation and accountability should apply to private and/or parochial schools. Strauss (2017) reveals two familiar privatization lines: (a) When proponents of school privatization have been pushed on the issues of accreditation and accountability, a well-known response is "Students could learn to read by simply putting a hand on a book" (p. 5) and (b) in terms of accountability standards, another oft-repeated line is "States can determine what kind of flexibility they are going to allow" (p. 5).

4. **Outdated, inefficient, inferior, inept, noncompetitive, and unchallenging**. Strong words to describe public education, but in fairness to the privatization agenda, proponents of for-profit schools claim that these terms are most representative of traditional public schools, which are all too often described by school privatization proponents as inherently inefficient, existing to survive, and only interested in meeting their own needs. Proponents of school privatization believe that their system of education provides a more competitive and challenging education as well as quality service to students. Proponents further claim that teachers in private institutions are free from bureaucratic norms, regulations, and top-down, outdated expectations. Thus, private education is much more apt to monetarily reward high-performance teaching and instruction. Public schools are moreover described by privatization proponents as simply enhancing and rewarding mediocrity and ineptitude (Debate.org, 2017).

Again, are the proposed changes new and improved and at what cost—or does it really matter? Put it another way, do the pros of school privatization outweigh the cons?

Pause and Consider

- Why do you believe the majority of states continue to cut public school funding, years after the Great Recession (2008–2010)? Specifically, consider the fact that 31 states (more than half the nation) provide less funding today, per pupil, than during the worst of recent economic times.
- How does underfunding affect your school—your students, faculty, staff, and administration?
- After examining the four above-noted considerations, debate the pros and cons of school funding relative to public and private education.

The Effects of Budget Cuts

In the wake of the Great Recession and with continued reductions in federal, state, and local education dollars, and in today's era of fiscal constraint and conservative funding, budget cuts have become commonplace in many states and directly affect faculty and staff and, just as importantly, students and student achievement, to include

- laying off teachers,
- initiating hiring freezes,
- increasing class size,
- cutting extracurricular programs or limiting activities,
- eliminating summer school,
- cutting instructional programs such as the arts and fine arts,
- eliminating field trips,
- reducing or eliminating teacher and staff stipends and/or bonuses,
- closing older/economically burdensome schools,
- implementing changes in benefits (for example, higher health care deductibles),
- introducing energy/utility savings initiatives,
- cutting professional development for teachers and staff, or
- revoking contracts, thus requiring teachers and administrators accept "at-will" employment status.

Following the confrontation of said cutbacks, school leaders have been forced to live with budgetary reductions. In many instances, school leaders have been required to address certain key budgetary considerations:

- Communicate with faculty and staff about how conservative funding affects schools, most notably the budgetary process, and how it must be reasonably, positively, and effectively addressed.
- Establish budget advisory teams and develop site-based guidelines and practices to include regularly scheduled budget and campus decision-making meetings.
- Collaboratively conduct a cost analysis of all campus-based programs and initiatives. Can certain expensive programs be replaced with similar inexpensive programs?
- Ensure that purchases are extended to the lowest bidder.
- Conduct a needs assessment to include an intensive data-analysis process.

- Develop and analyze a campus action or improvement plan with specific goals, objectives, strategies, action implementations, staff responsibilities, timelines, resource (human/material/fiscal) identifications, and formative as well as summative evaluative measures.
- Align the school budget with the campus action or improvement plan.
- Develop a priority-setting process and strictly fund the greatest of instructional priorities.
- Accumulate an expenditure history: Examine how campus funding, over a period of three to five years, has been expended, on what, and why.
- Appoint a budget manager (principal, assistant principal, secretary, clerk) who at predetermined intervals reviews and assesses the campus budget and provides reports to the site-based team.
- Address student achievement by asking pressing questions:
  - What are the most efficient methods of organizing our instructional programs and student-centered initiatives?
  - How can classes be better scheduled—and not at the expense of students?
  - What are specific and effective methods of presenting instruction in the differing subject areas?
  - What classes are crucial for all graduates?
  - What is the value of programs such as prekindergarten, dropout prevention initiatives, and the support of late graduates?
  - What class-size capacity can be reached without negatively impacting teaching and learning?
  - How can teacher quality, student learning, and instructional methodology be redefined in an era of technological norms and advancements?
  - What are the short-term and long-term impacts of conservative budgetary funding on student achievement?
  - What does the research reveal regarding current instructional programs and initiatives, and are schools still doing the same old things the same old ways? Can improvements come with fiscal constraints?
  - What are other school districts and other schools doing to be more instructionally innovative yet cost effective?
  - What additional or innovative fundraising or crowdfunding efforts can be implemented?

    o How can a school team communicate with state and federal legislators and provide them with a clear understanding of local conditions and the need for improved funding?

- Carefully monitor enrollment trends. Conduct at the campus level the cohort survival method process (see Chapter 6, p. 257).
- Implement attendance incentive plans.
- Monitor copier and paper usage (see "Case Study Application #1: Paper and the Copier").
- Carefully monitor and limit overtime.
- Reduce energy consumption.
- Limit travel expenses—especially out of state.
- Seek grant and foundation funding.
- Permit district personnel and campus experts to provide quality staff development.
- Utilize benchmarking procedures as a method of identifying and monitoring student progress and achievement, thus reducing the purchase of unnecessary materials as well as tutorial expenditures for students not in need of academic interventions.
- Develop community partnerships (Adopt-A-School, Friends of Education, etc.).
- Develop a materials center, an instructional resource center, where teaching and learning materials are stored for teacher/ student use. Material centers reduce cost duplications, create material check-out systems, serve as inventory depositories, better facilitate the sharing of materials, and reduce pilferage.
- Every "nonnegotiable" must become "negotiable" whereby evaluative measures are initiated at least once a year.
- Finally, maintain hope and a positive attitude. Create an optimistic work environment whereby a culture of confident determination and expectation—one of constancy of purpose— is the norm. This environment allows for continual improvement in all areas: services, products, and resource allocations. Here's how:
  - o Recognize that hope is not based on circumstances. A hopeful spirit is contagious and is a leader's gift to others. Pass on hope by speaking the language of hope. That means stop speaking in terms of negativity. Here's an example: Don't say, "Funds are tight." Instead state, "Let's find the funds. I have a few ideas as to where we can get additional dollars. Do you?"

- ○ Eliminate despairing thoughts, depressive mindsets, and negative responses. Donna Cover (2017) says, "Put hope on repeat and turn up the volume!" Stay positive in every discussion, budgetary meeting, strategy seminar, instructional planning session, and school-related event. Remember, people are tired of being tired. They're tired of false promises, unexpected outcomes, uncertainty in the workplace, artificial leadership, and constant reminders things aren't getting better. They want hope and they want it in a most positive manner. So, deliver!

- ○ Recognize that hope is the belief that everything is possible and actually probable, even in the direst of straits! Recall the old adage, "Show me the money!" A school principal that turns this phrase into a positive response, especially when there is no money, will state, "I'll find the money" or "Let's find the money!"

- ○ Understand that people want something or someone to believe in, something or someone to solve their issues or problems, and something or someone to bring on a brighter future. When a school leader, during an era of fiscal constraint, knows that students and faculty and staff need more, that leader develops a team of believers—a team that is responsible enough to not only believe in the principal but in each other. This type of team puts forth a vibrant energy of endless possibilities—a "do it together" mentality. The authors know a principal who, during this era of fiscal constraint, recognized that the teaching team desired an outdoor learning environment for the students. The team had researched this approach to instruction and learning. Money, however, was tight. The principal stated, "I've got an idea. While we don't have the money or the supplies and materials, I know who does!" The principal held hope and presented a positive attitude. The principal went to district leadership that had purchased an outdoor work environment for the district offices. The principal stated, "If you can have it, why can't we?" After presenting her case, the principal convinced the district leadership team to provide an outdoor learning environment for the school. But the district didn't have the money either. What the district did have was the outdoor equipment. The district took half of their outdoor materials and moved them to the principal's school. The students and faculty and staff were elated. Their confidence in their leader expanded, their hope became a reality, and instruction and learning increased—and outdoors to boot!

o Hope requires a school leader to make good choices with his or her team in order to sustain a positive work environment. Hope definitely does two things: (1) renews faith and (2) builds confidence. When fiscal times are tough, the best school leaders develop a sense of security for students and the team, a feeling that the worries and concerns will soon be eliminated. It's pretty simple: Individuals want to recapture that moment in time when they felt their best, when the school had minimal fiscal issues and other workplace problems. The best school leaders live by and readily share a constant: "We are either solving a problem or dwelling within a problem." Why waste time and energy within the quagmire of a problem when a solution is an idea away? Remember, hope and a positive attitude will alleviate any negativity! Place this quote on your desk: "Your success will be determined by how well you overcome hardship!"

Fiscal constraint and budgetary conservativism in schools are nothing new! The authors of this text have witnessed, over the years, numerous economic downturns and their effects on schools—from the high-inflation era of the 1970s to the oil industry collapse in the 1980s to the disintegration of tax bases in the 1990s to the Great Recession in the first decade of the 21st century and to the serious drop in crude oil prices and the politics of funding in the second decade of the 21st century. In response, the adage "this too shall pass" is appropriate. Again, remember there is and always will be hope! However, it is important to keep in mind that until any era of economic downturn and conservative funding lapses, effective school leaders must maintain a single and most essential visionary perspective: Students first and foremost, no matter the constraints in budgetary funding!

Allocation—The Key to the Budgetary Process

School budgeting is directly related to the allocation of those specified and, far too often, scarce sources of state and federal funding. To coin a financial term, the bottom line to adequately and effectively delineating between school finance and school budgeting can be summed up with one simple word: *allocation*. Allocation is the key to understanding the school budgeting process. Allocation, as well as efficient funding, is not only important to state public education systems, but the amount of money schools receive for budgetary purposes is also critical to continued student success and achievement.

Nevertheless, school leaders must realize and understand that the school budgeting process is much more than the technical skill associated with the term *allocation*. Exceptional school leaders recognize that effective budgeting must be an integrated approach incorporating team planning, visionary leadership, efficient time management, and data analysis to establish instructional priorities for necessary funding. This integrated approach to school budgeting was previously explored in Chapter 3 and will be examined in greater detail in Chapter 5.

Speaking of efficient time management, a critical examination of the text *The Principal's Guide to Time Management: Instructional Leadership in the Digital Age* (Sorenson et al., 2016) is well worth the reader's time. This text provides the school leader with the necessary skills, relevant information, and functional tools to promote effective time management, instructional leadership, and technological ideals into real school applications.

Sources of School Funding

The key to understanding sources of school funding is realizing that expenditures correlated with student educational needs are affected by whether federal, state, and local governments appropriately share in the responsibility of supporting schools (Brimley et al., 2015; Poston, 2011). Naturally, adequate and equitable funding during any fiscal era (upswing or downturn) becomes a critical issue not only with educators but with politicians and taxpayers as well. The reason why appropriate, adequate, and equitable funding is a contested issue in public education is related to the fact that our Founding Fathers failed to provide any arrangements for education in the federal constitution. As a result, the funding of schools has become the responsibility of individual states, whether by design or by default, and in most instances, not by choice. By placing the responsibility for public education funding in the hands of individual states, our nation has become, in reality, 51 systems of education and, more notably, 51 sources of school funding.

Education is the largest single budgetary component of state and local governments. School districts receive nearly all of their funding for instruction, either directly or indirectly, from federal, state, and local governments, although the majority of this funding comes from local and state revenues, as revealed in Table 4.1. While school districts depend, and most certainly place special emphasis, on the amount of federal funds received, the percentage of federal support for schools is relatively insignificant in relation to state and local funding. For example, many states provide well over 50% of school district funding. As further noted in Table 4.1, federal funding typically amounts to less than 10% to 15% of a district's funding dollars, with local revenue coming close to or exceeding that of the state funding allotments (Leachman et al., 2016; National Center for Education Statistics, 2016a).

Table 4.1   Percentages of Revenues by State for Education

State	Local Revenue	State Revenue	Federal Revenue
US	45.3	45.6	9.1
AL	34.2	54.5	11.3
AK	18.2	67.1	12.6
AR	12.5	76.2	11.3
AZ	37.3	36.2	14.6
CA	35.3	52.9	11.8
CO	50.0	42.1	7.9
CT	57.4	38.3	4.3
DE	32.2	59.8	8.0
DC	90.0	0.00	10.0
FL	49.4	38.3	12.3
GA	46.2	43.4	10.3
HI	2.5	84.2	13.3
ID	24.7	63.4	11.8
IL	52.5	35.4	7.9
IN	29.2	62.6	8.2
IA	40.7	51.7	7.6
KS	36.2	56.4	7.4
KY	33.1	54.9	12.0
LA	43.1	41.7	15.2
MA	52.3	40.2	7.5
MD	49.9	44.1	6.0
ME	54.7	40.2	5.1
MI	33.7	56.9	9.4

(*Continued*)

Table 4.1 (Continued)

State	Local Revenue	State Revenue	Federal Revenue
MN	30.5	63.5	6.1
MO	48.9	42.2	8.9
MS	34.1	49.9	16.0
MT	39.5	47.7	12.8
NE	58.3	32.1	9.7
NH	58.8	35.5	5.7
NJ	57.2	38.7	4.1
NM	17.0	68.3	14.8
NV	28.6	61.9	9.5
NC	25.6	62.0	12.4
ND	38.9	50.3	10.7
NY	54.6	39.8	5.6
OH	50.7	41.4	7.9
OK	38.6	49.2	12.2
OR	41.7	50.5	7.8
PA	56.3	36.1	7.6
RI	54.2	37.2	8.6
SC	43.8	46.3	9.9
SD	54.1	31.0	14.8
TN	40.8	46.1	13.1
TX	50.0	38.5	11.4
UT	38.5	52.0	9.5
VA	53.4	39.2	7.4
VT	4.5	88.4	7.1
WA	32.5	58.9	8.6
WI	47.5	44.8	7.7
WV	30.6	58.3	11.0
WY	41.3	52.0	6.7

SOURCES: National Education Association (2016), U.S. Census Bureau (2016).

NOTE: The totals for each row may not equal 100% due to rounding or due to states receiving intermediate revenue for education. *Intermediate revenue* is defined as receipts from county or regional governments that are typically quite small or frequently nonexistent in most states.

Naturally, a prerequisite for understanding the budgetary process is a keen realization of where the money comes from—the sources of money received to operate school districts. In financial circles, the appropriate terms are *revenue, income,* and *fiduciary* funding. The flip side of the "money received" coin is *expenditure,* or money spent. Income sources will be examined in greater detail later in this chapter. However, to better understand the relationship between revenue and expenditure, Figures 4.1a and 4.1b reveal, on a per-pupil basis, the revenue and expenditures of Texas schools during the fiscal year 2017–2018. The revenue amounts displayed in Figures 4.1a and 4.1b combine state aid and property tax levy figures from state agencies with the amounts in the budget for other sources of school revenue.

Notice in Figure 4.1a that the revenue figures are based on a funding starting point, an allocation simply known, from a school finance perspective, as the *basic allotment.* The basic allotment to school districts can be further adjusted incrementally with "adjustment allotments," such as

- *cost of education index*—a funding "multiplier" designed to compensate districts for geographic (rural schools) and cost (the percentage of economically disadvantaged students) differences beyond the control of the local school system.
- *small district adjustment*—small school systems are more expensive to operate due to diseconomies of scale. For example, districts with 1,600 or fewer students in average daily attendance could receive an increase in funding.
- *impact aid*—districts can receive additional funding for each student who has a parent serving in the military on active duty.
- *other weighted allotments*—for example, special education (districts could possibly be entitled to up to five times more funding for a student with special needs), bilingual education (possibly an additional 10% for English language learners [ELLs]), compensatory education (potential funding of 20% or more to pay for intensive or accelerated instructional services [tutoring, for example] for students who are performing below grade level or are at risk of dropping out of school), and so on.

Revenue is obtained primarily from tax collection and the sale of bonds. The tax collection funds provide the majority of money received and money expended for the instructional and operational

Figure 4.1a Revenue per Pupil, Texas School Budgets

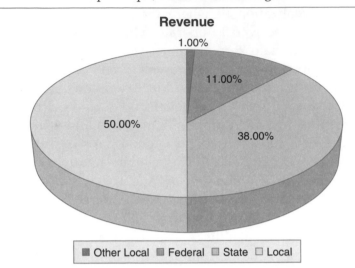

Revenue

1.00%
11.00%
38.00%
50.00%

■ Other Local ■ Federal ■ State ☐ Local

Figure 4.1b Expenditures per Pupil, Texas School Budgets

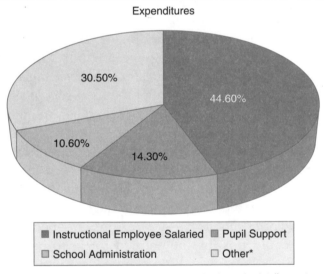

Expenditures

30.50%
44.60%
10.60%
14.30%

■ Instructional Employee Salaried ■ Pupil Support
☐ School Administration   ☐ Other*

*Other refers to but is not limited to general administration, instructional staff support, instructional employee benefits, capital assets, debt services, and payroll.

SOURCES: Figures utilized in this report were provided by Governing Data (2016), the Property Tax Division of the Texas Comptroller's Office (2017), the Texas Education Agency (2017a), the Texas Taxpayers and Research Association (2017), the U.S. Census Bureau (2016).

NOTE: As previously documented within this chapter, most states have continued to cut school funding during the period 2008–2017. In Texas, the figures identified in Figure 4.1a and 4.1b reflect a 2.4% decrease in 2015–2016 revenue and a 1.9% increase in 2015–2016 expenditures since 2012–2013 (Governing Data, 2016; Leachman et al., 2016; U.S. Census Bureau, 2016).

aspects of a school district. Bond sales provide revenue necessary for the construction of new school facilities.

Income is a particular funding category that is representative of funds received from the sale of goods and services. A perfect example of income funding is the district food services program. Since income can be generated from the sale of food items in the school cafeteria, district administrators must develop budgets that project sales and anticipate expenditures, and then they must implement and monitor a budget.

The *fiduciary* category refers to funds received from donations and thus must be managed by or entrusted to a school district in a most legal and ethical manner. While these dollars are important, such funds are generally not critical to the instructional operation of a school district. However, these same dollars may be very significant to a school that needs additional dollars to finance school-related initiatives and activities not normally funded by a school district. A perfect example of fiduciary receipts are monies generated from fundraisers and collected by student clubs, campus organizations, graduating classes, or booster clubs; as a result, the school district must agree to be the depository of these funds and must ensure that the funds are expended appropriately.

Expenditures are exactly that—money spent. Whenever money is spent, the expenditure must be charged against a revenue account and source. School leaders will invariably note that within their budget software listings or on their budget spreadsheets, the accounting term *encumbered* appears. *Encumbered* or *encumbrance*, by definition, is by no means the same as *expenditure*. However, both terms maintain a compelling correlation in terms of the budgetary process. For example, when a specified school account is used to initiate a purchase order, the funds are immediately set aside or *encumbered*, indicating that the dollars for products or services ordered have been committed, held back, or set aside. At this point, a school leader can expect the purchase order to be processed, and when the goods are received, a payment will be submitted. When the payment has been issued, an *expenditure* of district dollars has occurred.

The expenditure of funds must always be accounted for, and thus, a school leader may complain from time to time about the numerous business department forms that have to be completed, such as purchase orders, requisitions, travel reimbursements, amendments and transfers, and vouchers, all of which are examples of the paperwork commonly associated with district expenditures. Completing these forms may seem a nuisance, but they ensure fiscal accountability, and each may very well be the necessary documentation to keep a school leader out of a legal entanglement. Mutter and Parker (2012) in their book *School Money Matters: A Handbook for Principals*, note that financial forms and accompanying safeguards are "designed to meet three important school financial objectives: (1) to protect school staff from suspicion of theft or laxness, (2) to protect school assets, and (3) to fulfill the stewardship responsibility for public funds expected by the general public" (p. 1). When fiscal accountability is ignored, for whatever reason, the end result is less than attractive—much less. For example, consider the *Scheming Peg* scenario, a "no way out" situation involving a school budget clerk and based on a real-life event.

SCHEMING PEG

Sandy Cypress is a small town with a small school system that has a big problem. No one knows it yet because Peg Riley is getting away with murder—well, not murder, but she's operating a scheme that's making her lots of money and no one will ever figure it out!

Peg is the budget clerk at Digby O'Dell School and she has created eleven fake vendors as part of a fraudulent billing scheme that has netted her more than $475,000 in nine short years. Her principal and immediate supervisor, Otto Schmidlap, is past retirement age. He's been principal at O'Dell School for 44 years. Peg is his most trusted employee. He thinks Peg is the best and brightest employee he has ever supervised. Peg thinks Principal Schmidlap is too trusting, a sweet—but weak—school leader. In her mind, she's outwitted him all these years, and she's confident her scheme will go on for even more years!

Here's how Peg pulled off the scheme: She lined up eleven individuals, mostly relatives and a few close friends, who know how to keep their mouths shut and who are more than anxious to make a few bucks every month. These eleven individuals pose as school vendors. Using eleven different post office boxes, opened at various locales within a larger nearby city, Peg has created monthly vendor bills and she has the school system making monthly payments to all eleven fictitious vendors—those friends and relatives who are in on the take, getting a percentage of Peg's ill-conceived and completely illegal income. And, it works—until one day!

That one day comes when Principal Schmidlap doesn't return to work following Christmas break. He unexpectedly retires as he and his wife decide to move closer to their son and daughter-in-law and grandchildren who reside in a beach community in a much warmer state. Sandy Cypress School System immediately hires a new principal and with her employment, an instantaneous audit is triggered! The school system audit reveals more than $267,000 in suspect reimbursements—checks written to several vendors that the district's business office can't find physical addresses for. The school system shares this information with the district attorney, who begins working with federal investigators who, in turn, begin an undercover sting operation.

Four of Peg's relatives are detained within days, along with five close friends. Peg and her two sisters attempt to grab a quick flight to Costa Rica but are subsequently nabbed at a major airport during a layover. The rest of the story? The district attorney's office, working in conjunction with federal agents, indict Peg Riley and, upon her confession, arrest the other conspirators. All individuals, including Peg, are now serving prison sentences, and a percentage of the embezzled funds have been subsequently recovered and returned to Sandy Cypress School System to be used for the good of the students served.

The *Scheming Peg* scenario is an obvious example of how school-based budgeting is much more than a technical or managerial skill and process. One must understand that the budgeting process constantly overlaps into the arena of certain behaviors—visionary, integrity, fairness, trustworthiness, legal and ethical, for example. Recall that these extremely important behavioral concepts, along with their impact on school-based budgeting, were explored in Chapter 1 and will be reexamined in Chapter 6.

To recap, district revenue funds are generated, by and large, through taxes assessed on the general public and on for-profit businesses. As noted earlier in the chapter, school districts receive the vast majority of their revenue for instruction from federal, state, and local governments. Let's now examine each of these specific sources of generated revenue or income for school districts.

Federal Sources of Income

Federal revenue comes in the form of different and distinct sources of transfer payments known as *general, categorical,* and *block grants* aid. General and categorical aid, the major source of federal income for education, significantly impacts and expands the capabilities of school districts to enhance student achievement.

General aid flows from federal and state governments with few limitations to local school districts. General aid provides the largest proportion of financial support for school operations. Local school boards and district administrators largely determine how such income will be allocated to educational programs and other related expenditures.

Categorical aid is a source of funding to school districts that links funding to specific objectives of the government in support of specified programs, such as special education, gifted and talented education, career and technology education (formerly vocational education), and compensatory education. Unlike general aid, categorical aid must be utilized for certain groups of students (e.g., those with disabilities), a specific purpose (e.g., pupil transportation), or a particular project (e.g., construction of a school facility). Most often, categorical aid calls for annual applications, documentation of expenditures, and frequent program evaluations and audits. Categorical aid was once the predominant form of federal income to states and school districts. However, other forms of federal aid now serve as district income supplements, with fewer restrictions at the local level. In recent years, much of the categorical aid has been absorbed into block grants to reduce the local paperwork and personnel productivity burdens associated with federal funds to education.

Block grants provide funding for a wide range of services, with federal requirements for planning, implementing, and assessing programs being much less stringent than those associated with categorical aid. Block grants provide for local funding based on the number of students rather than through a competitive application process that identifies particular educational needs. Local school districts appreciate the greater latitude provided by block grants. This source of federal funding provides district administrators with more discretion in programmatic designs.

The largest of the block grant programs is Title I funding, which reaches 25 million disadvantaged students, with minority students accounting for two-thirds of the Title I participants (National Center for Education Statistics, 2016c). Title I monies, in the form of block grants, go directly to school districts and schools where they are most needed and fund, for example, extra teachers and innovative programs—all of which help students master reading, writing, and mathematics. Over the years, block grant funding has served to focus on and improve proven programs that have turned around entire schools and even school districts. Federal aid has certainly served to promote equity and equality in education over the last 45 to 50 years and has generally improved the quality of education for all students.

What a "Title" Means Descriptions of Title I; Title II–Part A, Part B, Part C, and Part D; and Title IV are available on the companion website at http://resources.corwin.com/schoolbudget.

> ### GROWING INTO EQUITY AND EXCELLENCE: TITLE I SCHOOLS WITH HIGH-ACHIEVING STUDENTS AND TEACHERS
>
> Title I schools where learning and personalization have combined to form high-achieving learning communities are exemplified and found in an excellent read, *Growing Into Equity: Professional Learning and Personalization in High-Achieving Schools* (2014) by Sonia Caus Gleason and Nancy J. Gerzon. Four schools are the focus and study of this text—Stults Road Elementary School (PreK–6) in Dallas, Texas; Social Justice Humanitas Academy (9–12) in Los Angeles, California; Montgomery Center School (PreK–8) in Montgomery Center, Vermont; and Tusculum View Elementary School (PreK–5) in Greenville, Tennessee. Each of these schools is a Title I school with a significantly high percentage of economically disadvantaged students, most of which are students of color. Each school serves to exemplify how personalized learning will not only improve academic achievement but also provide an equitable and high-quality education for all students. Each school focuses on the whole child, engaging every student, addressing social justice, and incorporating equity-driven practices. In doing so, these four Title I learning communities better ensure the raising of the academic bar and, moreover, narrow the achievement gap among student populations that, tragically, are all too often left behind in other schools. Federal funds well spent!

State Sources of Income

Most states have property taxes, sales taxes, or income taxes as their source of income. These income sources determine the amount of state funding for school districts. This revenue allotment is then typically distributed to the differing school districts across a state by means of a *state aid formula*. These funding formulas are generally driven by student enrollment and, again, this aid comes primarily from assessed taxes. While property taxation remains the major source of local revenue for many schools across the nation, the local tax base is typically insufficient to support a school district. Therefore, most states have developed state aid formulas as the basis for infusing some fundamental element of equity from district to district within a state. State aid formulas are the result of legislative choice and litigation force.

The purpose of state aid formulas is to counterbalance disparities in educational equity and opportunity that would most certainly be present if school districts depended solely on the local tax base. An example of such a disparity is illustrated below.

PORT GREGORY VS. NUECESTOWN: A CASE OF EDUCATIONAL DISPARITY?

The Port Gregory school system is located along a state coastline near a major seaport. This school system is the recipient of tax dollars generated by several major petrochemical corporations. These taxable entities generate significant per-pupil wealth on the basis of taxable property. A second school system, Nuecestown Public Schools, similar in size and population but located further inland, is solely dependent on the agribusiness industry, and thus this district receives only limited revenue from its economically depressed tax base.

Pause and Consider

- What type of funding mechanism might help alleviate the disparity between the two school systems identified in the scenario above?
- How is the financing of school systems in your state equalized?
- What has historically been the result of funding inequities of public schools in your state?

Another example is often evident in states with large urban centers that face vast disparities in their tax base due to ever-growing suburbs and the related citizenry and corporation flight to the nearby bedroom communities.

Most states develop foundation programs to facilitate the state aid formulas. These programs are the mechanism by which the equalization of resources from district to district can occur. Foundation programs allow for the difference in the cost of a school program and the amount each school district must contribute from local taxation.

Today, very complex state aid formulas advance the foundation programs, and such formulas are generally related to a fictitious "weighted student" consideration. After the foundation program cost is determined by formula, financing is equalized by determining the local share for each district and then the remainder is funded by state aid. State aid for individual school districts equals the foundation program cost minus the local share. However, it is worth noting that state aid formulas have come under intense scrutiny in recent years and, to date, legal challenges related to formula funding continue to come before the United States Supreme Court.

For example, the issue of equity in relation to educational opportunities for all students regardless of socioeconomic background and/or ethnicity continues to be a critical issue before the courts, both state and federal, as well as state legislatures. Inequities have long plagued public schools, particularly in the area of financing educational facilities with minimal funding reforms and state-led efforts. This is not to say the courts have completely ignored equity in public school financing. Consideration by the courts is most certainly revealed in several recent court cases in which lawsuits have demanded that states provide adequate and equitable educational facilities. Unfortunately, the operative term and process utilized in response to these legal entanglements has most often been nothing more than *adequate*.

Court cases from Texas (*San Antonio Independent School District v. Rodriguez* [the landmark U.S. Supreme Court decision affecting school finance programs across the nation], 1973; *Edgewood v. Kirby*, 1986; and *West Orange Cove CISD v. Neeley*, 2007); California (*Serrano v. Priest*, 1971 and *Williams v. California*, 2000), Kansas (*Montoy v. State of Kansas*, 2003), Ohio (*DeRolph v. State of Ohio*, 2002), New Jersey (*Abbott v. Burke*, 1990), New Mexico (*Alamogordo v. Morgan*, 1995), New York (*CFE v. State of New York*, 2003), West Virginia (*Pauley v. Bailey*, 1994), and Tennessee (*Small Schools v. McWherter*, 1988) serve to exemplify just a few decisions that have impacted equitable facilities and funding for all students (Alexander & Alexander, 2012; Brimley et al., 2015). An excellent source relative to school finance reform is *School Law and the Public Schools: A Practical Guide for Educational Leaders* (2015) by Nathan L. Essex, especially Chapter 13, "School Finance."

Local Sources of Income

The majority of school districts in the United States obtain their locally generated income from at least one of the following sources: ad valorem (property) taxes, sales taxes, income taxes, or sumptuary (sin) taxes.

Property tax is the most common source of income for school districts. Typically, a tax is levied on property such as land and buildings owned by individuals and businesses. A property tax is generally determined on the basis of a percentage of the true market value of each piece of property assessed. These assessments are rarely accurate since local assessors either over- or underassess the value of the property. Typically, the assessed value of the property is adjusted to an agreed-upon percentage of the market value when it is sold (Brimley et al., 2015).

Property taxation remains a largely complicated and particularly controversial source of local income for school districts because numerous complexities are associated with the assessment process. Homestead exemptions, tax abatements, legal entanglements, taxpayer associations, and underassessments of property all serve to erode the true tax base for individual school districts. However, property taxation continues to be the most stable income base as well as a dependable source of income for school districts.

Another form of taxation that serves as a revenue source for many school districts is the sales tax, which is quite popular in many states. This tax is assessed on the price of a good or service when it is purchased by a consumer. The seller of the merchandise or service collects the sales tax dollars, which are included in the purchase price, and transfers the amount of the sales tax to the state comptroller offices. Since this tax is based on sales, its yield is quite elastic. As a result, a sales tax as a form of revenue for school districts is only as stable as the economy.

Some school districts acquire their local source of income from a state income tax that is levied on corporations and/or individuals. Income taxation is the most widely accepted form of taxation for schools, and it is considered the most equitable of any source of taxation. Over the years, several states have initiated income taxation as a source of funding education. In a majority of states, the taxing of income is considered the most appropriate mechanism for property tax relief. In addition, income taxation provides a high revenue yield and creates minimal social and economic disruption (Brimley et al., 2015).

Very few school districts derive income from sumptuary taxes on items such as tobacco, alcohol, and gambling. This type of taxation is somewhat different than income and property taxes because it is based on "sin" sales. Due to this dependency, the tax yield is quite elastic and thus, it—much like a sales tax—is only as stable as the economy. Also, the tobacco and alcohol industries extensively lobby state legislators, and, as a result, this type of taxation has not necessarily served as a viable taxing alternative (Owings & Kaplan, 2013).

Another source of educational revenue can be dollars received from a lottery—an assessment on legalized gambling. Many individuals believe that the proceeds from a state lottery system provide great sums of income for education. Nothing is further from the truth. This argument has been used for years by proponents of the legalization of state lotteries. The individuals most susceptible to the promises of a lottery are those in the lower income bracket, which further makes the proceeds from this form of state income regressive (Brimley et al., 2015). There is no evidence that any state lottery has significantly supported or benefited any school district or, for that matter, public education in general (Brady & Pijanowski, 2007; Jones & Amalfitano, 1994; Strauss, 2012). Other studies conducted by Garrett (2001) and Erekson, DeShano, Platt, and Zeigert (2002) found that increased lottery revenues failed to provide any discernible increase in public school funding and, moreover, revealed that as lottery revenues increase, less state funding is appropriated to public schools. In Texas, for example, the lottery was sold to the public, as in most states, as a voluntary tax that would fund public education. Just the opposite has been the case. In 1996, the Texas lottery proceeds paid for about two weeks of schooling. By 2010, the proceeds paid for about three days (Strauss, 2012). Today, chances are, the proceeds pay for even less. Richard S. "Kinky" Friedman, American Texas country singer, songwriter, novelist, humorist, and politician, has said of the Texas lottery:

> It's a shell game, instead of facing issues directly . . . for example, to pay for education, legalized gambling will produce $6 billion to $8 billion a year. That's why you see this Texas campaign from the lottery that claims the money goes to education. Why the campaign? Because every Texan knows it's a lie. (Negron, 2006)

Now that we have explored several of the possible sources of income for school districts, it becomes apparent that wherever the funding is derived, allocations to individual schools at the district level are made, and thus school leaders have as one of their many responsibilities the task of developing a budget. Developing a school budget can be an arduous undertaking, but it can be completed with some sense of ease and satisfaction when a school leader is able to utilize specific steps or methods to collaboratively, effectively, and efficiently plan for a successful school budget.

Ten Steps to Budgeting Success

There are 10 important steps to successful budgeting. These steps are identified below with brief descriptors explaining why each step is critical to a school leader's success in developing, implementing, and evaluating a budget.

1. Determine the Allotment

Before deciding what educationally related expenditures to make, it is important to know the specified funding allotment that has been appropriated within each budgetary category. Furthermore, certain budgetary allotments can only be used for a variety of specified services and expenditures at the school level. As a result, some funds are more restrictive than others. These restricted funds are often associated with

Title I, bilingual education, and special education dollars and programs, for example. Restricted funds are further examined in Chapter 6.

2. Identify Fixed Expenditures

Recognize and note those expenditures that do not vary from year to year. Set aside the necessary funds in the amount of the fixed expenditures before building the school budget.

3. Involve All Stakeholders

Whether at school or home, everyone should be involved in the budgetary decision-making process. By involving as many stakeholders as possible, a school leader can more effectively ensure ultimate buy-in as related to the school budget and funded programs and initiatives. Stakeholders include, for example, faculty and staff, parents, students, community members, and any other interested individuals. When all stakeholders are provided with the opportunity for input, with their particular issues being given noteworthy consideration, buy-in is more likely and any plans, preparations, or budgetary considerations are less susceptible to interference or possible sabotage by a disgruntled member of the learning community. The collaborative involvement process as related to stakeholders is examined in Chapter 6.

The Principal's Guide to Managing School Personnel (Sorenson & Goldsmith, 2009) is an effective source and reliable desk reference for practicing or prospective school leaders who desire to learn more about collaboratively working with school personnel. While each of the eight chapters within this text serves as an excellent guide for school principals when interacting with campus personnel, Chapter 3 "Personnel and the Principal" (pp. 47–68), Chapter 4 "Personnel and Communication" (pp. 69–84), and Chapter 5 "Personnel and Conflict Resolution" (pp. 85–101) provide essential guidance, necessary information, and an examination of human resource skills critical to the successful principal–personnel relationship.

4. Identify Potential Expenditures

The effective school leader reviews past budgetary records to better identify and predict future expenditures. Knowing which expenditures are necessary and imperative will help faculty and staff avoid making impulsive purchases.

5. Cut Back

Most newly created school budgets are overbudgeted. A school leader is responsible for examining all potential expenditures and must determine where cutbacks can occur. Remember, cutting back too severely can build discontent among faculty. School budgets that are continually out of balance lead to greater fiscal sacrifices and may very well lead to a financial point of no return. Cut back as necessary and be aware that budgeting is an exercise in self-discipline for all parties. A simple yet effective way to cut back involves implementing a thorough physical inventory. School administrators should do more than just go through the motions when completing a physical inventory. Such an inventory will identify areas where unnecessary purchases can be avoided. Consider the following: Why continue to purchase supplies such as dry-erase markers, staples, paperclips, and the like when these items can be found in abundance in a classroom or office closet or central warehouse?

While cutting back is important in the school business, the creative school administrator is always seeking windfalls. Additional funding sources are available to those administrators who are willing to put forth the time and effort to seek financial assistance. For example, one school in a property-poor district utilized the campus leaders, site-based team members, and the parent–teacher organization to canvas the community seeking Adopt-A-School partners. A partnership with a large retail corporation proved extremely successful. The school was able to acquire not only essential supplies and merchandise for student use and consumption, the corporation also provided funding for computers and other important resources that otherwise would not have been available to either students or staff. An excellent source for finding, raising, and attracting extra dollars for a school or school system is *Achieving Excellence in Fundraising* by Eugene Tempel, Timothy Seiler, and Eva Aldrich (2015).

6. Avoid Continued Debts

The effective budget manager knows exactly what funds are out of balance and where debt is or has accumulated. Many school leaders fail to list and total their debts during the course of the fiscal year and thus wait until the end of the school year to make necessary budget revisions to amend for such shortsighted calculations. This is a poor practice. Most states and school districts do not allow individual school sites to acquire debts on a monthly or annual basis. Such a policy is not only worthwhile but wise. Nevertheless, debt reduction is readily achieved by avoiding unnecessary purchases. Recall the old, wise advice that was shared with you and your spouse when first married: "Most unhappiness is caused by giving up what you want most for what you want at the moment!" Life as a school leader is stressful enough without further complicating matters by overspending at the expense of the school budget, if not the student population. Remember, the most important word to use as a school administrator, specifically in connection with the school budget, could be *no*—especially when it comes to unwise or inappropriate spending!

7. Develop a Plan

Any budget—school, home, or business—should be based on a plan. From a school perspective, an educationally centered action or improvement plan must be developed to target and prioritize instructional goals and objectives along with school programs and activities. In addition, a second plan of action (school budget plan) is designed to identify budgetary priorities, focusing on appropriations and expenditures. Furthermore, such a plan is designed to determine what programs and activities match the budgetary allotments for the school. Campus-improvement plan and budget-plan development are examined in Chapters 3, 5, and 6.

8. Set Goals and Manage Time Efficiently

Many would insist that "setting goals" should be first and foremost on any list of budgetary considerations. No argument here. However, it is important for the effective school leader to do all the preliminary work of determining what funding is available before planning to spend the fiscal resources. This process requires the school leader to appropriately manage time. Remember, the way we spend our time defines who we are. Moreover, setting goals (whether management or instructional) and efficiently managing time are two fundamental steps all self-disciplined administrators utilize. Setting goals is frequently the one step most are—unfortunately—inclined to skip. Managing time is one step that most allow to escape attention.

As the budgetary process is developed and established, it is imperative that deliberate thought be given to those two considerations as issues, demands, and dictates can simply overwhelm the school leader and the development and management of the school budget.

Involving all stakeholders is a most reliable and effective method of ensuring goals are identified and established. But remember, setting goals takes more than money; it takes time, effort, determination, and considerable thought and preparation. How does a school leader, working in collaboration with a learning community, set goals? Listed below are five essential considerations.

1. Establish priorities—ascertain what is instructionally important—and recognize that instructional leadership in this digital age requires the instructional leader to effectively and efficiently manage time.

2. Decide, in a timely manner, what can wait until later in the budget cycle or until the next school year.

3. Assess what is important today but will not be tomorrow.

4. Determine what priorities are timely and meaningful as compared to those that are mandated.

5. Submit various proposed budgets (by department, grade level, etc.) on a timely basis to the site-based committee that serves in part to determine if the allocated dollars within each budget correlate with the established goals of the school.

Finally, remember that goals can and will change. Therefore, as the school leader and budget manager, it is imperative that you, in collaboration with the school's decision-making team, regularly assess and evaluate each budgetary goal and make any necessary changes as the school year progresses.

9. Evaluate the Budget

After a plan has been developed, it must be put into action. Take time to meet at least once a month with the decision-making team to evaluate the budget process and to better determine if the established goals and the budgeted dollars are equitable and compatible.

Planned budgeting and goal evaluation go hand in hand. Always seek answers to the following questions:

1. Is the budget within the allotted limits, or do adjustments (transfers and amendments) need to be made on the basis of alternative needs or vision changes?

2. Is timely progress being made toward the established goals?

3. Are purchases coinciding with planned goals?

4. Has the budget process been successful when compared with the established plan and goals?

5. What improvements can be made in the future?

10. Abide by the Budget

Abiding by the budget means living by the budget. A school leader must set the example in all areas of instructional leadership for others to follow. This is most certainly true in relation to the school budget. "Time on task" is an old adage in our business, but nothing rings truer in terms of the school budget and the necessity for the instructional leader to monitor, evaluate, and abide by the budget and the accompanying action or improvement plan.

The Principal's Guide to Time Management: Instructional Leadership in the Digital Age (Sorenson et al., 2016) is a must-read for every practicing or aspiring administrator who wishes to take a fresh look at time management issues while maintaining a focus on the principles of effective instructional leadership and the applications of emerging technology. Important elements of the text include an examination of essential instructional leadership skills as well as technological and digital applications, all designed to enhance the school leadership role.

Final Thoughts

School leaders must invest the necessary time and energy to deal with appropriated funds as well as the learning community. Wise budgeting will bring a sense of accomplishment and even fulfillment—most notably when the instructional program improves and student achievement excels. However, before budgeting, plan. *Planning* is defined in this context as meaning the development of a vision, the establishment of goals, the determination of objectives, and the initiation of strategies for school implementation. This is critical if a leader expects a continuing effort to increase student achievement. Each of these planning indicators is an essential element in the development of an effective budget using an integrated and collaborative approach to budgeting. Remember, failing to plan is nothing more than planning to fail!

A budget is not a once-a-year event, something developed and never examined again. A budget must be abided by, reviewed, and amended on a regular basis as the needs of its academic counterpart change. This requires ongoing evaluation and revision. Nothing in life is perfect, and the same holds true for school budgets. Academic goals—while imperative to the budgeting process—must, from time to time, be reorganized and adjusted. Action planning and goal development, academic improvement, and budget management must be integrated if school leaders intend to bring about educational excellence and increased student achievement. Certain standards as analyzed in Chapter 1 must be emphasized and incorporated by the school leader if the budgeting process is to meet with success. Abide by the budget, implement necessary changes, and always follow up with ongoing evaluation. Allow self-discipline, trustworthiness, transparency, integrity, and collaboration to be guiding factors in budgetary decision making. Finally, remember: An integrated budget and academic action plan will not work unless you do!

Discussion Questions

1. Consider each of the local sources of income that support school districts. What are the advantages and disadvantages of each in relation to equity, yield, and taxpayer acceptance?

(Continued)

(Continued)

2. Why is it important to integrate the school budget and the academic or action plan? How can the budget and academic planning processes be integrated?

3. Which of the budgeting myths pose a more fundamental obstacle to the school administrator in relation to the development of a campus budget? Why?

4. What might be considered a serious risk factor a school administrator could face in relation to fiduciary receipts?

5. What are the commonalities and differences of the three federal sources of district income?

6. Should any one of the 10 steps to budgeting success be considered more important than the others? Which one and why?

7. To better understand the percentage of revenues, as exemplified in Figure 4.1a, contact the official state education website (conduct a Google search or utilize your favorite search engine) as well as the school business administrator or superintendent of schools to determine the sources of income for the school district.

Case Study Application #1: Paper and the Copier

The application of a case study or case studies is presented at the conclusion of each chapter to provide applicable and relevant workplace scenarios so the reader can apply, in a practical manner, the knowledge acquired through textual readings.

Dr. Kate Bradley, principal at Homer Bedlow School, sat thinking to herself: "It all started during the Great Recession and it has yet to stop!" Then Kate mused out loud, "What's with this stinkin' thinkin'? It doesn't solve the problem, does it, Kate?" Principal Bradley pushed her chair back from the desk that late September afternoon, stood up, and walked over to her secretary's office. Kate asked her secretary and budget clerk, Jo Carson, to print out current enrollment figures as well as a current budget report. The school secretary did so, handed the reports to Dr. Bradley, and watched her walk down the hallway back to her office. The school secretary knew exactly what was taking a toll on Principal Bradley this day, something no principal really wants to address—budgetary cuts in paper and photocopier usage!

Here's how it all began. With a continual decline in student enrollment because of population shifts, along with an ever-eroding tax base and a state legislature playing politics with public school finance and funding, the results were to be expected: Deep budget cuts in the amount of $40,650! Principal Bradley had already trimmed all nonessential expenditures. What she had failed to cut were the two items teachers scream most about—"Don't take away my paper supply or my use of the copy machine!" Dr. Bradley thought to herself, "This is a catch-22 proposition!"

Dr. Bradley examined the budget report and noted the following:

Budget Code	Description	Allocation	Expended	Total
199-11-6269.00-102-FY-11	Rentals/Operating Leases—Copier	$14,580.00	$1,620.00	$12,960.00
199-11-6399.00-102-FY-11	General Supplies—Paper	$46,170.00	$5,130.00	$41,040.00

Remember, *allocation* relates to the dollar amount allotted at the beginning of the budget cycle, *expended* to the dollar amount spent to date, and *total* to the amount remaining to consume until the conclusion of the budget cycle.

Application Questions

1. Examine the abbreviated budget report above. Think deeply and place yourself in the shoes of Dr. Kate Bradley. How would you handle this catch-22 proposition? Budget cuts are required. What's a principal to do? Here are some options worthy of exploration:

   _____ Negate any budgetary cuts in paper or copier expenditures.

   _____ Cut funds to one or the other (paper or copier).

   _____ Cut funds in other areas. Which other areas?

   _____ Make minor cuts to paper usage and install a smaller, less expensive copier.

   _____ Take a position at the district office and be rid of all this headache.

   _____ Collaboratively develop a paper and copier use policy to cut costs and distribute the new regulation for campuswide implementation.

   (Continued)

(Continued)

_____ Place staff in charge of constantly monitoring paper and copier usage, looking for instances of waste.

_____ Recognize that you are the one who has been hired to make these kinds of budgetary decisions. Isn't that what you're being paid for?

_____ Work with team to implement an appropriate budget and campus action plan that affords hope and proper cuts in budget funds and creates a win–win for all parties. How?

_____ Other idea(s)?

Relate your answer(s) to the ten steps to budgeting success as noted within this chapter and to the Professional Standards for Educational Leaders (PSEL) identified in Chapter 1. Which one or more of the ten steps and the PSEL apply? Explain.

Case Study Application #2: Fiscal Issues and the New Principal

Part I: "Boy, Do I Have a Lot to Learn!"

Dr. Ryan Paulson, new principal at Mountain View School, arrived at Vista Ridge Independent School District from a neighboring state. While Dr. Paulson certainly recognized and understood certain aspects of the fiscal and budgetary processes in his former state, he realized he needed a refresher course in budgeting, especially as it related to the fiscal issues he might face in his new state and school district.

Dr. Paulson decided to stop by the administrative offices of Vista Ridge Independent School District and visit with the superintendent, Dr. Mildred Dunn, as well as the associate superintendent for school finance, Dr. Gene Corley. Certainly, these two individuals could bring him up to speed on the fiscal expectations of his new state and school district. As good fortune would have it, the first two individuals he encountered as he stepped into the main offices were Dr. Dunn and Dr. Corley. Dr. Corley, a most gregarious individual, was the first to see the new principal and hollered out at him, "Hey, hotshot, did you get to eat some of that good barbeque I told you about?" Dr. Paulson responded he had not yet had the opportunity, but he was looking forward to getting over to Elginton for a tasty plate of sausage and ribs. Dr. Dunn then spoke up and asked what was on the young man's mind.

"Well, since you've inquired," replied Dr. Paulson, "I need some guidance about the state's fiscal policies and the district's budgeting practices."

Dr. Dunn suggested that all three step into Dr. Corley's office for, as she put it, "a quick review of School Budgeting 101."

"School budgeting and finance, in this era of accountability, change, conservative funding, and fiscal restraint, can be a real juggling act," noted Dr. Dunn. "However, let's start with the basics and get you on the right track before school starts." Thus began an afternoon of one learning experience after another. By the conclusion of the meeting, Dr. Paulson had come to realize that costly political wars, an economy that had been hit hard by the Great Recession, and federal and state accountability standards, mandates, and funding cuts, as well as numerous other conditions, had negatively influenced the ability of both the state and local districts to raise tax revenues to meet the demands of educating today's students. These challenges most notably and negatively reflected on each school's list of priorities and each district's ability to finance them.

The bottom line of the first meeting among the three parties revolved around the realization that education must be viewed as an investment in human capital. Resource allocations to public schools are the responsibility not only of the federal and state governments but of the local school district. Moreover, funding the rapidly increasing costs of education is an ongoing challenge for schools, and such funding is becoming more frequently associated with accountability expectations and standards at all levels—local, state, and federal.

A most interesting point made by Dr. Dunn related to the proposition that educational services and funding must be provided with equality, but could they be provided equitably?

"Wow," thought Dr. Paulson to himself. "Does anyone have an answer to that question?"

Furthermore, Dr. Paulson recognized that even though the cost of education continues to increase annually, this burden is eased when one realizes that while the cost of public schooling involves money, mostly in salaries, much of the cost is readily returned to the marketplace, thus benefiting the economy, consumers, local households, individual citizens, and, most importantly, local students. This meeting reminded Dr. Paulson of a fact that had been drilled into his head by a former professor in his principal certification program at Union State University: "While the cost of education may be high, the defining and measuring result must always be quality in learning."

Finally, Dr. Paulson had been directed to the state's website regarding operating accounting codes and structures. It was essential that he quickly learn the proper budgetary coding procedures as dictated by the state's education agency. He had already memorized the website address and was now ready to adapt to the new coding structure and fiscal practices associated with his new school system and campus budget. As he left the district's administrative offices, he could not help but think, "Boy, do I have a lot to learn!"

Application Questions

1. What is meant by the following terms: *adequacy, equality, equitable, human capital, quality?*

2. How is the theoretical concept "education must be viewed as an investment in human capital" realized in your community? Provide concrete examples.

3. Can educational services and funding be provided with equality and equity? Support your answer.

4. What is meant by the quote, "While the cost of education may be high, the defining and measuring result must always be quality in learning"? How does this proposition relate to the concept of vision development?

Part II: "Well, It's My Money!"

Dr. Ryan Paulson, now into his second semester as principal at Mountain View School, had just developed—in collaboration with his site-based decision-making team—the campus budget for the next school year. He had learned much since that initial meeting with Dr. Dunn and Dr. Corley the preceding July, but, as is always the case, much more was yet to be realized. The budget for Mountain View School included funds to retain three special education aides who assisted with the support facilitation program. These aides worked with special-needs students who warranted considerable assistance and who required significant support and class time to complete the assigned academic tasks.

When the budget was submitted to Olga Bitters—the associate superintendent for instruction—for approval, she cut the aide positions and transferred the funds to the appropriate account for the purchasing of active-learning technological tools for students in the gifted and talented program. Such tools included portable e-devices, robotic telepresence technologies for virtual learning, virtual reality headsets and smartphones, and droids with app-enabled wrist bands. These state-of-the-art e-tools were part of a digital educational promise program for students to learn about technology product design and filmmaking through digital activities, projects, and challenges. Dr. Paulson realized the importance of purchasing these items for students, and he understood the importance of superior technology in the hands of the gifted and talented students. However, he thought the school district should fund such items for *all* students, not simply one subpopulation of students. He further believed that the functioning of the special-needs students in the support facilitation program would suffer by the budgetary reduction of the three special education aide positions. He was quite irritated by the recent turn of budgetary events, and he knew he must address the situation, and soon. Additionally, he thought to himself, "Well, it's my money and I should be able to spend it how I please!"

Application Questions

1. Regarding his concerns about the transfer of funds as made by the associate superintendent of instruction, how should Dr. Paulson address this budgetary issue and decision-making consideration? How is this particular issue related to a trio of concepts: integrity, fairness, and ethics?

2. What are the potential implications as related to the decision made by the associate superintendent in relation to the site-based decision-making team? To the school community?

3. Identify the possible repercussions as related to the special education department. What legal issues must be considered as related to the removal of the special education paraprofessionals as well as the maintenance of services to the students in light of Individual Education Plans (IEPs) and associated stipulations? Can funds that were originally designated for the special education paraprofessionals be transferred and used to purchase e-devices and other technological tools? If such action is legal, is it fair or ethical? Support your conclusions.

4. Immediately after the budget changes are made public, Dr. Paulson receives several telephone calls from the parents of a number of the students who were being served in the support facilitation program. These parents are disturbed about the effects on the learning environment in their children's classes as a result of the loss of the aides. How can Dr. Paulson best respond to these parents?

5. What did Dr. Paulson infer by stating, "Well, it's my money and I should be able to spend it how I please"? Could such a statement be justified in relation to the ten steps to budgeting success? Support your answer.

5

Effective, Efficient, and Essential Budgeting Practices

I find all this money a considerable burden!

—J. Paul Getty, American industrialist (Lazear, 1992, p. 342)

The Budget Plan

J. Paul Getty (1882–1976), at one time the world's richest private citizen, no doubt found his extensive personal wealth to be a "considerable burden," as he was married and divorced five times at great personal, professional, and financial expense. His monetary woes continued later into life as his 16-year-old grandson was kidnapped and held for ransom. J. Paul Getty refused to pay the ransom. Finally, after the kidnappers mutilated the grandson—his ear being delivered to a newspaper—J. Paul Getty decided to forfeit only a portion of the extorted demand—a maximum amount that was tax deductible. Getty then loaned the rest of the required extortion money to his son at 4% interest. The grandson was then released by the kidnappers but soon lapsed into permanent drug addiction, a consequence of the trauma he had suffered, which ultimately resulted in a stroke leaving him speechless, blind, and partially paralyzed for the remainder of his life. Now, that said, it is not our wish or our intention for the school budgeting process to be nearly as complicated or problematic or even traumatic for the educational leader! In fact, our greatest desire is for the school administrator, as the budget manager, to find the practice of school budgeting to be efficient, effective, and far less complicated than one might assume. With this thought in mind, let's turn to the first rule of school budgeting: The secret for successful budgeting is threefold: visionary demonstration, consistency in planning, and an interwoven relationship with school goals, objectives, and the school budget.

Theoretically, and most certainly appropriate in practice, the school academic action or improvement plan should be developed in tandem with the budget plan, which serves to identify the costs necessary to support the academic plan and instructional program. The budget plan is then converted into fund-oriented accounts (a school budget) as associated with the fiscal allotment provided to the school by the local district. The rationale for such planning makes sense because the obligation of any school administrator is to—first and foremost—plan for the specified needs of the students and not permit the available funds to dictate nor confine any aspect of a school's instructional program (Brimley, Verstegen, & Garfield, 2015). Unfortunately, and all too often, a lack of integrated budget and academic planning at the school or district level results in the selection and application of programs and services that are short sighted, insufficient, and ineffective in meeting the varied needs of the students served—resulting in wasted revenue and poor academic performance.

The purpose of the budget plan is to support the school's action or improvement plan and consolidate it into dollar appropriations. Basically, an action or improvement plan must be worth more than the paper it is written on if it is to be integrated with the budget plan. Table 5.1 specifies the necessary steps a school administrator and decision-making team should follow in relation to the budgetary process, which includes training, planning, and development.

The budget plan must be developed with the following questions in mind:

1. Prior to any budget planning and development process, has the school leader provided professional development

Table 5.1   The Budgetary Process—Training, Assessing, Prioritizing, Goal Setting, Objective Development, Monitoring, and Evaluation

1	2	3	4	5	6	7
Professional Development	Planning and Needs Assessment	Causal Barriers Identification	Prioritizing School-Based Needs	Goal Setting and Objective Development	Budget Development and Implementation	Budget Monitoring and Evaluation

8
◄ Have all stakeholders been actively engaged and involved? ►

The budgetary process, from training to planning to goal setting and objective development to actual budget implementation, is a constant course of action that requires a principal to engage the decision-making team in a collaborative and problem-solving effort.

This table illustrates how a principal can transform the budgetary process through a series of step-by-step essential elements that clarify the complexities associated with budget development, specifically as correlated with goal alignment and attainment.

training that is essential to understanding how visioning and planning impact programmatic considerations and the school budget?

2. Has a needs assessment been conducted to address what impact programmatic initiatives—federal, state, and local—have on student achievement? Levin (2011) suggests that school leaders want to know which particular interventions are most promising for increasing student achievement and cost the least, because monetary resources are often in short supply. In other words, it is essential to ensure the effectiveness of school resources by incorporating methods that will promote an age-old adage: *Get the biggest bang for the buck!* This is what a needs assessment is all about.

3. Have student needs and academic achievement been addressed in the form of a school action or improvement plan that emphasizes goal development?

4. Following the needs assessment and goal-development process, have specific instructional as well as nonacademic programs been identified for implementation, improvement, or exclusion?

5. Have learning community representatives been provided with forms and figures that are indicative of previous budgetary allotments and expenditures for at least one prior year, preferably three to five years?

6. Has the learning community (specifically the teaching staff) been asked by school administration to submit requests for supplies, equipment, and facilities that are essential, if not critical, in meeting the academic needs of the students and that are necessary in relation to the dictates imposed on the school or district academic programs by state and federal mandates?

7. Have budgeted dollars been allocated to support the action plan, and have the budget manager and team regularly and collaboratively monitored and evaluated budgetary expenditures in relation to programmatic effectiveness and student academic gains? This is more than a "wish list" approach to instruction and school budgeting—this is an integrated visionary process, through a needs-assessment process, that readily identifies priorities that are necessary for programmatic and student success.

8. Finally, have faculty, staff, students, parents, and community members been actively involved in the decision-making process leading to the development of the school action or improvement plan as well as the campus budget?

These eight components represent essential budgeting theory, which better serves to ensure that the ideas and recommendations of the learning community are actively sought and incorporated into budgeting practice via the budgetary process.

Analyzing the School Action and Budget Plans

The school action or improvement plan, as previously examined in Chapter 3, serves as the vehicle that drives not only the instructional program but also the budget development process. Effective budgetary planning must allow for the school budget to be based upon the educational programs designated within the confines of an action or improvement plan. In other words, funding should be allocated to the educational programs as identified in priority order in the school action or improvement plan. There are numerous aspects or designators often associated with an action plan. In the state of Texas, for example, there are 13 components to be addressed within an action plan, as mandated by the Texas Education Agency (2017b). These 13 designators are identified as (1) student performance, (2) special education, (3) violence prevention, (4) parental involvement, (5) professional development, (6) suicide prevention, (7) conflict resolution, (8) dyslexia treatment programs, (9) dropout reduction, (10) technology, (11) discipline management, (12) accelerated instruction, and (13) career education. While each of these components is mandated in one particular state, it is noteworthy to recognize that as a whole, they are quite representative of school planning issues that any state, district, or school might encounter.

Budget plans must be developed in tandem with an action or improvement plan. The budget plan serves effectively to (1) project all anticipated income, (2) identify all needed programs, and (3) project current and future average daily attendance or membership for the purpose of seeking a district allocation that will serve to meet the needs of all the students enrolled.

The purpose of the budget plan is to anticipate, project, and predict potential sources of income, program development, any financial deficit, and potential areas for budgetary reduction or additions. The development of the budget plan, much like that of the action plan, should be made in collaboration with a school's site-based decision-making team. This team, following the guidance of the school leader, is most often involved in decisions related to educational planning, curriculum development, instructional issues, staffing patterns, professional development, school organization, and, of course, budgeting.

Prior to developing the budget plan, the effective school administrator must insist on and ensure that a professional-development program has been initiated to train the learning community in the methods of generating and completing a needs assessment (see Table 5.2). A needs assessment and an information or quality analysis both effectively correlate with campus action or improvement planning procedures as well as budget development processes. When utilized appropriately, a needs-assessment instrument and a quality analysis can do exactly what their names imply. Furthermore, each—working in tandem—can be the essential impetus for prioritizing school-based needs with the following caveat: Students and the academic program are always in the forefront of any budgetary consideration.

Performing an Information Analysis

An information analysis, sometimes identified as a *quality analysis*, is a thorough examination of a campus action or improvement plan with implications associated with the campus budget–development process. Information analysis is a four-step process whereby certain campus underlying or problematic factors can be identified via a three-point assessment:

1. Establish performance objectives.

2. Conduct a needs assessment.

3. Scrutinize an instructional problem (Sorenson & Cortez, 2010).

Information analysis must focus on a review and analysis of data, followed by the implementation of best-practice strategies. This is a principal-oriented and practice-based method of data scrutiny that guides a school leader and team in determining the problems or factors that are contributing to low student performance in particular subject areas for specific student populations (Sorenson, Goldsmith, Méndez, & Maxwell, 2011). Information analysis requires a principal, prior to developing a school budget, to seek "soft" or qualitative data and "hard" or quantitative data. Such data come from inside and outside the school or district. Consider the "What's a Principal to Do?" and the "Technology in Schools Today" scenarios, and reflect upon the four-step information analysis that follows as a means of determining how to solve an issue or problem.

WHAT'S A PRINCIPAL TO DO?

Whitten Van Horn is principal at Broadway School. He has a problem at school. A significant percentage of the students at Broadway School are struggling academically. Some are failing multiple classes. These students are English language learners (ELLs), and many are unable to read with comprehension or write in the English language with clarity. The ELL students are testing as English learners and are barely passing the English state accountability exam. These students, however, have received passing grades in previous years. The ELL students seem bored, are often disengaged, and, based on their behaviors, are uninterested in school. Principal Van Horn, thinking to himself, is reminded of a lyric from the Johnny Cash/Bob Dylan song, "Wanted Man" (Columbia Records, 1969): *"I've had all that I wanted of a lot of things I've had, and a lot more than I needed of some things that turned out bad."* He then mused, "What's a principal to do?"

Pause and Consider

- What is Principal Van Horn to do relative to the scenario presented? Need a helpful hint? See the following two sections—"Steps to Performing an Information Analysis" and "Conducting a Needs Assessment."

- Principals will all too often think of "things that turned out bad." Investing properly in students and their achievement is a good thing that prevents things from turning out bad. What would you do, if you were Principal Van Horn, from a funding perspective? In other words, what program(s), initiative(s), and/or personnel would you invest budgetary dollars in to better ensure the academic success of the students noted in this scenario?

Now, read, pause, and consider, this next scenario.

Technology in Schools Today!

Budgeting funds for technology continues to increase to the point that half of the nation's school systems will maintain last year's technology budget increases. Approximately 46% of school systems expect to increase their technology funding and spending this next school year. Here's an illustrative story.

Rita Sheridan had read, and moreover consumed, the empirically based research regarding technology in schools. As principal at Warner Pope School, Rita understood what the research stipulated—most notably from a budgetary perspective:

1. Principals must make every effort to expand technology in schools to keep up with workforce demands.

2. Insufficient numbers of students are engaged in high-quality, digitally oriented coursework.

3. Principals must lead curriculum reform efforts to better ensure more digital instruction and permit technology coursework to count as either a math or science requirement.

4. School systems must increase the number of qualified technology teachers.

5. Technology coursework in schools most underrepresents female and minority students.

6. Instructional models must use technology in early literacy learning.

(*Continued*)

(Continued)

7. Seven in ten students surveyed stipulate that campus technology needs a major overhaul.

8. Teachers are failing to keep up with mobile devices as instructional tools in schools.

9. Technologically reconfigured, redesigned, and repurposed school facilities must be a norm.

10. Of the top 10 skills that need to be taught in schools to ensure that students are hired in the real world, nine of those skills are technology-related/digitally based.

What Principal Sheridan did not understand was how to make the empirical research a budgetary and instructional reality in her school. A principal colleague from a neighboring school district had recently shared with Rita a process of analyzing a school's action or improvement plan, performing an information analysis, and conducting a needs assessment. These procedures could very well aid Principal Sheridan and her team in developing a strong technology-oriented, digitally focused school.

Pause and Consider

- How can Principal Rita Sheridan and the team at Warner Pope School incorporate the following sections ("Steps to Performing an Information Analysis," "Conducting a Needs Assessment") and utilize Table 5.3 to ensure a stronger technologically centered instructional program?
- Principal Sheridan recognizes that her campus budget is limited relative to increased funding for technological reforms and enhancements. What can she and her team do to find additional, if not essential, funding sources? (Hint: Read "Generated Income Sources," p. 168). Be specific in your answer.
- According to "Accounting Procedures" (see p. 178), the number-one priority for Principal Sheridan and the funding of technological improvements is to "monitor all incoming funds and outgoing expenditures in relation to the attainment of the school's vision, goals, and objectives." If you were Principal Sheridan, by what means would you follow this accounting priority?

SOURCES: Devaney, 2016; Guernsey & Levine, 2016; Schaffhauser, 2016; Sorenson, Goldsmith, & DeMatthews, 2016; Stansbury, 2016.

Steps to Performing an Information Analysis

Step 1: Qualitative or Soft/Outside Data and Information

Principals and site-based decision-making teams must examine "soft/outside" data sources by

- reviewing the research literature;
- enlisting the support of district and professional facilitators who understand the problem at hand;
- consulting educational research laboratories;
- determining which best practices, when implemented, will solve the instructional problem;
- providing teachers with release time to participate in essential and relatable professional development; and
- permitting teachers the opportunity to make site visits to schools (local and distant) that are effectively implementing the required best practices.

Step 2: Quantitative or Hard/Outside Data and Information

Principals and site-based decision-making teams must examine "hard/outside" data sources by deriving information from state and federal agencies in the form of statutes and reports, to include

- the State Education Agency codes, statutes, or official rulings;
- the United States Department of Education regulations;
- the Office of Civil Rights directives;
- Every Student Succeeds Act (ESSA);
- academic performance reports or other state education agency assessment reports; and
- Individuals with Disabilities Education Improvement Act (IDEIA) parameters.

Step 3: Qualitative or Soft/Inside Data and Information

Principals and site-based decision-making teams must examine "soft/inside" data sources by

- analyzing survey results;
- initiating focus groups and gathering relevant information;
- conducting interviews of teachers, parents, and students;
- initiating observations of effective teaching practices;
- surveying organizational climate and culture;

- examining student profiles;
- seeking teacher opinions; and
- conducting brainstorming sessions with members of the learning community.

Step 4: Quantitative or Hard/Inside Data and Information

Principals and site-based decision-making teams must examine "hard/inside" data sources by reviewing records, such as

- student academic records (to include cumulative folders),
- state assessment and accountability records,
  - Fiscal Education and Information Management System (FEIMS) records,
- school board policies,
- administrative regulations and procedures,
- school district attorney opinions,
- attendance records of school meetings, and
- classroom assessments and other benchmarking reports.

Conducting a Needs Assessment

A needs assessment must be initiated relative to the development of a campus action or improvement plan and the development of a school budget (see Table 5.2 and Table 5.3, pp. 169 and 171, respectively) for programmatic and student success to occur. Such an assessment requires a principal and team to ultimately prioritize school needs to positively impact the instructional program. To do so, the authors of this text—as former principals—strongly recommend four essential phases be addressed in the assessment process. These phases are addressed in Table 5.2.

Generated Income Sources

"If you can conceive it, you can achieve it!" Do you recall this old adage? School leaders are designated many responsibilities, the budgetary process being obviously one and, as a result, are often called upon to put such adages to work. The effective school administrator quickly learns to generate additional sources of income for the school beyond those funds already allocated by district administration. The district allocation is just one of numerous income sources that must be generated if a school is to establish a comprehensive, high-quality, and cost-effective program.

Table 5.2   Conducting a Needs Assessment

Phase	Work to Accomplish
I. Initiating the inquiry process 1. What needs improvement? 2. Why is improvement needed? 3. What data support the need to improve? 4. Do additional data need to be gathered to support areas in need of improvement?	1. Review the district's and school's mission or visionary statement to determine if the campus vision meets the written vision as well as the district's vision. 2. Analyze the current campus action or improvement plan. 3. Identify sources of data such as previously conducted studies and district and statewide test results, along with teacher, student, and parent surveys. 4. Identify other needed sources of data that may not be readily available, such as a longitudinal analysis of state and district indicator systems reports. This is a relevant approach to identifying instructional area(s) in need of improvement. Then determine what methods or procedures are needed to collect any particular data.
II. Deriving consensus 1. Can consensus or agreement be reached regarding the needs or problems that must be addressed? 2. Does the needs assessment process find areas that are important to bringing about organizational change and improvement? 3. Consider the following: Have the principal and site-based decision-making team overlooked any programmatic concerns, issues, or problems?	1. Review all pertinent sources of data in a transparent manner whereby all parties are collaboratively involved in the consensus-building process. Such a procedure better ensures buy-in within the site-based team and across the learning community. 2. Consider all instructional and curricular concerns, problems, and targeted needs that have been identified. 3. Arrive at a high level of consensus and then narrow down the list of needs. This is a priority-driven process.
III. Organizing and analyzing the data 1. What data need to be collected and why?	1. Following any analysis of data and an initial prioritization of perceived needs, the principal and team must discuss each area of concern, note problems, and then outline specific actions to be initiated. This particular phase is all about answering the question, "Why do we do this?"

(Continued)

Table 5.2   (Continued)

Phase	Work to Accomplish
2. From where will the data be collected? 3. What do the data reveal?	2. Principals must be prepared to share action or initiation proposals of data collection with members of the learning community. 3. Never avoid or ignore initiating a careful review of the research literature. Do not consider, and never implement, any organizational initiative that cannot be validated in the research literature or by empirical studies.
IV. Focusing on priorities 1. What is the greatest priority? The second greatest? The third greatest, and so on? 2. Priorities must be determined in accordance to the following criteria: What human, fiscal, and/ or material resources (including release time) are required? Are internal or external (or both) levels of expertise available and/or required? By what means will the priorities be addressed, solved, and/ or resolved? 3. Is there a sound research base in the professional literature for addressing each prioritized concern/ problem/need and for supporting the proposed actions and/or implementations?	1. Conduct a full examination of instructional priorities and hold open, collaborative, and transparent discussions with the site-based decision-making team. These discussions must address each priority consideration proposed. 2. Present team-determined recommendations to the district administrative leader (superintendent or designee) along with the priority rankings of each identified need. 3. Most importantly—work together as a team in a most transparent and collaborative manner, reaching a fair and equitable consensus. Always remember: Students come first and foremost!

SOURCES: Sorenson et al. (2011), Tanner & Tanner (2006).

Brimley et al. (2015), U.S. Census Bureau (2016), and Leachman, Albares, Masterson, and Wallace (2016) report that tax limitation efforts in many states, along with funding reduction at federal and state levels (all too frequently the result of political gamesmanship), continue to threaten or reduce local revenue. As a result, school

Table 5.3   A Step-by-Step Guide to Effective, Efficient, and Essential
            Funding

1. Examine!   The 13 Components   +

   Determine which of the 13 components are not a basic part of the
   campus action or improvement plan (see pp. 162–163).

2. Identify!   The 25 Data Sources   +

   Ascertain which of the data sources will be required to be analyzed as
   a beginning point in the needs assessment process (see pp. 89–91).

3. Review!   The Campus Action or Improvement Plan   +

   Pinpoint instructional gaps, holes, missing goals, objectives, and/
   or actions that must be addressed and resolved when analyzing the
   campus action or improvement plan (see pp. 162–163; pp. 227–228).

4. Conduct!   A Campus Instructional Needs Assessment   +

   Perform an assessment examining all state- and/or district-
   mandated curricular components and data sources to determine what
   instructional needs must be addressed (see pp. 169–170; 229).

5. Prioritize!   The Campus Instructional Needs   =

   Rank the campus instructional needs in order of most significance to
   best improve student achievement (see pp. 170; 229–230).

6. Effective, Efficient, and Essential Funding!

officials must increasingly seek nontraditional sources of funding for
schools. Such nontraditional income sources include grants from governmental entities and private foundations and gifts from business
(Adopt-A-School) partnerships, individuals within the community,
and various corporations that are most interested in maintaining their
commitment to education and to educational organizations. Income
from many of these sources can be generated locally when a school
administrator and team actively seek to make contact with potential
contributors.

Grants

Grants often provide an additional source of income for schools
but are typically obtained on a competitive basis. This practice
becomes even more intense and competitive during periods of fiscal conservatism. Grant funds are generally tied to a Request for
Application (RFA) process whereby a great deal of time and effort,
not to mention tedious research and data collection, must occur for
an application to be seriously considered. Most grants are categorical in nature, as noted in Chapter 4. As a reminder, *categorical* refers

to funds that are restricted to certain categories or activities, such as technology, science, mathematics, or accelerated instruction. These funds can only be utilized within the particular category in which they were awarded and must further be monitored and accounted for by the local school and district. Just as important, the instructional program funded must be frequently evaluated, often by outside sources (evaluators) or agencies, to ensure that the grant dollars are appropriately allotted, utilized, and expended. Listed below are a number of important attributes associated with grant funding.

- Grants are generally time sensitive—funded dollars must be appropriated and spent within a specific period of time.
- Grants are generally available from state or federal agencies and are often related to certain educational acts or initiatives.
- Grants and funding information can be identified and located by accessing governmental, commercial, nonprofit, and educational organization websites or home pages. Six resources for educators seeking grant funding are
  - *The Grantwriter's Internet Companion: A Resource for Educators and Others Seeking Grants and Funding* by S. L. Peterson (2001);
  - *Simplified Grantwriting* by Mary Ann Burke (2002);
  - *The First-Time Grantwriter's Guide to Success* by Cynthia Knowles (2002);
  - *Finding Funding: Grant Writing From Start to Finish, Including Project Management and Internet Use* by E. W. Brewer and C. M. Achilles (2008);
  - *Show Me the Money: Tips and Resources for Successful Grant Writing* by L. Starr (2008); and
  - *Writing Proposals: A Handbook of What Makes Your Project Right for Funding* by E. B. Zane (2016).
- Grants are generally restrictive—"in-kind" funds, for example, may be required whereby the funding agency expects the school or district to match the granted allotment with either dollars or services—transportation, custodial, equipment, or facilities usage are typical examples. Often the granted funds are further restricted and may not be used for furniture or travel or, in some cases, salaries. Such restrictions must be adhered to or a school or district risks losing the grant and thus the badly needed dollars.

An example of grant funding is the National Professional Development Program grant (https://ed.gov/programs/nfdp/index.html). This grant provides funding to ensure school personnel are well prepared to provide services to ELL students.

Finally, one of the best sources for locating grant funding is the internet. The internet provides numerous sites containing excellent information regarding grants. Such information ranges from daily announcements to useful statistics to tips and techniques for writing grants to current programs that are funded by grant dollars. Brewer and Achilles (2008) identify "101 Hot Sites for Grantwriters" (p. 108), several of which are listed below. The following internet sites and their corresponding URLs could very well provide the school leader and team with the funding necessary to initiate a program or programs that could impact student success and achievement. Review this "baker's dozen" listing and bookmark your favorite site(s). A tidbit of advice for the grant seeker: The sites identified and recommended often undergo changes and, as a result, the term "under construction" can very well indicate that a particular site may not be available. If so, move on to another site and source and, as always, best of luck in your search for additional school funds!

1. National Science Foundation—https://www.nsf.gov/funding/education.jsp? fund type=4

This is an excellent site for grant writers interested in science and mathematics funding.

2. Apply for a Grant—https://www2.ed.gov/fund/grants-apply.html? src=pn

3. U.S. Department of Education Grants for Teachers—https://www.ed.gov/category/subject/grants

Bookmark Sites 2 and 3, as noted above, if you are a novice grant writer seeking direct information to education grants.

4. Foundation Center—http://foundationcenter.org/

This site links grant writers to private foundations and corporations that provide funding. Additionally, as a service of the Foundation Center, Grantspace.org provides easy-to-use self-service tools and resources to help school personnel become more viable grant applicants.

5. FedStats—https://fedstats.sites.usa.gov/

Statistics are provided by more than 70 federal agencies, and the site also includes a wealth of information for the grant seeker.

6. Fundsnet Services—http://www.fundsnetservices.com/

This website provides an extensive array of links to grants and fundraising resources.

The following grant-related websites are specific to STEM funding:

7. Grants and Related Resources—http://staff.lib.msu.edu/ harris23/grants/0fdncoll.htm#2

8. Bill and Melinda Gates Foundation: Grantseeker FAQ— http://k12education.gatesfoundation.org/grantseeker-faq/

9. Battelle STEM Grants Program—https://www.battelle.org/ battelle-stem/battelle-stem-grant-program?gclid= CPvo496mtNQCFYy2wAod_owLyg

10. Grant Wrangler—http://www.grantwrangler.com/stemres ources.html

11. STEMfinity—https://www.stemfinity.com/STEM-Education-Grants

12. U.S. Department of Education—https://www.ed.gov/stem

13. STEM Grants for Teachers—https://www2.ed.gov/fund/ grants-apply.html? src=p

Fundraising and Crowdfunding

Additional school site income is frequently generated through the fundraising efforts of school-sponsored groups such as parent–teacher organizations and booster clubs, to name a couple. Parental involvement is essential for most school fundraising efforts. Parent groups and organizations provide a wide range of valuable services and activities, both inside and outside the school. However, the role of parents and parent–teacher organizations are seldom specifically defined and, as a result, problems—especially in the fundraising arena—often arise. What we do know and appreciate as school leaders is the involvement of parents in schools that can result in support for obtaining additional resources. The importance of parent organizations most often relates to their desire to obtain quality services and resources for their schools. These efforts are typically reactive rather than proactive; thus, proper training and guidance from school leaders is essential to ensure that parental efforts do not become administrative burdens or problems.

Fundraising events typically involve the sale of merchandise ranging from consumable items (candy, cookies, pizzas, or Thanksgiving turkeys, for example) to nonperishable items such as Christmas gift wrap, T-shirts, raffles, candles, senior rings, yearbooks, school picture sales, and just about anything else the fertile mind can imagine.

Crowdfunding is an alternative method of raising dollars in schools and has gained expanded support and use in recent years. Funds are raised, typically via the internet, to enhance schools and classrooms in terms of supplies and materials but also for more creative work, such as startup funding for student films, music, innovative projects, student small business ventures, and even field trips. Several well-known, highly publicized, and incorporated crowdfunding websites include GoFundMe, Kickstarter, Crowdcube, and Indiegogo. While crowdfunding is praised in many circles for its ability to raise cash fast, there are also numerous pitfalls—especially for schools and educators. Listed below are six pros and six cons associated with crowdfunding.

The Pros:

1. Anyone can reach a global audience to raise funds and find financial success.

2. It's been proven to be a very successful method to test the feasibility of a school idea or classroom project in need of funding.

3. It provides an easy way to generate cash—and fast.

4. It eliminates gender stigma by frequently eliminating the glass ceiling for the good of a project.

5. Except for board policies and school regulations, there are no limits to what funds can be raised.

6. Success leads to more success. Investors typically are willing to fund school- and student-oriented projects.

The Cons:

1. It is lots of work, often with limited to no positive results (funding).

2. Crowdfunding platforms take a commission of funds raised.

3. A great deal of time and effort is necessary to ensure a successful funding campaign.

4. Other schools, and even entrepreneurs, can copy teacher or student ideas when they are not protected.

5. A lack of accountability (policies and regulations) by schools and districts can create bad actions combined with inadequate directions and poor decision making, which frequently promote serious problems to include but not limited to misappropriation of funds.

6. Prepare for excessive emails.

Fundraising and crowdfunding can generate significant income for a school, income above and beyond the standard district allocation. Fundraising and crowdfunding can also serve as monetary sources for purchasing items such as stage curtains, playground equipment, instructional supplies, and even air conditioning for the school gym. However, if fundraising and crowdfunding efforts are not properly planned and organized, schools can be faced with numerous financial pitfalls (Mutter & Parker, 2012). For example, fundraising and crowdfunding—while financially compelling and potentially rewarding—can quickly turn sour with lost, missing, or stolen merchandise and/or generated funds. This can publicly tarnish a school or embarrass an administrator in the eyes of the community, not to mention the district superintendent or school board.

To avoid such problems, the effective school leader must either carefully follow designated district policies and procedures or proactively establish guidelines and regulations that allow for the proper management of crowdfunding dollars and fundraising merchandise, the selection of merchandise vendors, the designated responsibilities of those individuals involved, and the necessary bookkeeping systems. Such policies, procedures, and/or guidelines must be in place to protect a school's generated income, potential profit, and reputation. By neglecting to do so, a school administrator is breaking one of the cardinal rules of school budgeting: safeguarding school interests through the responsible stewardship of public funds and setting and adhering to internal fiscal controls, both of which are best business practices necessary to protect school assets and personnel. Question: How does fundraising and crowdfunding relate to the Professional Standards for Educational Leaders (PSEL) as documented in Chapter 1? Remember to consider the PSEL as your read the remainder of this chapter!

Expenditure Accountability and Control

One of the most important aspects of the school budgetary process is the accounting for and control of school expenditures. While expenditure accountability and control vary from state to state and from district to district, three closely related factors must be followed with strict and complete propriety: appropriate visionary planning, careful budgeting, and effective expenditure of school funds. Each is crucial to ensuring that students benefit from a school's instructional program (Guthrie, Hart, Hack, & Candoli, 2007). District and school site expenditure accountability and control are aided by the use of a FEIMS, appropriate accounting procedures, campus activity income collection, deposit guidelines, timely payment of bills, and budget amendment practices. These factors will be examined, and further consideration will be given to how the interweaving combinations of all factors contribute to effective, efficient, and essential school budgeting.

Fiscal Education and Information Management System

The FEIMS is an accounting and auditing process that is implemented in most states to control school and district budgets by utilizing a classification or codified structure (Governmental Accounting Standards Board [GASB], 2016). School districts as well as state departments of education need easy access to information directly related to the resources required to provide a fiscal infrastructure to support student learning. This codified information and management system electronically links revenues and expenditures, for example, from school to district office to state departments of education through an accounting process that traces and audits funding, examines programmatic considerations, and even reviews student achievement and accountability standards as well as other important issues related to individual schools and districts. FEIMS can also detect material errors in the fiscal data of a school district and can further recognize and analyze the state-adopted fiscal accounting system that is required by state education code. Again, while certain aspects of a FEIMS may be utilized at local option, the overall structure is to be uniformly applied to all school districts in accordance with the Generally Accepted Accounting Principles (GAAP) as directed by the United States Department of Education and the GASB (2016) in an effort to monitor and control expenditure accountability.

Accounting Procedures

The responsibility for wisely spending school funds to provide for a high-quality education for each student is further challenged by the precept that school dollars must also be actively and accurately accounted for and protected. The term *accounting* can be readily described as the process by which the effectiveness, legality, quality, and efficiency of budgeting procedures must be measured by the documented stewardship of all public funds. While such a notion may have once been considered simply good business by schools and school districts, this same consideration, by today's budgetary standards, is a practical—if not essential—fiscal imperative.

Accounting procedures are defined as the *fiscal imperative* method of determining whether a school has provided a fiscally valued and educationally valuable service to its clientele by emphasizing that school accounting procedures must serve to do the following:

1. Monitor all incoming funds and outgoing expenditures in relation to the attainment of the school's vision, goals, and objectives.

2. Protect public dollars from any potential loss attributable to irresponsibility, wrongful utilization, theft, and/or embezzlement by any individual associated with the school or school district.

3. Provide for an assurance that public funds are being used to better ensure the academic achievement of each student.

4. Ensure that all legal requirements are followed implicitly.

5. Inform the general community of any and all facts and information regarding the fiscal solvency of the school site and district.

In an effort to meet these accountability standards, the GASB (2016) issued a statement that emphasizes that accountability is the paramount objective of any budgetary process and, as such, all fiscal accountability reports must include information that (a) compares actual financial results with the legally adopted budget; (b) assesses the financial condition of a school or system; (c) complies with finance-related laws, rules, and regulations; and (d) assists in evaluating the efficiency and effectiveness of a school's or district's fiscal budget and educational program.

Finally, the National Center for Education Statistics (2016d) identifies four standard accounting practices that guide schools and districts in their common goal of accounting for public funds in relation to the budgetary process:

1. Define and utilize account classifications and codes that provide meaningful financial management information.

2. Comply with the GAAP as established by the GASB.

3. Recognize and utilize accounting technology and safety and security procedures.

4. Comply with all state and federal laws and fiscal accountability reporting requirements.

By adopting and following these standards, school leaders allow for the continuous monitoring of expenditures as well as accountability and control of budgeting procedures—all of which are most definitely considered to be best practices for further ensuring that students are benefiting from school appropriations. Equally important, all school personnel are protected from any potential legal entanglements that are often associated with the mishandling of district dollars.

Collection and Deposit Structures

The school leader, as budget manager, quickly realizes that the basis for effective budgeting is not only the planning aspect of the budgetary process but also the proper accounting of revenue collected and deposited. Good budgeting must be based on a structure of collections and deposits that further establishes an accounting control mechanism to preclude any monetary mistakes and possible theft or embezzlement.

Such a structure is imperative, since most schools have activity accounts that are based on the collection of funds from school clubs, booster organizations, general fees, and numerous other dollar-generating initiatives.

The School Activity Account

The school activity account is one important area of the budgetary process in which sound financial practice must be exercised. Many administrators will confide that there are two problematic areas that can get a school leader in serious trouble: sex is one and money is the other, romance and finance—especially when an activity account is involved (Sorenson, 2007). The school activity account is one budgetary consideration that poses the most serious financial complications and implications. For example, the activity account at many schools (high schools in particular) can generate significant income from revenue sources such as fundraisers, crowdfunding, vending machines, school pictures, athletic receipts, library and textbook fines, student clubs and organizations, numerous student fees, school store operations, field trip receipts, and appropriated district funds; the list can go on and on.

In most states, thousands of dollars flow through a school's activity account. As a result, administrators have the primary fiscal responsibility of not only managing such a budget but also complying with federal and state laws and district policies and procedures (Brimley et al., 2015). School activity funds must be safeguarded, and prudent verification of all accounts within the activity fund must be monitored and audited for the purpose of ensuring such monies are appropriately utilized for student benefit.

FRAUD AND EMBEZZLEMENT: HOW THE MONEY VANISHES!

Go to a favorite search engine and type in "embezzlement and the school activity account" and chances are, you'll find more than 8.6 million results! Why? This particular act of fraud and theft at the school-site level is rampant across the United States today. Probably not in your state or school system, you think? Think again!

The authors selected the first ten postings as a sampling of where the most recent embezzlement of school activity accounts have occurred—Washington DC, New York, Florida, Texas, North Carolina, Wisconsin, California, Connecticut, Michigan, and Oklahoma. That's just ten of the fifty states. Is this type of criminal activity occurring in the remaining forty states? Absolutely! Why? And what will stop it? The *why* elicits a simple response: (1) There's opportunity, (2) financial pressure is a very common incentive, and (3) thieves can readily justify their stealing—even from students!

Consider the following real scenario, along with recommendations to stop the embezzlement of funds from school activity accounts, because yours just might be next!

There's No Right Way to Do Something Wrong!

The principal embezzled, from the school's activity accounts, more than $700,000 over a period of seven years. This amount was from the collected funds of students and parents, monies to be used to benefit students. The principal also robbed the students, faculty, administration, and parents and families of their self-worth and dignity by falsifying standardized test scores. The principal was ultimately charged with embezzlement of more than $750,000 in student activity account funds, four charges of fraud, and one account of conspiracy. When the judge's gavel fell, the principal had to pay back $500,000 of the $750,000 embezzled dollars and serve a 40-month sentence in federal prison—avoiding a 15-year maximum sentence! How did it all happen?

Patty Ann Landers was hired as a teacher by the Cleaver Consolidated School System in the month of June. By August, she was promoted to an assistant principal position. Within two years, she was a principal. Later, before her embezzlement escapades were discovered, Patty Ann was promoted to assistant superintendent.

Principal Landers was admired and respected. She worked diligently, yet unethically, to turn around a school where test scores were regularly low. She was actively involved in the community where she served as a school administrator, and she, her husband, and their adult children were pillars of honesty and decency in a local church. Principal Landers, using student funds, purchased expensive clothing for herself and her family, took her family and friends to vacations in the Caribbean, remodeled her home and that of one of her sons, and purchased at least two luxurious automobiles. Life was nice—really nice—especially on a principal's salary!

The nice life began to unravel right after Patty Ann Landers was promoted to assistant superintendent. An automatic board policy–mandated audit of the campus budget and funds occurred. Over the next few months, ex-principal Landers was investigated, arrested, and charged. Following a total of four years of court appearances, plea-bargaining, and verdicts, Patty Ann Landers was sentenced for the criminal acts she committed, all at the expense of the students she was charged to serve and protect.

Now, for the rest of the story: Prior to the U. S. Marshals Service taking Patty Ann into custody and transferring her to prison, she broke down and cried out, "My actions are nothing more than hurtful and shameful. I'm especially shamed that my mother, father, and my husband and family had to witness all of this." Next, her husband, Charles, cursed the media in an interview and then went on to divorce his wife of

(Continued)

(Continued)

40 years. Additionally, Patty Ann Landers was ordered to pay 25% of her retirement income to repay the $500,000 debt as part of a plea agreement. Tragically, the criminal efforts, investigations, and ultimate conviction of Patty Ann Landers led to criminal convictions of embezzlement for five other individuals who had worked for or with the ex-principal.

The Top-10 Embezzlement Preventions

1. Understand that lax control of the school activity account opens the door to embezzlement.

2. Recognize the warning signs:
   o Continued deficit balances
   o Corrective actions bringing no improvements
   o Lack of communication with the district business office
   o Lack of organization at the school site business office
   o Failed school leadership oversight

3. Create annual budgets that are monitored and reconciled by a group of people, especially the in-flow and out-flow of club (activity account) dollars.

4. Dictate that more than one person maintain the activity accounts, creating a division of duties that ensures separate and independent oversight.

5. Regularly rotate club officers responsible for financial control processes.

6. Require that all monies collected be immediately deposited.

7. Direct that a two-signature process be implemented relative to all written checks.

8. Stipulate that annual independent audits occur with all outside school-related clubs.

9. Ensure appropriate accounting and record-keeping procedures.

10. Demand that all individuals who touch school/student monies are bonded to prevent losses from embezzlement. Ensure that the school district purchases fidelity bond insurance: $1 million per occurrence and $2 million aggregate are common recommendations.

More detailed procedures and recommendations are noted in the "Accounting and Auditing Procedures" section of this chapter (see pp. 194–204). Remember: Be honest, think sincerely, and act with integrity!

School administrators must understand that the school activity account can quickly become a nightmare if appropriate bookkeeping practices are not in place, followed, and maintained. Funds collected from various school-related activities must be accounted for, as money received and spent, in relation to the different activity accounts in which said dollars have been allocated. For example, money collected from ticket sales related to the school athletic banquet must be placed in the athletic account; money collected from the sale of school pictures for the purpose of postal services must be placed in the postal account. Now, let's return to bookkeeping practices and the development of an income collection and deposit structure.

Components of the Collection and Deposit Structure

The purpose of any collection and deposit structure is to establish budgetary controls to prevent general accounting mistakes, blatant theft, and/or embezzlement of funds. This structure is composed of several components that identify key personnel who should be bonded prior to collecting, accounting for, and depositing funds. The term *bonded* relates to a legal process known as *surety bonding*, which is frequently defined as a guarantee of performance. In other words, a bonding agency will reimburse a school district for any financial loss related to fraud, theft, or embezzlement that might occur as a result of an individual who has been entrusted with the handling of funds (Brimley et al., 2015). Returning to the components of collection and deposit, a carefully crafted budgetary structure should include and ensure the following:

Cash receipts collections—When generated dollars, typically in small denominations, are brought into the school office by an activity sponsor, at least two bonded individuals should collect, count, and account for the funds. In this manner, the total amount of cash and checks submitted should accurately match the receipts presented and also match the amount listed on the receipt given to the sponsor.

Activity account postings—Following the cash receipts collection, the monetary amount should be counted and double counted, again by bonded personnel, and then entered into the bookkeeping system. If the system is electronic, a summary cash receipts report is automatically generated and provides the bookkeeping staff and school leader with a listing of the receipt entries, as designated by date, along with the dollar amount of said receipts and the specified activity account (athletics, school pictures, or library fund, for example) into which the collected receipts are to be entered.

Bank deposit procedures—Following any account posting, a bank deposit slip must be prepared immediately. Then, a third bonded individual (someone different than the two individuals who are collecting, accounting, and preparing the deposit slip) should be selected to place the funds in a deposit bag and promptly directed to make the bank deposit. Many school districts require two individuals take any deposits to the bank. Other districts contract the bank depositing process with an armored collection and transport service. While such procedures are not absolutely necessary, each is a wise practice. Proper bank depository procedures help ensure that the amount of money received totals the daily deposit. Furthermore, such procedures reduce the possibility of human error, theft, and/or embezzlement.

Bank reconciliation processes—The bank reconciliation process reveals much about the management of a school's budgetary practices. Proper reconciliation of bank statements and records is considered one of the most important fiscal safeguards available to a school leader. Bank reconciliation is nothing more than a check-and-balance system that ensures that the school's bank statement matches the data recorded in the school's financial records. This process, while tedious and time consuming, provides an opportunity for the school leader to identify differences that may exist between bank records and school records. This process goes beyond the trust factor to a method of verification by providing for a monthly analysis of the school's financial records. School leaders should be cognizant of the possibility that problems associated with the school's bank statement could very well signal financial problems elsewhere—in other school accounts, for example, or with the school's accounting procedures. Mutter and Parker (2012) have noted "repeated, irreconcilable differences between a bank statement and the school's books may indicate incompetence or fraud" (p. 17). Nothing could come closer to the truth, and every school leader must recognize that such possibilities can and do exist in schools, and, as a result, the administrator, as the budgetary manager, should be ever vigilant. Applicable to today's school budgetary accounting process, and a motto every principal should adopt, is a quote attributed to President Ronald Reagan when speaking about the U.S. relationship with the Soviet Union and intermediate-range nuclear missiles during the 1980s: "Trust but verify" (Reagan, 1987). Exactly! Avoiding any political connection, the authors highly recommend that a principal must trust but verify all accounting procedures. Another truism: "Inspect what you expect" (Miranda, 2012). Both quotes make good business sense!

Understanding each of the specified components as well as the need for income collection and deposit is an essential element of the budgetary process and one that must be mastered by the school administrator to prevent fiscal problems that could lead to the ending of what may very well have been a successful and most satisfying administrative career.

Timely Payment of Bills

One of the most overlooked aspects of expenditure control is the timely payment of bills. Timely payment of bills can be a source of revenue, as this practice often translates to the collection of a discount. In other words, vendors often offer discounts for early payment. For example, many vendors provide for a 15% discount if the bill is paid within 30 days or a 10% discount if the bill is paid within 60 days. For any school administrator to avoid or ignore the possibility of early payment of bills is to neglect the potential of controlling expenditures and, more important, keeping school money in school pockets. When a vendor discount is earned, that is money saved, and money saved is simply ensuring there are funds for further allocation to meet other important educational needs.

Some administrators might suggest the payment of bills accrued by each school is the responsibility of the district's business office and there is little that can be done beyond the school site. We beg to differ! The effective school administrator must work to ensure his or her bookkeeping clerk regularly contacts the business office department in charge of payment of bills. This method of reminder can very well encourage business department personnel to speed up the payment process and, as a result, a discount is collected, an additional expenditure is controlled, and the money saved remains at the school level.

Budget Amendments

Flexibility is an operative term associated with school budgeting. Those administrators who carefully manage and monitor the school budget realize that all purposeful planning combined with the best of intentions can go by the wayside when academic goals and objectives change for the betterment of the students served. For example, consider the following scenario.

When amendments or transfers are necessary, the school administrator must move funds from one account to another to correct a

THE ABOVE-BASIC ALLOTMENT ARRIVES
AT CLARK ANDREWS SCHOOL

During the second semester of the recent school year at Clark Andrews School, Principal Teresa Méndez appreciated the fact that additional funds were allocated to the school due to a significant increase in unexpected student enrollment. An above-basic allotment of $60,000 was transferred to the school by district administration at the conclusion of the first semester to make up for the financial strain the increased enrollment was imposing on the educational program, most notably in the area of technology. Dr. Méndez had only recently learned from an administrative colleague in an adjacent school district about an exciting digital initiative—one in which active-learning technological tools were being utilized to enhance student achievement. Such tools included portable e-devices, a robotic telepresence for virtual learning, virtual reality headsets and smartphones, and even droids with app-enabled wrist bands. All excited, Dr. Méndez and her site-based committee were determined to bring about a digital vision to their school.

As a first step of several planned digital steps, the campus computer lab had been abandoned earlier in the first semester of the school year as each student was issued an e-tablet. Due to the increased student enrollment, funding for the virtual reality headsets and smartphones fell short by about 33 students. Moreover, funding for e-tablets for all students was inadequate by 12 students. The digital equipment funding shortfall equaled approximately $16,500. Therefore, Dr. Méndez was ecstatic in recognizing she and her team could use the above-basic allotment to supplement the technology account to purchase the additional, but necessary, e-tablets along with some of the other digital equipment. Subsequently, she made an amendment or transfer within the school budget, as such was needed to facilitate the incoming new dollars and to further account for the new funds.

Pause and Consider

- Utilizing Forms 5.1 and 5.2 as guides, what justification could you provide for the budget amendment/transfer? Explain.
- Reflect upon the digital equipment being considered for purchase for the Clark Andrews School. Think now as an instructional leader, and select and determine how the one digital equipment piece, the droids with app-enabled wrist bands, might be actively incorporated into the learning environment, notably into the following subject areas: English, mathematics, science, computing, and design technology. Provide a few instructional strategies as

examples. Need a few helpful hints? See the digital piece (the droid) exemplified as an instructional strategy and incorporated into the learning environment, as noted at the conclusion of this chapter (p. 213). How do these hints/instructional strategies match up with your instructionally conceived ideas/approaches? How do they differ? Explain your own instructional and budgetary thinking.

Budget amendments are an essential part of the budgetary process and are utilized in an effort to move funds from one account to another and, at times, to correct an accounting error that has been made. It is recommended the school leader follow district budget amendment instructions and procedures by making wise decisions with regard to income and expenditure adjustments and transfers and by completing the appropriate paperwork involved in the budget-amendment process. While budget amendments are sometimes necessary, the effective school administrator readily learns that the overuse of the adjustment and transfer process can send questionable signals to and raise serious inquiries from business department personnel, district-level administrators, and even school board members, who in many systems have final approval over budgetary changes.

previous posting by transferring a portion, if not all, of a balance from one account to another. Consider the technology-oriented scenario above, and note that an "above-basic" allotment has been provided to the school to adjust for the unexpected increase in student enrollment. This allotment (over $10,000) is transferred from the district level to the school and placed in the technology line item account. At the school site level, the funds are needed for e-tablets for each student. Therefore, an adjustment or amendment must be submitted, with the funds being transferred to the proper accounts—technology equipment/software. To facilitate the transfer of any funds and to further amend the school budget, administrators utilize either standardized forms or memoranda that have been approved by the school district (see Forms 5.1 and 5.2). These forms, typically completed online, serve as a method of budgetary accountability and provide the necessary documentation, ensuring that the adjustment and/or transfer will occur.

Form 5.1   Sample Budget Amendment Request (Standardized Form)

Cullen Place Independent School District

Budget Amendment Form

School or Department: Fannin Middle School

From Account # 199-11-6399.00-041-11	Amount $50,000.00	Previous Budget $78,055.00	Current Budget $28,055.00
To Account # 199-11-6395.00-041-11	Amount $50,000.00	Previous Budget $2,200.00	Current Budget $52,200.00
From Account # 199-11-6399.00-041-11	Amount $16,500.00	Amount $52,200.00	Current Budget $35,700.00
To Account # 199-11-6396.00-041-11	Amount $16,500.00	Amount $1,000.00	Current Budget $17,500.00

Campus Action Plan Goal/Objective/Activity or Need Addressed

Goal IV: Provide an intensive, technology-centered curriculum that emphasizes the learning and application of technological communicative skills at all grade levels.

Objective 1.6: Explore and implement a technologically oriented instructional program with the utilization of digital equipment to better increase student achievement.

Activity 2.3: Upgrade technology instruction by abandoning the computer lab and providing each student with enhanced digital equipment.

Justification for Budget Amendment

Fannin Middle School plans to amend a portion of its allocated funds from the supplies and materials account and transfer said funds to the technology supplies/equipment under $5,000 account to purchase e-tablets and to the furniture and equipment account to purchase other digital equipment to better meet the campus need for additional technology equipment as related to the recent increase in student enrollment. Consequences of non-approval would hinder our ability to increase student achievement in the area of differing subject areas because the current computer hardware and furnishings are inadequate, again due to the significant increase in student enrollment. Implementation would begin immediately during the second semester of the current school year.

_____   _____
Originator   Date Requested

_____   _____
Principal   Date Approved

_____   _____
Director of Budgeting   Date Approved

Form 5.2   Sample Budget Amendment Request (Letterhead
Correspondence)

Fannin Middle School

"Committed to Excellence"

TO: Director of Budgeting, Cullen Place Independent School District

FROM: Dr. Hamlin Brown, Principal

DATE: January 12, _____

SUBJECT: Budget Amendment Request

The following transfer of funds is being requested:

Amount	From Account Number	To Account Number
$50,000	199-11-6399.00-041-11	199-11-6395.00-041-11
$16,000	199-11-6399.00-041-11	199-11-6396.00-041-11

Campus Action Plan Goal/Objective/Activity or Need Addressed

Goal IV: Provide an intensive, technology-centered curriculum that emphasizes the learning and application of technological communicative skills in all subject areas, at all grade levels.

Objective 1.6: Explore and implement a technologically oriented instructional program with the utilization of e-tablets and other digital equipment to better increase student achievement.

Activity 2.3: Upgrade the technological equipment by abandoning the computer lab and providing each student with a personal e-tablet.

Budget Amendment Justification

Fannin Middle School plans to amend a portion of its allocated funds from the supplies and materials account and transfer said funds to the technology supply/equipment under $5,000 (per unit cost) for extensive student-oriented technological upgrades. Additionally, funding from the supplies and materials account will be transferred to the furniture/equipment under $5,000 (per unit cost) account to purchase e-tablets to better meet the campus need for additional digital equipment as related to the recent increase in student enrollment. Consequences of non-approval would hinder our ability to increase student achievement as well as technologically oriented communication and learning, as the current number of e-tablets is inadequate, again due to the significant increase in student enrollment. Implementation would begin immediately during the second semester of the current school year.

Approved by: _____

Budgeting Director, Cullen Place Independent School District

Budgetary Systems

Chapter 4 outlined the differences between school finance and school budgeting. School finance is often associated with stringent fiscal policies and accountability procedures. School finance, simply put, is the process by which funding to support public schools is raised and distributed (Guthrie et al., 2007). On the other hand, budgeting has been defined by Brimley et al. (2015) as a process that involves planning, allocation, and expenditure of funds and a continuous monitoring and evaluation of each of the pieces within the process. This working definition correlates effectively with "The Budget Plan" section previously examined in this chapter.

The school budget serves numerous functions, often depending on which system of budget administration a school district uses. The most common budgetary systems, which are typically prescribed by state education code or local board policy, include function/object budgeting, zero-based budgeting, and school-based budgeting. Each system has particular strengths and weaknesses, but all are intended to serve important functions, including a projection of proposed sources, allocations, and expenditures of funds for the next fiscal year. While budgetary administration and budget systems go hand in hand, it must be noted that each varies from state to state and all must be appropriately administered and evaluated within the confines of standard accounting practices as defined by the National Center for Education Statistics in *Financial Accounting for Local and State Systems* (2016d) and correlated with the GAAP as established by the GASB.

Function/Object Budgeting

This particular administrative system of budgeting is based on a process whereby anticipated expenditures are entered into the budget ledgers through a codified and electronic process. Funds within this administrative system are budgeted according to *function* (instruction or administration or health services, for example) and *object* (supplies and materials or payroll or professional and contracted services, for example). This system is used by many school districts across the nation since it is the required format of most state and federal education agencies (see Table 5.4). The function/object budgetary system also closely aligns with the FEIMS of each state.

The strength of function/object budgeting correlates with the administrative need of schools and districts to exercise the maximum

Table 5.4   Function/Object Budgeting and Coding

199-11-6395.00-041-Current Year-30

The *function code* is an accounting entity that identifies the purpose of any school or district transaction.	The *object code* identifies the nature and object of an account or transactions. For example: payroll, supplies and materials, capital outlay.
Function 11 refers to *instruction*. Thus, this particular code represents a transaction that will impact the instructional program of a school or district.	Object 6395 refers to *technology equipment/software under $5,000.00 (per unit cost)*. This particular object code is found under the main object heading (6300) entitled: *Supplies and Materials*.

amount of fiscal control over funds, especially when numerous individuals are responsible and accountable for the budgeted dollars. The function/object budgetary system readily provides for quick and easy administration of the school budget and further allows for sensible decision making in relation to the general analysis of cost and benefit factors associated with evaluating specific instructional programs and programmatic expenditures relative to student academic gains and achievement.

A weakness frequently attributed to the function/object budgeting system is the system's strongest point. Function/object budgeting, while providing for analysis and assessment of programs and expenditures, unfortunately lacks specificity as well as depth and detail necessary to aid with the often essential and ongoing analysis that is so critical in mandated evaluations of differing instructional programs.

Zero-Based Budgeting

Following the 1977 U.S. Supreme Court ruling *Serrano v. Priest*, a budgetary system known as *zero-based budgeting* gained popularity in states such as California, New Mexico, Texas, and others where educational inequities existed in state funding formulas, processes, and procedures (Alexander & Alexander, 2012; Dayton, 2002; LaMorte, 2011). This system of budgeting is based on the most advantageous concept of involving all parties in the budgetary decision-making process, with school administrators and teams carefully analyzing budgeted line items, whether each is currently in place or is being newly proposed. Beginning the budget-development process with zero dollars, the learning community, with administrative guidance, is charged with ranking all budgetary considerations in priority order, then choosing potential alternatives based upon funding allocations and further annually evaluating all programs that are associated with the accompanying budget.

The downside to zero-based budgeting is the significant amount of time, effort, and paperwork associated with the process as well as the fact there are only so many dollars appropriated by the school district. Many school districts and administrators—often to the dismay of the learning community—decide that this particular budgetary system is too cumbersome and complicated, especially when compared to other budgetary preparation systems.

School-Based Budgeting

School- or site-based budgeting is a system similar in concept to the zero-based budgetary system. It, too, incorporates the idea of involving all parties in the budgeting effort for the betterment of student achievement and school reform. This system of budgeting gained credible recognition during the late 1980s and early 1990s. The system provided the learning community—especially faculty and staff—with serious and legitimate input into the school budgeting process. School-based budgeting has been described as a decentralized system of providing appropriations for all aspects of the school program (Brimley et al., 2015). For example, school staff can often impact the final decision as to what areas of the school budget will be funded and for what amount. Such areas can include the instructional program, instructional supplies, technology equipment, textbooks, library books, travel, professional development, and, in some instances, the distribution of school personnel salaries.

One potential benefit of the school- or site-based budgeting system is the ongoing analysis of student needs in relation to teaching resources and budgeted dollars. The effectiveness and efficiency of this system relates to the essential planning and recognition, by all parties, of those educational factors (socioeconomic status or ethnicity, for example) that can impact or influence student achievement (Sorenson & Cortez, 2010). Such a budgetary system is advantageous because it enables the school site team to exert significant influence not only on the budget development process but also on school policy and programmatic decisions. In addition, this particular system is considered to positively impact the morale and climate of a school, since many individuals within the learning community are actively involved in the decision-making process. Finally, school- or site-based budgeting, much like site-based decision making, can very well serve to increase the academic achievement of students (Sorenson, Cortez, & Negrete, 2010; Ubben & Hughes, 2016; Yukl, 2012). One can only be reminded of a most correlating quote from Guthrie et al. (2007, p. 235): "The dead and heavy hand of centralized, tightly drawn decision making stifles innovation and results in a one-size-fits-all instructional mentality." The authors of this text agree!

Another important consideration associated with the school- or site-based budgeting system relates to an understanding that district administrators must rethink the top-down approach to school budgeting and decision making and assume a more facilitative or collaborative role at the school level in the budget-preparation and decision-making processes (Sorenson, 2008). Typically, district administration continues to determine, monitor, and evaluate allocated dollars associated with maintenance, cafeteria, and transportation services. Responsibility for these areas of educational management often requires additional and more specified expertise that extends beyond that of the instructional leader and site-based team.

The downside to the school- or site-based budgetary system relates to three considerations: (1) The addition of parents and community members in the budgetary decision-making process requires significant training and learning for all constituents involved; (2) equity among differing schools may be endangered, as some schools' budgetary decision-making process reflects greater participation and advocacy of the constituents; and (3) certain budgetary decision-making procedures as related to personnel, for example, can bring potential legal entanglements.

The advantage of any or all of the budgeting systems identified within this chapter relates most importantly to the implementation and utilization of the site-based decision-making model and process and to an understanding that while each budgetary system can be effective, no single system is necessarily better than the other. The bottom line is this: school systems should never settle for one of the budgetary approaches when a combination of fiscal practices can be incorporated for a more systematic and comprehensive evaluation, on a cost and benefit basis, to best enhance the instructional programs and learning activities offered students.

Accounting and Auditing Procedures

Proper accounting and auditing procedures serve as a protective process for school district administrators and personnel. Such is absolutely essential as two terms, *accounting* and *auditing*, go hand in hand and serve as the critical elements in best safeguarding individuals and organizations from financial wrongdoing, suspicion, accusation, and even innuendo (Sorenson & Goldsmith, 2006). Auditing serves four functions:

1. Auditing makes good business sense—audit investigations are essential to determining if appropriate and legal expenditure of funds has occurred.

2. Auditing and the accompanying regular investigations provide written documentation to school administrators, superintendents, and board members who must be kept abreast of the financial dealings of the district and schools. Such documentation provides proof to the educational constituency (parents, taxpayers, state and federal governmental agencies) that the fiscal integrity of a school or district is sound, intact, and following the dictates of law.

3. Auditing helps to detect human and technical error in the accounting process. In any school system, large or small, errors will occur, and the audit investigations delineate between accidental and intentional errors.

4. Auditing can be the guiding force that brings about necessary change to accounting procedures and financial operations in need of improvement.

Several types of auditing procedures have been developed to provide a system of checks and balances to an educational organization. The two most common are internal and external auditing.

Internal auditing is a self-checking process that typically provides monthly reports to the school board. These reports detail the financial status of the school district and, in most instances, reveal expenditures of the differing schools within a district. Internal auditing is generally a continuous examination of a school's and district's accounting system in which a multiple-approval process is incorporated to safeguard against error or fraudulent practices.

External auditing is the formal accounting process by which a school's financial records are examined by a qualified and independent accountant—typically a certified public accountant. External audits are generally ordered on an annual basis, with an accounting firm spending anywhere from three to nine weeks conducting an extensive and exhaustive investigation that checks revenues and expenditures and further compares cash balances against encumbrances. External auditing ensures all statutory and legal requirements are in good order. External audits provide reports and findings in written and presentation formats as well as fiscal and accounting recommendations to superintendents and school boards. Audits serve as a measurement of the trust factor in any educational organization by validating the fiscal management (good or bad) of a school system. The auditing process is more than good business, it is money well spent to better ensure the sound fiscal stewardship of a school and school system.

Fraudulent Practices

Fraudulent practice in the education business may not be an everyday occurrence. However, newspaper accounts regularly reveal that dishonest and unethical employees manage to divert thousands of dollars from a school's activity account into the pockets of the unscrupulous embezzler. When school personnel hear district gossip about such capers but realize that these types of dealings are not making the local newspaper or evening newscast, this is usually associated with the fact that school systems do not want to provide unsolicited attention and unsettling fodder for community consumption. However, if you are a school leader of any tenure, you quickly recognize that embezzling can very well happen during your watch. Therefore, the possible advent of such fraudulent actions makes it worthwhile to learn about the subject. School leaders would be well advised to examine the school's recordkeeping and auditing procedures to best negate any tempting prospects and looming loopholes.

Fraudulent practices are closely akin to an individual's ethical decision-making process as revealed in Chapter 1 and Chapter 2. Beckner (2004), for example, examines the topic of responsibility and two relatable considerations: discretion and accountability. Johnson (2017) examines character and integrity. Both note that a school leader must exhibit discretion and accountability by exemplifying levels of

Figure 5.1   The Fraud Triangle

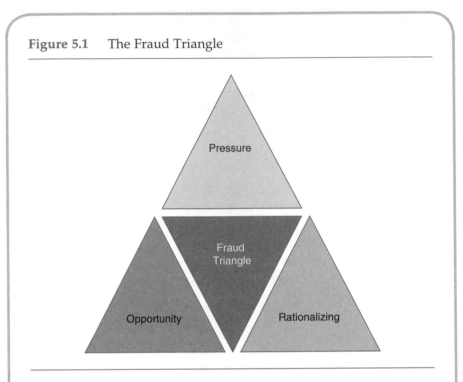

What is the fraud triangle? The triangle visually represents a framework for identifying high-risk fraudulent situations or circumstances. The corresponding corners of the triangle represent pressure, opportunity, and rationalizing. Each is described as follows:

1. *Pressure*—A financial need exists and serves as the catalyst that motivates an individual to commit a fraudulent act. For a school employee, for example, pressure to commit an illegal act may be related to a family member losing their job, having his or her house in foreclosure, medical bills that are continuously increasing due to a sick family member, or credit card abuse.

2. *Opportunity*—Serves as the open door or ability to commit an act of fraud. Opportunity increases with a lack of oversight or accountability. Opportunity occurs when fewer steps to commit the crime are more likely, when there are limited or no restrictions on access, oversight, and/or accountability. Simply, opportunity is viewed by the employee as the ability to execute a devious plan without being caught.

3. *Rationalizing*—Occurs when a school employee recognizes that committing a fraud can be justified—in his or her mind,

of course. Most individuals who commit frauds consider themselves, and are viewed as, honest and trustworthy. However, they also view themselves as being victims of unusual or unjust circumstances and thus rationalize or explain within their own minds that the fraudulent behavior or illegal activity is acceptable. Common rationalizations, verbalized after the fraudulent actor is caught, include the following:

- "I needed the money."
- "I deserved it."
- "I'm only borrowing the funds and intend to pay it all back."
- "I'm underpaid, overworked, and my principal is at fault because [he/she] doesn't pay any attention."
- "I have family obligations."
- "I must take care of my [child, parent, spouse, etc.]."
- "My spouse is a gambler or can't control [his/her] spending habits."
- "My medical expenses are astronomical."
- "Our credit card debt is massive and creditors are demanding repossession of goods or properties."

honesty, trustworthiness, and responsibility that appropriately and discretely follow school policies and procedures.

Accountability standards exemplifying the highest levels of ethical conduct must also be maintained. A perfect example was unfortunately showcased in a school district in which an associate superintendent for business and financial affairs entertained colleagues at a local men's club and subsequently charged lap-dancing expenses, to the tune of $2,000 in a single visit, to the school district's credit card. The expectation for responsible behavior and personal ethical standards quickly went by the wayside. The cost for such a personal indiscretion is serious: the loss of the associate superintendent's professional reputation and the subsequent public humiliation of the individual and his family. The district also suffered both internal turmoil and external criticism. This, in turn, negatively affected the public's confidence in the school district's leadership team and several school board members. Ultimately, the community outcry resulted in numerous administrative resignations, and several school board members who ran for reelection went down in defeat (Osborne, Barbee, & Suydam, 1999).

"IT SHOULDN'T BE A PROBLEM!"—CREDIT CARD FRAUD AND ACCOUNTABILITY QUESTIONS

Millicent Lowe, principal of Shermer Boynton School, was perceived by the school community as an outstanding instructional leader. That is, until she was arrested and charged with three counts of theft by embezzlement for using a school credit card for personal expenditures. Principal Lowe used a district credit card for more than $15,000 worth of purchases for personal use and another $28,200 that was, at the time of her arrest, unaccounted for, according to Grace Harper, Cade County police investigator.

Detective Harper noted that a random audit by the Northern Lakes School District turned up a charge on the school district credit card issued to Principal Lowe at a store on the island of Maui, in Hawaii. The auditor continued to examine numerous charges over a 12-week period and found other credit card charges that were not school-related expenses. The auditor, in the company of a district business officer, contacted Principal Lowe about the charges and Lowe stated she must have accidentally used the wrong credit card and then offered to write a personal check to cover the $4,300 in charges found during the 12-week period of the school audit.

The auditor and school district business officer both declined to accept the check and returned to the district business offices to uncover the remaining credit card charges dating from an almost three-year period. To make the scheme work, Principal Lowe would simply log onto the district's budget and fiscal accounting system, upload associated receipts, add a corresponding budget code, and then click the "approve" button.

In addition to the Maui store charge during a summer trip to Hawaii, Principal Lowe also used the district credit card to purchase gift cards for family members and friends; auto rentals; summer European tours to England, France, and Italy; alcohol purchases; cellphone services; computer and laptop purchases for family members; clothing; and numerous food purchases at differing restaurants within the Northern Lake School District and in Hawaii and at differing cities across the nation as Principal Lowe and husband followed the Grand Lakes University football team, attending games each fall.

When Principal Lowe was asked by Detective Harper why she committed the credit card fraud, she responded, "I accidently used the district credit card for a purchase of shoes and when I realized nothing happened, it just became an easy thing to do. You know, no one was watching, no one seemed to care. So, I just kept on doing it. I was planning on paying the money back as soon as my husband returned to work following his layoff at the Grand Lakes Steel Mills three years ago; it shouldn't be a problem. I know other principals and teachers are doing the same thing!"

Pause and Consider

- Examine your school regulations and district board policy to determine how fraud and, more specifically, credit card fraud is addressed. How can said policy be enhanced or improved in the form of a school site regulation(s)?
- How does the fraudulent incident and Principal Lowe's explanation for theft as detailed in this scenario relate to the fraud triangle in Figure 5.1? Explain.
- How does this scenario violate the PSEL as identified in Chapter 1?
- Principal Lowe stated, "I know other principals and teachers are doing the same thing [committing credit card fraud]!" How might a school principal and/or district ensure that fraud is not committed by school employees entrusted with credit cards? Need a few hints? See the section below entitled, "Credit Card Fraud."

A second example of fraudulent behavior involved the superintendent of an urban southwestern school district. Conspiring to defraud the school district by securing a $450,000 sole-source contract under false pretenses, the superintendent was arrested at his office, handcuffed, and subsequently escorted by Federal Bureau of Investigation (FBI) agents to a federal courthouse, where he was charged with conspiracy to commit mail fraud and aiding and abetting theft from instructional programs receiving federal funds. Charges called for up to 20 years in a federal prison. The superintendent resigned in disgrace to await federal prosecution and sentencing (KFOX 14 Television, 2011; Schladen & Kappes, 2012). At the time, the same superintendent was leading numerous school officials in a scheme to fraudulently boost the district's test scores and attendance and graduation rates to meet federal accountability standards. Six years later, the associate superintendent, along with multiple other school leaders—including principals and assistant principals—continue to plead guilty or are facing charges of conspiracy to defraud the United States (Martinez, 2017). What makes this fraudulent activity so blatantly wrong, if not immoral, is the fact the entire scheme was based on pushing students out of school, placing them in wrong grade levels, improperly denying services to ELLs, or deliberately and unashamedly denying students credit—all because these school leaders believed certain students would be unable to pass a state accountability exam.

Three points to recognize and remember:

1. The effects of corrupt and fraudulent behaviors are frequently irreversible and typically long-lasting.

2. No one is above the law—no matter title or position.

3. School leaders have a moral obligation to ensure that students are never placed in harm's way by any unethical, immoral, or illegal means or activity.

Credit Card Fraud

Credit card fraud in schools has become a regular occurrence. Sad, but true! As more school systems move from campus checks and bank reconciliation processes to online automated banking, the number of district credit cards issued to principals—and teachers, too—has increased. With the increase of credit card distributions, an alarming increase in credit card fraud has occurred. Such fraud has raised not only accountability issues but also problems related to cultural norms—or in the case of credit card fraud, cultural abnormal behaviors! It would take too much time and space, and consulting with psychiatrists and psychologists, to address the issue of abnormal behaviors in society today. However, what can and must be addressed are methods by which accountability standards and preventions can be put in place to better ensure that credit card fraud does not occur. List below are a few recommendations.

*   Limit the number of credit card users in the school district.
*   Ensure that district policy and campus regulation changes are made, reviewed with school district credit card holders, and enforced. When said changes fail to make sense or simply work ineffectively in terms of good business sense, reform them.
*   Establish a credit card usage code of conduct. Statements related to clearly stipulated rules and procedures—what behaviors will not be tolerated—must be included within any code of conduct.

- Audit regularly (monthly) for purchases that are not approved before payment or not approved at all.
- Monitor employee behaviors. Investigate immediately any behaviors that do not look or feel right. If something doesn't appear appropriate, it's probably not!
- Have great confidence in the accounting system. If this does not occur, make changes in software and implement human detection processes as well.
- Examine spending practices at the district and school levels. Restrict certain credit card purchases such as food, travel, lodging, and so on unless preapproved by district business officers.
- Implement districtwide virtual conferences detailing accountability procedures and related consequences for inappropriate credit card usage.
- Limit types of purchases and where said purchases can be made.
- No personal meal purchases on district credit cards. Meals can be reimbursed by the school district at a later date after proper forms have been completed and approved.
- Ensure that credit card purchases are from authorized vendors.
- Establish guidelines for purchases of electronic hardware and software. No items in this category should be made with district credit card—only through approved requisition forms (Halsne & Koeberl, 2016; Worth, 2015).

Embezzlement

Embezzlement has been defined as the fraudulent appropriation of property by an individual to whom it has been entrusted (Office of Management and Budget, 2005; Sorenson & Goldsmith, 2006). The operative term within this definition is *entrusted*. The embezzler is usually a trusted employee who is taking advantage of a school leader's confidence or a school leader's lack of attention to detail. Embezzlers have a method of operation, a thinking process that is frequently thrust upon unsuspecting schools or school systems and school leaders. Embezzlers often believe they are smarter than the school leader, and they generally perceive themselves as being someone who can outwit a less-than-sterling school business department. Embezzlers are more likely to be

- female (64% of the time);
- employed as either a clerk in a school business, finance, budgeting, bookkeeping, or accounting office or department; a school club (booster) official; or a school principal;
- acting alone (84% of the time);
- well dressed; and
- hidden in a single office or cubicle (Green, 2016; Worrell, 2011).

Common schemes are typically quite simple to employ because the trusted employee has generally won the confidence of a school or district leader. In fact, the best embezzlers are often the individuals who are given more authority than a position dictates. These same individuals have also realized that the ability to embezzle is only limited by their own imagination. Most embezzlement at the school level involves the pocketing of cash received through activity fund–related dollars coming into the school office—especially in relation to fundraising and crowdfunding programs and efforts.

The theft of cash is quick and easy, and it is often difficult to detect. An act of embezzlement is accomplished by a trusted employee who simply doesn't enter the cash receipt in the accounts-receivable records. A perfect example involves cash received from a school activity or from a club sponsor who is less interested in the details associated with recordkeeping and, thus, simply trusts the administrative office clerical staff: "Count this for me, please; I've got to get back to class—my students are taking a test!" To prevent this scenario and the associated monetary temptation, a school principal should insist, if not demand, that all cash received be accompanied by a written receipt of the calculated dollar amount, and a cash receipt must be provided by the "trusted" employee to the club or activity sponsor immediately upon receipt of the cash funds.

Another preventive step is the spot-check process instituted by the school leader. This process further assures that cash received is cash recorded. In other words, the school leader needs to purposefully check on a regular basis with differing school activity or club sponsors to determine when funds are coming into the school and, most notably, into the school office. The school leader should also carefully monitor the bookkeeping records, always looking for suspicious signs of fraud and theft. The school leader should also understand that unexpected internal audits by district business office personnel can often prevent employee embezzlement efforts.

Finally, never underestimate the vulnerability of a school or district to an act of embezzlement. An ounce of prevention may very well be the cure for the common scheme. Effective school leaders must recognize the following 10 precautionary practices that can inhibit and discourage embezzlement.

1. Ensure that the individuals who expend monies are not the custodians of accounting for said monies.

2. Review all bank statement reconciliation procedures.

3. Keep two separate and independently maintained sets of bookkeeping records as related to receipts and expenditures.

4. Provide for effective and appropriate reconciliation of receipts and accounts.

5. Never sign blank checks before leaving for a conference or vacation.

6. Develop and utilize bookkeeping policies or regulations.

7. Utilize bonded employees only.

8. Cross-train office personnel to perform bookkeeping responsibilities.

9. Utilize an independent accountant to conduct regular internal and external audits.

10. Review on a regular basis the detailed expectations for appropriate and ethical office bookkeeping standards and procedures with office staff.

Other Risk Factors

While an incident of monetary theft or embezzlement may not be directly tied to the school administrator, a public perception will definitely exist that such a fraudulent practice occurred on the administrator's watch and, therefore, the administrator shares responsibility. Some school leaders take a lax approach to the budgeting process by delegating all or part of the budget process and accompanying tasks to others or simply deciding that "instruction is my bag" and, as a result, either neglecting or ignoring important budget details. Such thinking or action can very well be considered a costly risk factor, if not an ultimate criminal mistake.

Hughes, Ginnett, and Curphy (2015) examined a Center for Creative Leadership report that studied the topic of career derailment; in other words, how leaders fall short of the personal success predicted earlier in their careers. Three different but quite compelling causes of career derailment quickly came to light when examined in relation to fraudulent practices at school: (1) failure to constructively face an obvious problem, issue, or circumstance; (2) mismanagement; and (3) inability to select trustworthy subordinates. Reflect upon the three noted causes for career derailment and then consider three interesting questions related to the risk factor of monetary theft or embezzlement: (1) Do you perceive the fraudulent problem as being the result of the leader's actions or inactions? (2) Do you perceive that the leader was aware of the consequences of his or her actions or inactions? (3) Which of the three causes do you perceive would most likely lead to the career derailment of an educational leader from the perspective of a fraudulent practice at school?

Appropriate auditing and accounting procedures, while never completely foolproof in eliminating the potential for fraud and embezzlement, do serve to assure the educational clientele of the fiscal state of a school and district, and such procedures further discourage unethical practices. Effective school leaders understand that any misuse or misappropriation of school funds can quickly destroy the public trust. Most importantly, the effective school leader acknowledges that any and all unethical, immoral, and fraudulent activities can very well derail, if not promptly conclude, a career that was once perceived to be most promising and long lasting.

The Leadership Role: Ethical and Moral Behaviors

We live in an era in which cultural norms seem to be shifting from a society built upon genuine respect for one another to one in which far too many individuals are abusive to those who lead our governing institutions, schools, and school districts. The latter group often prefers a scorched earth approach to social interaction. Why build people up when it is easier to tear them down? Why offer a simple truth when a disparaging lie is more convenient and, of course, damaging? We hear stories of community members blatantly attacking school leaders, working to destroy credibility and character simply because these "concerned" citizens don't get their way. Regrettably, we learn of ethical and moral school leaders who become burned out and are willing to escape their leadership role, not because of more money elsewhere, but because they are tired of the abuse.

Cooper (2012) has proclaimed, "Modern society is preoccupied with action, to the exclusion of reflection about values, morals, and principles" (p. xi). Question: What is important about Cooper's statement? Answer: We know Cooper is correct! We also recognize that something has to give, something has to change, some cultural normalcy must prevail upon our society and help individuals in their actions within our schools and school systems. We also know a Biblical truth: "Neither shall you allege the example of the many as an excuse for doing wrong!"

MISTAKES WERE MADE!

"Yes, that's correct, they misappropriated federal funds, changed enrollment data, and manipulated state testing outcomes." These were the words of the principal at Dewey Chetum School. The principal further noted that "mistakes were made" as he explained the illegal activities. The principal showed no signs of regret or remorse, and he maintained blame at arm's length, finding others to hold accountable but never admitting that he had personally been involved, had done anything wrong, or was responsible to any degree. It was a complete failure of accepting any accountability.

Here's what a school leader must recognize: Some "mistakes" are just that—mistakes that are unintentional, simply human error: "I turned the wrong direction on a one-way street;" "I forgot and worked too late, missing dinner with my spouse and a few friends;" "I miscalculated my credit card receipts and statement and overlooked a required payment;" or "I forgot to take the car in for an oil change and the discount no longer applied." All of these are unintentional and typically excusable mistakes.

However, there are purposeful acts that go beyond a simple unintentional mistake. These deeds are ethically and/or morally wrong. They are deliberate, calculated, and determined.

Pause and Consider

- Cooper (2012) relates that "principals must direct the activities of those under their supervision . . . and monitor performance. In turn,

(Continued)

(Continued)

> principals are accountable for clearly defining the assigned duties and are held accountable for the fulfillment of any assignment" (p. 68). How does this quote relate to the principal in the scenario above? How not? Explain.

- Tschannen-Moran (2014) asserts that it is the principal who is responsible for advancing a school's vision in an ethical, moral, and trustworthy manner. Explain how you have observed this at your school.
- *PSEL 2: Ethics and Professional Norms* should have been effectively implemented in this scenario. Explain how.
- What ethical questions are raised in this particular case?
- Which of the following behaviors, as detailed by Johnson (2017), relate to the principal in the scenario? Explain.
  - *Deceit*—Lying and giving false or misleading information
  - *Selfishness*—Blaming followers and making them out to be scapegoats
  - *Disregard*—Ignoring normal standards of responsibility; an obvious disdain for followers
  - *Deification*—Creating a master–servant relationship. In this instance, school leaders believe they can do whatever they desire because they are superior to their followers.
- Closer to home, describe the key principles or values that define your personal vision of good moral and ethical behaviors. How does your personal vision relate to the Chapter 1?
- Consider your own district regulations or school board policies. Which might apply to the situation in the above noted scenario?

Therefore, we return to the question that has been posed in previous chapters: "What's a principal to do?" Might the authors—who have each been in the education business more than 45+ years—recommend the following as a guide to answering the question. The very best, the most exceptional of school leaders offer a character and example based upon acting and being:

- *Genuine and caring. Genuine* is much more than a passing term when it comes to leadership. It is a *we* thing, a statement of what *we* must be as school leaders: *We* make a living by what *we* get. *We* make a life by what *we* give. Are you genuinely giving or duplicitously getting? Being genuine and giving and caring is the right way to lead!

- *Dependable and reliable. Dependability, reliability,* and *responsibility* may very well be three of the most important words in a school leader's tool kit of appropriate actions. School leaders are frequently confronted with issues that demand prompt action. School leaders are depended upon to make decisions that are in the best interest of students and the entire learning community. School leaders must be reliable in identifying a problem, confronting an issue, and deciding a response. Thus, a school leader defines her or his administrative responsibility based on a simple question: "Am I dependable and reliable?"

- *Trustworthy.* A trustworthy person is defined as one who is ethical and moral in all aspects of life, personal and professional. There's an old saying, a most demeaning one about those of us in education: "There are those who do, and then there are those who teach." We are much more than that! Our credo must be that of longtime educational leader, Jane Wilhour (1998): "I teach, I lead. While students may not always recall what I taught, they will remember what I stood for as a teacher and leader!"

- *Transparent.* Simply defined, a school leader is transparent when her or his actions are clear, obvious, apparent, aboveboard, and/or visible. The authors believe that transparency in leadership is key to restoring our faith in school principals. When transparency is ignored, there develops a distrust of the school leader and a critical sense of insecurity by followers. Recall the words of Mother Teresa: "Honesty and transparency make you vulnerable. Be honest and transparent anyway" (AZQuotes, n.d.).

- *Task and relationship oriented.* Task-oriented school leaders focus on planning, scheduling, coordinating meetings and activities, and providing necessary resources, supplies, and technical assistance. Relationship-oriented principals are supportive and helpful, exhibiting trust, confidence, friendliness, good humor, and consideration. They care, keep faculty and staff informed, and show appreciation. Today, school leaders must be all this and more! These leaders must be sincere in building and maintaining the personal worth and importance of others but never negating realistic task-related goals and expectations.

- *Evenly tempered.* Personality affects leadership and followership. School leaders who have a calm disposition and do not belittle others or issue personal attacks are much more likely to receive competent and timely information from faculty and staff. Authoritative leadership lessens legitimacy and increases in others a decreased sense of psychological identification. Uneven temperament is much more likely to result in two things: (1) a demand for loyalty (What do the best leaders do? They *earn* loyalty by showing respect, care, and interest) and (2) a faculty and staff that run scared. If people are working in fear, they will make bad decisions to the detriment of the leader and the organization.

- *Student centered and achievement oriented.* Effective school leadership is all about placing students first and foremost in all thinking and decision making. No ands, ifs, or buts! The best administrative leaders never overlook their students. The authors repeatedly shared with faculty that students always come first, then faculty, and then parents. Being student centered is an absolute. However, school leaders must also be achievement oriented. This means exhibiting leadership behaviors that are demanding yet supportive, setting challenging academic goals, and continually seeking methods to improve performance and achievement.

Research conducted by O'Donnell and Sorenson (2005) revealed that educational leaders face numerous dilemmas of differing dimensions on a regular basis. The best leaders recognize these dilemmas as opportunities for doing what is right, not necessarily what is expedient. School leaders have an obligation to set ethical and moral examples for the organizations they serve. Those leaders who do not honor integrity, those who fail to establish truth and who further negate moral reasoning, are the same leaders who fail to inspire honesty and ethical practice in others. Such inappropriate behaviors in the education business lead to moral abandonment, pure selfishness, and the ultimate in career derailment.

Several years ago, a Harris Poll reported that 89% of workers and leaders surveyed believed it was important for leaders to be upright, honest, and ethical in their behaviors. However, only 41% indicated their current leader had such characteristics (Vamos & Jackson, 1989). Such an indictment serves to underscore the need for strong character and ethical behavior in the school leadership business. Followers place their trust in a leader who models integrity, and when leaders compromise their moral and ethical values, they risk losing the respect they so readily deserve (Nelson & Toler, 2002). Recently, in a school district in an urban center in the Southwest, four ethically and morally oriented misbehaviors on the part of a district leader allowed for a culture of corruption, manipulation, arrogance, and rule (policy) exemptions. The four behaviors were (1) inappropriate sexual conduct, (2) fiscal mismanagement, (3) forged documentation, and (4) data manipulation. To the credit of the newly named interim superintendent of the district, he appropriately noted the days of playing fast and loose were over!

What is known about ethics is striking: "Ethics has to do with what leaders do and who leaders are" (Northouse, 2015, p. 378). "Fast and loose" behaviors frequently lead to devastating professional and personal consequences. While the daily pressures of life and career are often overwhelming, the effective school leader must remain an individual of committed character, integrity, and personal ethics. Leaders can ill afford to ignore strong moral and ethical margins because the aforementioned stresses can compromise the decision-making processes. When such a compromise occurs, a leader's character is terribly strained, revealing flaws, cracks, and defects that in turn allow a leader to be susceptible to deception (lying and cheating), inappropriate behaviors (sexual affairs), questionable or illegal actions (embezzlement), and a general lack of personal accountability (Goldsmith & Sorenson, 2005; Nelson & Toler, 2002; Sorenson, 2007). See "Case Study Application #2: Sex, Money, and a Tangled Web Woven" (pp. 215–217) for a real-life account. Remember, truth is often stranger than fiction!

Professional behavior, personal integrity, and appropriate ethical and moral conduct must be the defining qualities of any leader. Nothing less will do. If trust and integrity serve as the paramount bond between school administration and faculty, what guidelines or principles should serve as the focal point to better ensure ethical conduct and moral leadership? Here are five targeted areas for serious leadership consideration.

1. Show respect—True leaders earn respect by showing respect. When leaders fail to respect followers, they fail to understand the main goal of leadership, which is leading. This may seem quaint, but effective leaders epitomize affirmation, listening, esteem, care, and concern—all inherently related to respect. Respect has been described by Northouse (2015) as granting credibility to the ideas of others and treating others in a way that makes them feel valued and competent.

2. *Demonstrate integrity*—Whatever qualities, skills, or talents a leader may possess, lacking integrity is an absolute flaw. Yukl (2012) advances the theory that leaders who demonstrate high levels of integrity are more credible, more open, more collaborative, more receptive to receiving bad news or negative feedback, and less likely to be consumed with impressing their superiors at the expense of others.

3. *Exhibit honesty*—Honesty is best defined in relation to what it is not, what an effective leader cannot be: deceitful, untrustworthy, and fraudulent. The leader who exhibits honesty reveals a genuine honorableness in character and action.

4. *Resist temptations*—The moral and ethical strength of any school leader is often tested by the many temptations in life. Resistance is often accompanied by endurance. When a leader is close to temptation, a loss of perspective has occurred. Resisting temptation serves to make a school leader more respected, honest, and endearing to others who furthermore perceive the leader to be an individual who possesses the highest level of integrity.

5. *Provide service*—The effective school leader is one who is involved in servant leadership. The servant leader is one who is willing to empathize and understand by listening, by observing, and by assisting others within the learning community (Greenleaf, 2002). Servant leadership provides for a level of tolerance by recognizing the strengths and talents of others when their weaknesses and mistakes may be more than obvious (DePree, 2003). Servant leadership can help others overcome their own weaknesses and mistakes by targeting those areas for personal and professional growth while at the same time emphasizing their not-so-apparent strengths and talents. In turn, followers are more likely to be just as tolerant of a leader when mistakes are made and when weaknesses are exhibited (Beckner, 2004; Shapiro & Stefkovich, 2016).

Now, some serious advice for the educational leader: The best of school leaders always make appropriate decisions by upholding legal, moral, and ethical behaviors, even in an era when a general cynicism exists regarding the integrity of individuals in leadership positions, especially those leaders who actually espouse personal ethics and moral values. All school leaders would be wise to consider and remember the following adage, as no words of advice could ring truer:

> *It's important that people know what you stand for. It's equally important that they know what you won't stand for.*

> —Mary Waldrop (AZQuotes, n.d.)

Final Thoughts

The budget development process, with its numerous components, is a legal mandate in most states. Effective, efficient, and essential budgeting practices are dependent upon skillful school leaders who know more than budgetary management. School leaders must not only understand fiscal accountability and control, they must also be aware of collection and deposit structures, budgetary systems, and accounting and auditing procedures. Moreover, school leaders must realize how the visionary component of school-based planning integrates with the budget development process and how each collaboratively functions to build a stronger academic program that, in turn, positively impacts student achievement.

The budget development process is more than implementing and utilizing effective, efficient, and essential fiscal practices. The budget development process is an integral part of visioning and planning from which all members of the learning community have a voice, a stake, and a right to impact the academic success of students. Many decades ago, long before the concept of school-based budgeting gained popular acceptance in schools, Roe (1961) revealed that the school budget is the translating of

> educational needs into a financial plan which is interpreted to the public in such a way that when formally adopted, it expresses the kind of educational program the community is willing to support, financially and morally, for a one-year period. (p. 81)

Such sentiment couldn't be expressed any better half a century later, except to say this: Unlike J. Paul Getty, as noted in the introductory quote, it is hoped that educational leaders find allocating money to support academic goals and student achievement to be a considerable pleasure!

Discussion Questions

1. What is the purpose of a budget plan and how does it interact in relation to the school action or improvement plan?

2. Identify at least two sources of income a school leader and team can generate, discuss the pros and cons of each, and further explain how these sources relate to the visioning and planning aspects of the school budgeting process.

3. Which of the components of the collection and deposit structure are essential to the budgetary handling of the school activity account? Support your answer.

4. Consider the purposes of accounting procedures and explain how such practices can assist school leaders in their quest of accounting for the expenditure of public funds.

5. Which budgetary system has your school or district adopted? Discuss how this particular system further commits your school or district to the site-based decision-making and management approach.

6. What precautions should a school leader take with regard to the possibility of embezzlement? In what ways is your school vulnerable to this budgetary risk factor and how would you as a school leader address the identified vulnerabilities?

7. Fraudulent practices have been described as being closely akin to an individual's ethical decision-making process. How does PSEL 2, identified in Chapter 1, support this statement?

8. You have recently been named a new school leader. Outline your responsibilities as related to effective, efficient, and essential budgetary practices and further explain how the learning community (faculty, students, parents, external patrons, etc.) should be involved in the development of the school budget.

THE ABOVE-BASIC ALLOTMENT ARRIVES AT CLARK ANDREWS SCHOOL

<u>Helpful Hints</u>: Instructional strategies and suggestions for using a droid in the classroom. As a reminder, feel free to refer to pp. 186–187.

The students will

English

- utilize the droid as a character in fiction writing.
- write a story from the point of view of the droid.

Mathematics

- use the droid to review compass directions by making it move in different directions—north, south, east, and west.
- create a large coordinate grid on the classroom floor and move the droid to specific locations.
- conduct races recording how much time it takes the droid to travel a certain distance. This can be a data handling or statistics activity.

Science

- interact in groups strategizing how the droid "head" remains attached to its base. Such an activity can be used to initiate a learning session relative to magnetism.

Computing

- utilize the droid for a control technology activity. For example, can the students guide the droid safely from one location to another?
- Discuss how the droid works: (1) What features does it have? (2) How does the droid operate and move? (3) What functions does the app perform? (4) How does the app communicate with the droid? Use these questions as reference points for other discussions about robotics in professions, how robotics help society today, and how robotics can improve life today and in the future.

Design Technology

- design and create a maze in which the droid can travel.
- create different courses for the droid to explore, using the movement as means of examining distance, time, and angles.
- develop schematics of a new droid version with enhanced features.
- create a life-size model of the droid. Research life-size droids and their use in differing professions.

SOURCE: Warner (n.d.).

Case Study Application #1: Love That Principal!

The application of a case study or case studies as related to campus visioning, planning, and budgeting is presented at the conclusion of each chapter to provide applicable and relevant workplace scenarios so the reader can apply, in a practical manner, the knowledge acquired through textual readings.

Dr. Margaret MacDonald, principal at Maynard G. Krebs School, spent the morning hours of a cold, snow-laden, wintry day recognizing that school funds were very limited. However, additional dollars were needed for instructional supplies and materials dedicated to science, technology, engineering, and mathematics-related projects. She called her assistant principal, Bob Collins, into the office, along with Zelda Gilroy (her budget clerk); the school's parent–teacher association president, Charmaine Schultz; and the school's academic booster club president, Thalia Menninger. Principal MacDonald hoped these individuals would be able to stimulate ideas for funding the following science, technology, engineering, and mathematics (STEM) needs:

- manipulatives and teaching/learning kits
- cooperative learning centers
- e-tablets
- professional development for teacher training/support
- use of hands-on robotics kits
- development of cybersecurity projects
- drones and high-altitude balloons for designated payloads
- telescopes to study planetary systems
- field trips to the NASA space flight center
- rockets constructed to complete a variety of space-inspired missions

Dr. MacDonald and team were excited to begin the work at hand. In fact, Charmaine Schultz whispered to Bob Collins, "Love that principal!" Bob grinned and said right back:, "You bet! She means business and we'll find the money to help our students and teachers!"

Application Questions

Utilize the "Generated Income Sources" section of this chapter and the specific segments regarding grants, fundraising, and crowdfunding to respond to the following queries.

1. Consider the circumstances at Maynard G. Krebs School and determine what potential grants (see pp. 171–174) might help alleviate the financial burden Principal MacDonald and her team face when it comes to funding the STEM efforts on campus. Be specific in support of your answer(s).

2. Determine potential crowdfunding endeavors to help bolster the school's STEM efforts. How might crowdfunding be of benefit? Be specific and determine a crowdfunding example/process to incorporate at Maynard G. Krebs School. Then, detail the advantages and disadvantages of using crowdfunding in this particular example.

3. Both Charmaine Shultz and Thalia Menninger are determined to raise funds for the STEM projects at Maynard G. Krebs School. Generate ideas of potential fundraisers. Identify the pros and cons of your identified fundraising example(s) as related to this situation.

4. From the perspective of the budget clerk, Zelda Gilroy, think about what's right with the fundraising and crowdfunding approaches to the STEM-related project. What's wrong?

Case Study Application #2:
Sex, Money, and a Tangled Web Woven

Dr. Edgar Buchannen was principal at Fullerton Peak High School in the suburban community of Gibsonville. He had been in this position of instructional leadership for nearly five years. Previously, he had experienced a very successful principalship at Woodson Middle School in a major metropolitan area just north of the state capital. Dr. Buchannen had worked diligently with his new faculty to raise student academic achievement from low performing to a significantly higher state department standard of accountability. Such a task had not been easy, but Dr. Buchannen was convinced that he and his team—along with the students at Fullerton Peak High School—had jumped a most difficult hurdle.

In the interim, Dr. Buchannen had developed a great working relationship with Lisa Nicoles, the school's bookkeeping and attendance clerk. The two had clicked from their first day together, and they really appreciated each other's work ethic. One Saturday morning, Eddie—as he had asked Lisa to call him—came in early to catch up on some budgeting issues while Lisa was completing the student demographic information needed for the next scheduled round of statewide testing. Both were pleased to see one another working on the important tasks at hand, and soon, they took a break to enjoy a morning doughnut and cup of coffee. Lisa complained of a neck ache from working all morning to enter the demographic data into the computer system, and Eddie quickly offered to massage her neck. Lisa did not object or complain.

Well, you've heard this type of story before—all too common in our business—and we need not go any further other than to reveal that such an act quickly led to serious complications. Over the next few months, a steamy affair developed, although the two tried to keep any suggestion of impropriety away from the office.

Unfortunately, Lisa's marriage was falling apart, and although Eddie was married with three children of his own, the two carried on their secret romance. With Lisa's failing marriage, she had developed—along with her husband, who had a serious gambling problem—credit card debts to the tune of $225,000. She was in deep trouble, since these financial complications were in her name, and the collectors were demanding payment or repossession of tangible assets. What she needed was cash, and she needed it fast. While the romance grew, so did a little problem Lisa had at work—she was regularly taking money from the school's different activity accounts such as athletics, drama, band, choir, and even the "cola wagon," which took in hundreds of dollars at the varsity football game each Friday night.

Dr. Edgar Buchannen had no idea of these embezzlement efforts until one evening when Lisa broke down in tears and told him he needed to help her get out of this financial predicament. He grew furious and stated, "Help you? Wait a minute, aren't you the one stealing from the district? Don't involve me in your petty theft crimes!" Lisa, with a steely-eyed stare, retorted, "Don't play games with me, Mr. Self-Righteous. You're the one cheating on your wife, you two-faced fraud. You help me or else!"

Thus, began a criminal partnership conceived in a mutual distrust of one another and based on some very questionable ethical and moral standards. From that point forward, a dangerous game of "borrowing" money, with every intention of paying back the stolen funds, escalated to a point of no return. The "borrowed" dollars never found their way back into the accounts, and the cover-up only lasted until someone in the district business office caught on to a scheme built on lies, deceit, misjudgment, and unethical practices.

Application Questions

1. What probable repercussions will Dr. Edgar Buchannen and Lisa Nicoles face as a result of their actions? Explain the risk factors associated with their behaviors.

2. Cooper (2012) examines two approaches to maintaining responsible conduct in organizations: internal and external controls. *External control* has been described as responding to an unethical situation by developing new rules, rearranging the organizational structure, or establishing more cautious monitoring procedures. *Internal control* is often described as increasing preservice and in-service training programs or placing ethical leadership discussions on local meeting agendas. Which of these two policy perspectives would best be associated with this case study and why?

3. What legal implications are at issue in this case study? Which laws, education codes, or board policies have been broken or infringed upon? Give specific examples and explanations.

4. From the perspective of a school leader, how could the act of embezzlement presented in this case study have been prevented? Identify specific precautionary practices you would incorporate.

5. Northouse (2015) defines *ethics* as a "system of rules or principles that guide us in making decisions about what is 'right or wrong' and 'good or bad' in a particular situation." He further stipulates that ethics provide "a basis for understanding what it means to be a morally decent human being" (p. 424). Is Dr. Buchannen a morally decent human being? Support your answer and relate to the PSEL.

6. What is the possible impact of such actions, as described in the case study, in relation to the school district? Support your response from both a budgetary and political perspective.

6

Building the School Budget

All of us are smarter than any one of us!

—Japanese proverb attributed to
W. Edwards Deming (2000, p. 114)

Site-Based Decision Making

Leaders of the 21st century must be knowledgeable about how to work within the political functions of organizations and, moreover, highly skilled in operating in arenas of competition, conflict, problem solving, and decision making—all in a timely fashion (Norton, 2005; Sorenson, Goldsmith, & DeMatthews, 2016; Ubben & Hughes, 2016). Such thinking exemplifies the parameters by which school leaders utilize differing strategies for working with the learning community and readily correlate with the collaborative statement attributed to W. Edwards Deming in the introductory quote. Deming identified personnel as the key to program quality. He believed that working collaboratively with employees to help them perform better, making decisions and solving problems as a team, and placing importance on the gathering of data were the essential keys to organizational and individual improvement (Hughes, Ginnett, & Curphy, 2015; Razik & Swanson, 2010; Sorenson & Goldsmith, 2009; Sorenson, Goldsmith, Méndez, & Maxwell, 2011).

One of the most effective strategies to be incorporated by a school leader is the site-based decision-making (SBDM) process, as this approach to school leadership is superior to the autocratic process (followers do not play a role in defining the problem or in generating a solution or decision) and exceeds the consultative process (followers are consulted but the leader makes the decision) yet is reflective of the group process (followers in collaboration with the leader reach a consensus relative to a solution to the dilemma or decision presented). What we do know about decision making relates to the concept that a high-quality decision has a direct and measurable impact on an organization (Hoy & Miskel, 2012). When the SBDM process is properly implemented, there is a total quality component to a decision—generally one in which the decision made has improved services to the clientele (the students, parents, faculty and staff, and the overall learning community). Visioning, planning, developing, implementing, and continuously evaluating a school budget must be an extension of the leader–follower collaborative decision-making dimension. Recall the words of Edward L. Bernays: "I must follow the people. Am I not their leader?" (AZQuotes, n.d.). He might have added, "I must lead the people. Am I not their servant?"

During the 1980s, public schools began to shift to a business-purpose approach, incorporating business principles into program planning, daily operations, and an overall reform movement in response to concerns about the quality of American education (Urban & Wagoner, 2014). This paradigm shift, as applied to school fiscal matters, was associated with the decentralization of district budgets. During the late 1980s and early 1990s, W. Edwards Deming's total quality principles were infused into the mainstream of public school reform efforts. The term *quality*, like integrity, fairness, and ethics—as discussed in Chapter 1—was then and continues to be difficult to define, although everyone claims to know quality when they see it. John M. Loh states that the definition of quality is quite simple: "It is a leadership philosophy which creates throughout the entire enterprise a working environment which inspires trust, teamwork, and the quest for continuous, measurable improvement" (AZQuotes, n.d.). While Loh's definition serves as a starting point for understanding the school budgeting process, a more practical and working definition of quality might be identified as a continuous process that is achieved through a change in organizational culture. In other words, a school leader must ensure that the budgeting process, in collaboration with site-based decision making, is never ending (continuous) by transforming the shared norms, values, or beliefs (culture) of a school into one in which the leader becomes a facilitator and the followers become active participants. Therefore, the school leader, for the betterment of the organization, must place emphasis on total quality through the empowerment of others by utilizing participative decision making, by articulating a vision, and by involving many in the planning and development stages of a school budget. Hence, all of us are smarter than any one of us. This change process makes the work of schools more intrinsically motivating and thus more appealing, rather than one of a controlling nature in which the members of the learning community are extrinsically motivated as a result of a top-down attitude and approach (Hughes et al., 2015).

Why Site-Based Decision Making?

The SBDM process is crucial to building an effective school budget. First, all actions regarding the budgetary process are considered, assessed, evaluated, and approved in a public forum with all stakeholders involved. Site-based decision making is essential in an era of intense scrutiny, transparency, accountability, and fiscal conservatism. Effective school leaders welcome the opportunity to showcase the sensitive subject of public fund expenditures and the overall school budget in an open forum. Second, when utilizing site-based decision making, the budgetary process is above board or transparent. In other words, there are no hidden funds or secret accounts. Third, all stakeholders are involved and thus private and personal agendas meet with little merit and have a tendency to go by the wayside. Fourth, decentralizing four key resources (power, information, knowledge, and rewards) enhances organizational effectiveness and productivity (Hadderman, 2002). Hadderman further stipulates,

> highly involved schools need real power over the budget to decide how and where to allocate resources; they need fiscal and performance data for making informed decisions about the budget; their staff needs professional development and training to participate in the budget process; and the school must have control over compensation to reward performance. (p. 27)

Finally, budgetary decisions must be made on a student-first basis. For these reasons alone, it only makes sense to incorporate the SBDM model into the budget development process.

Who Builds the School Budget?

Recall the eight components of the Sorenson-Goldsmith Integrated Budget Model in Chapter 3. Specifically, think about Component 2, which briefly examined the site-based committee size and structure. Taking this precept further, the authors of this text strongly support the idea of all stakeholders being actively involved in the development of a school budget. This requires a collaborative process involving the school leader doing more than calling a group of representatives together for the purpose of reviewing the already completed school budget. Appropriate training, supervision, guidance, and direction—in a most confident, energetic, intelligent, creative, tolerant, adjustable, dependable, and social manner—must be the leadership norm in a systematic budget development process. Note the words of Alex Cornell: "The real world is a messy place—yet, even a messy place should be attacked systematically" (AZQuotes, n.d.). Building a school budget must involve all parties who, by working collaboratively, develop the budget from a more specific, systematic, and decision-making perspective.

Chapter 3 and Chapter 5 noted that the academic action or improvement plan is useless unless it is directly integrated with the budget plan. Working collaboratively with the school leader, representatives of the learning community begin determining the educational needs of an organization in relation to the allocated funds. Sound budgeting theory dictates the involvement of all stakeholders serving in a representative capacity. Unfortunately, the active participation of the learning community members in the budgetary process has been given significant lip service by far too many school leaders when, in fact, such collaboration is often minimal in practice. Considering this assessment in a more detailed manner, let's examine which stakeholders should be involved in the budget development process and further identify their respective roles and responsibilities.

The School Leader

The school leader at the site level is the most important individual in the budgeting process. School leaders today can be described as having slightly fewer years of teaching experience (12.2 years, compared to a 25-year high of 14.0 years in 2000) prior to assuming their first administrative position (National Center for Education Statistics [NCES], 2016b). Principals today are increasingly female at both the elementary and secondary levels, making up to 54% of all school principals when compared with 12% in 1988 and 7% in 1978 (NCES, 2016b). Administrators of color continue to be under-represented in our public schools, with only 8% African American (NCES, 2016b) compared with 2.6% African American in 2000, and 5% Hispanic (NCES, 2016b) compared with less than 1% Hispanic in 2000 (Banks, 2000).

School leaders for years have viewed their role as being hurried, overburdened, and frustrated with more responsibility, less authority, and increasing stress (Sergiovanni, Kelleher, McCarthy, & Fowler, 2009). Specifically, principals today are leaders in the middle, caught among high expectations, constant pressures, managing a daily barrage of administrative and instructional demands, and handling unremitting stressors.

What is needed in terms of school leadership reform is a distributed leadership model as described by the Be the Change Group at the Harvard School of Education (Be the Change Group, 2017). This model closely correlates with the SBDM process in which leadership does not reside in specific roles or with specific persons, but in the relationships developed between the differing individuals in social, cultural, and instructional roles and responsibilities. In other words, leadership at the school level must be collaborative, participative, and shared. Keeping these descriptors in mind, the school leader, as well as the campus team, plays a very important role in the budgeting process. Delving deeper into the differing roles and responsibilities as related to the development of the school budget is required.

School Site Administrators

Differing administrators with differing titles and responsibilities—principal, assistant principal, site specialist, campus facilitator, or instructional coach—often make budgetary decisions. These individuals may very well serve as the school's budget manager. As previously noted within this chapter, budgetary decision making can occur as follows:

1. By autocratic method and manner ("My way or the highway!")

2. By involving a select group of individuals ("those who understand best")

3. By working in collaboration with a SBDM team ("All of us are smarter than any one of us!")

The latter is the best approach to building a school budget because those who have worked collaboratively in developing an academic action or improvement plan must be responsible, along with the school leader, for determining the budgetary needs of the organization. In this process, the school leader or designated leader provides the SBDM group with the necessary forms and figures indicating previous and current year budget allotments and expenditures. Budget histories are very useful in providing fiscal information to all stakeholders. This information is essential in understanding how budgetary allotments and expenditures influence and impact student achievement over time.

Next, the school leader must seek teacher and staff input by asking for the submission of inventory requests for specific supplies, materials, and other educational needs essential to the establishment of an exceptional instructional program. Faculty and staff accustomed to an autocratic approach to the school budgeting process may not initially be thrilled about this new approach to building the school budget. It may seem a waste of valuable time, since their ideas and suggestions have never been sought or implemented before. However, with the passage of time coupled with proper guidance, the team will realize that the process is worthwhile and that their input is actually being sought, valued, and utilized to determine what expenditures are important in providing the best possible learning environment. Moreover, the team soon learns that the school leader is genuinely interested in their ideas and input.

Interestingly, as time goes by, the school leader realizes that the faculty and staff are, in many respects, the best persons to evaluate optimal considerations for the teaching and learning process. With proper training, guidance, and leadership, budgeting team buy-in comes quite easily. The days when the budgeting process was described as too complex, a time when a chosen few were the only ones able to develop a budget, or the "tight-ship" era when authoritarian rule was the norm must be over. A new era of collaborative decision making and participative leadership and teamwork becomes boldly institutionalized within an organization's culture.

Finally, once the necessary input has been collected, a budget meeting is scheduled and the process of bringing recommendations for budgetary expenditures begins in earnest. Building a school budget, from a school leader's perspective, is a step-by-step process culminating in a document developed in collaboration with representatives of the learning community. This document, when properly prepared, contains more than just the budgeted dollars. It is a document that allocates funds for the best instructional methods and programs that further ensure the academic success of each student.

Other Committee Members

Question: What is the one query often posed by school leaders in relation to the budgetary process? Answer: Which individuals should serve as stakeholders on the budget development team? Such a determination varies from school to school. Some states and school districts define, in policy, the parameters of the SBDM process and the stakeholders who will serve on the budget development team. For the sake of a further explanation, the SBDM/budget development team membership is defined as those individuals (elected and/or appointed and voting and/or nonvoting members) who are representative of the learning community. Such contributing members could be teachers representing grade levels or departments as well as band, choir, orchestra, drama, and athletic directors; paraprofessionals; custodians; parent–teacher organization representatives; parents; military liaisons; community members (chief of police, for example); school administrators; and central office administrators (directors of curriculum, special education, bilingual education, gifted and talented education, maintenance and transportation, and business operations, for example) as well as comptrollers or business managers and even the superintendent of schools. The key to identifying committee members is inclusive representation of the learning community. A closer examination of the differing members and their roles is required.

School Site Directors

Band, choir, orchestra, and drama directors should be automatically represented on the budget development team, since these individuals often serve as budget managers with responsibilities related to instruction, extracurricular issues, purchasing musical instruments and materials, uniforms, costumes, and the cost of transportation. The building-level athletic director can very well serve on the team to help coordinate expenditures related to the athletic program and to further supervise costs associated with transportation, coaches' salaries and stipends, officials, uniforms, ticket takers, police, ambulance, doctors, and meal and lodging expenses.

Teachers and Grade-Level or Department Chairs

Teachers and other certified personnel must be an integral part of the school committee. These individuals know and understand the students and the instructional programs, and they are the professionals who most affect a school's culture and climate, which directly impacts students' ability to excel and achieve. Grade-level or department chairs are generally the most informed and best prepared to lead the instructional program and thus, their areas of expertise qualify them to effectively make budgetary decisions.

Central Office Administrators

Administrators may be required at times to serve on the school committee when their particular area of expertise and advice is needed. Central office administrators are generally nonvoting members who can provide helpful advice when certain topics outside the committee's level of expertise are being discussed and examined.

Students

Often overlooked, students (typically Grades 6 and above) can provide legitimate advice and consideration as related to the budgetary process. Who knows better what is most relevant, timely, and workable in relation to student issues and, in some instances, programmatic considerations? We fail as school leaders when we do not listen to others—most notably, our students!

Community Members

Community members often provide insight only an outsider can visualize. Many times, school administrators, and faculty are myopic when it comes to school and programmatic issues. Sometimes, whether educators like it or not, the outsiders—the community members—can present a long-overlooked or often ignored perspective that, when addressed, can have a positive and long-lasting impact on school reform, improvement, and—most important— student achievement.

School Budget Applications

Ovsiew and Castetter (1960), in their classic text, *Budgeting for Better Schools,* suggest that there are several integrating aspects of a school budget that ensure better budgets for better schools. Their book—while more than half a century old—may be dated; however, their message is not. Examine the budgetary components and applications essential to building an effective school-based budget. By following this prescribed step-by-step process, the school leader experiences a sense of security in that the proposed budget will meet with appropriate recognition and approval at the district-level budget hearing and defense session. Below are several budgetary components and applications essential to building an effective school-based budget.

1. *Descriptive Narrative*—A detailed description of the school (years of operation, location, demographic information such as percentage of free and reduced-price lunch population, federal program eligibilities and identifiers, and other important descriptors such as socioeconomic backgrounds and poverty status of the student population) identifies in narrative form the areas of budgetary need and consideration.

2. *Programmatic Identifiers*—Identifiers relating the grades of the school, total students enrolled, ethnic distribution, and other programmatic considerations (special education, gifted and talented, bilingual education, vocational education, etc.) along with the number of faculty employed—teachers, counselors, nurses, administrators, librarians, paraprofessionals, clerks, secretaries, and so on—are detailed in this narrative.

3. *Mission Statement*—A statement of introduction as related to the school's goal or philosophy about the nature of learners, learning, and the purpose of the school serves to explain the rationale of the organization and how it impacts the decision-making and budgetary process.

4. *Student Enrollment Projections*—A chart or table utilizing the cohort survival method (see "Projecting Student Enrollment" in this chapter) is used to project student populations critical to any school budget as future student enrollment increases or decreases. Increases or decreases in student enrollment are indicative of the funding necessities essential for a school's success. Many school districts, especially in urban areas, will project student enrollment out as much as 30 years. The reason? Districts must know the locations of potential population growth patterns to purchase land for the construction of future schools and/or to make decisions regarding school closures.

5. *Analysis of Academic Action or Improvement Plan*—When analyzing the academic action or improvement plan of a school, consider the following questions:

1. What aspects of the instructional program need improvement?

2. What pertinent sources of data verify any areas of improvement?

3. Which of the concerns, problems, or needs are most significant for improving the overall instructional program?

4. Which proposed improvement efforts are within the school's
budgetary scope and capability for effective action and
implementation?

5. Which concerns, problems, or needs are of the highest priority, and is there a sound research base for addressing each
prioritized concern, problem, or need?

Additionally, numerous states identify components to be
addressed in campus action or improvement plans. For example, as
previously identified in Chapter 5 but important to review again, the
state of Texas has 13 essential campus action or improvement plan
components as stipulated by law (TEC §11.252 and §11.253—Texas
Education Agency, 2017b):

1. Student performance

2. Special education

3. Violence prevention

4. Parental involvement

5. Staff development

6. Suicide prevention

7. Conflict resolution

8. Dyslexia treatment programs

9. Dropout reduction

10. Technology

11. Discipline management

12. Accelerated instruction

13. Career education

A careful analysis of a campus action or improvement plan should
reflect the inclusion of these and/or other important components as
identified by a state or school district. Such components are essential
to a campus action or improvement plan serving as the vehicle that
drives the direction of a school's instructional program, positively
impacting student academic achievement.

6. *Needs Assessment*—A needs assessment serves to identify what areas or aspects of the school program need improvement after a review of all pertinent sources of data (e.g., academic action plan, previous studies, local and statewide test results, and surveys of teachers, students, and parents). In addition, a review of the research literature along with collaborative team discussions regarding each area of instructional and/or programmatic concerns is particularly useful and beneficial.

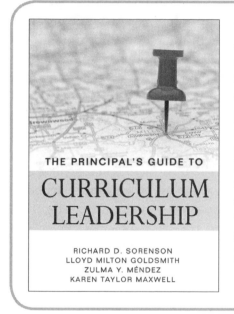

THE PRINCIPAL'S GUIDE TO

CURRICULUM LEADERSHIP

RICHARD D. SORENSON
LLOYD MILTON GOLDSMITH
ZULMA Y. MÉNDEZ
KAREN TAYLOR MAXWELL

The Principal's Guide to Curriculum Leadership (Sorenson et al., 2011) is an excellent source and reliable desk reference for the practicing or prospective school leader. Chapter 3, pages 54–83, of that text provides a step-by-step, expectation-oriented guide to the identification of a site-based team, vision development, quality analysis, needs assessment, and needs prioritization process as well as instructional enhancements and a how-to approach to conflict polarization.

7. *Priority Analysis*—A priority analysis immediately follows a needs assessment. The principal and team interacting collaboratively determine the campus instructional and student-centered priorities and then ordinate the priorities. In other words, list in order what is the most important need, followed by the second most important, then third most important, and so forth. The funding of needs must be in priority order. Listed below are several examples of identified priorities from a needs assessment recently conducted at a public school in an urban center located in the southwestern United States:

- Staff development will be initiated with all faculty, with a concentration in research-based strategies proven to be effective in assisting English language learners (ELLs) to acquire the language and skills needed to be successful in all content areas. Forms of assessment must be empirically researched and utilized to monitor the progress of this particular subgroup in order to best determine if the implementation of instructional strategies is effective relative to increasing student test scores and improving academic achievement. This training will be conducted and facilitated by the Hispanic Educational Learning Program (HELP) initiative.

- Staff development will be initiated with all faculty with a concentration in research-based strategies proven to be effective in assisting and motivating male Hispanic students to best experience academic success in the classroom in all core areas. Teachers must be provided additional training regarding the analysis of student data to determine the academic progress of this subgroup. Consultants from the Southwestern Regional Research Laboratory (SWRL) will conduct this training.
- To increase special education (SPED) test scores to 80% > and ELLs' test scores to 90% > in mathematics, seventh- and eighth-grade mathematics teachers will continue to utilize the Closing the Gap academic initiative to best provide SPED and ELL students with academic achievement–oriented instruction. Teachers will also utilize district-determined best teaching and learning practices and strategies during classroom instruction to target programmatic objectives in which SPED and ELL students are at risk of failing.
- To further increase SPED and ELL student test scores and to improve the teaching and learning of students in these subgroups, teachers will incorporate differentiated instructional techniques utilizing the research-based EdScope-At-Risk Student Analysis program, to be purchased by the school.
- Student attendance rates, most notably of ELL students, must be increased by implementing the empirical, research-based, and more efficient student attendance monitoring system, StudentTrak, to be purchased by the school. Research reveals this particular tracking system of student attendance provides for a more efficient collaboration with parents and guardians, community members, assistant principals, attendance clerks, teachers, and counselors.

8. *Teacher/Student Distribution Table*—Table 6.1 indicates the distribution of students by grade level or subject area (secondary schools) in relation to the number of staff dedicated to serving students from a programmatic consideration (e.g., bilingual classrooms, inclusion-monolingual classrooms, and monolingual-only classrooms). This table provides a visual understanding of why and how an increase or decrease in student enrollment impacts the budgetary allotment for teacher salaries, paraprofessional assistance, and program development.

Table 6.1 Teacher/Student Distribution Table

	Bilingual	Inclusion-Monolingual	Monolingual Only			
PreK	15 t & ta	15 t & ta				
K	22 t	5 + 10 t & ta	21 t	22 t	22 t	22 t
Grade 1	21 t	5 + 10 t & ta	22 t	22 t	20 t	21 t
Grade 2	20 t	5 + 10 t & ta	21 t	22 t	22 t	
Grade 3	22 t	5 + 10 t & ta	22 t	22 t	20 t	21 t
Grade 4	20 t	4 + 10 t & ta	22 t	21 t	22 t	
Grade 5	28 t	5 + 15 t & ta	31 t	35 t	33 t	32 t
SPED			43 2 t & 5 ta			
# Students	148	29 + 65	197	144	139	96
# Staff	7 t 1 ta	6 t 6 ta	9 t 6 ta	6 t	6 t	4 t

NOTE: t = teacher; ta = teacher aide or assistant.

9. Faculty Apportionment Table—Table 6.2 reveals the apportionment or distribution of the entire faculty in relation to the number of assigned personnel to a school. This table allows the school leader and team as well as district office and business department administrators to visualize areas of need in relation to the student enrollment projections.

10. *Above-Basic Personnel Request and Justification*—The above-basic personnel request narrative is another necessary component of the budgetary process, as this particular section of the school budget justifies the need for increased faculty and staff. Furthermore, this narrative seeks those critical funds for additional personnel that may be above the basic school allotment.

Table 6.2   *Faculty Apportionment Table*

Position	No. Assigned to Campus
Principal	1
Assistant principal	1
School secretary	1
Fiscal Education and Information Management System (FEIMS) clerk	1
Instructional facilitator	1
Counselor	1
Nurse	1
Nurse assistant	1
Librarian	1
Total faculty	**9**

Position	No. Assigned to Campus
Gifted and talented teacher	½
Speech therapist	½
Physical education teacher	1
Music teacher	1
Office aides	2
Title VI aides	1
Custodians	4
Food services	5
Total faculty	**15**

11. *Allocation Statement*—The allocation statement serves to provide in tabular form (see Table 6.3) a brief but descriptive distribution of funds. Within this statement, the total student population count is noted along with the average daily attendance (ADA) or average daily membership (ADM) rate. In addition, the statement identifies the ADA or ADM funding on a per-pupil basis along with the SPED, gifted and talented, bilingual/English as a Second Language (ESL), Title I, and state compensatory funding allocations. Finally, a total allocation is listed. This total allocation is the basis for building the school budget.

12. *Salaries for Personnel Table*—This section of the school budget details in tabular form (see Table 6.4) the exact identification and distribution of salaries for personnel.

Table 6.3   Allocation Statement

		State Allocation				Campus Allotment
Student population	=	818				
Average daily attendance (ADA)	=	90%		818 × 0.90	=	736.2 = 736
ADA funding	=	736	×	$2,537.00	=	$1,867,232.00
SPED	=	72	×	$7,125.00	=	$513,000.00
Gifted and talented	=	45	×	$285.00	=	$12,825.00
Bilingual/ESL	=	148	×	$237.50	=	$35,150.00
Title I (82%)	=	671	×	$262.50	=	$176,137.50
State compensatory	=	671	×	$475.00	=	$318,725.00
Total Allocation					=	**$2,923,069.50**

Table 6.4   Salaries for Personnel

Personnel Salaries		
Teachers, nurse, librarian	=	$47,500
Principal	=	$101,000
Assistant principal	=	$87,000
Counselor	=	$55,000
Diagnostician	=	$57,000
Instructional facilitator	=	$60,000
Speech therapist	=	$52,000

(Continued)

Table 6.4   (Continued)

Personnel Salaries		
Testing coordinator	=	$49,000
Security officer	=	$41,000
Secretary	=	$35,000
Instructional/clerical aides	=	$31,000
Nurse assistant	=	$31,000
Custodian (head)	=	$37,000
Custodian	=	$30,000
Food services	=	$12,100
Consultant(s)	=	$2,500 per day

Supplements (Stipends) = $2,000	
Resource (SPED)	Head nurse
Bilingual	Head counselor
Math	Head custodian
Science	Department chairs
Librarian	Diagnostician
Home economics	

13. *Salary Distribution Table*—Table 6.5 reflects salaries and supplements (stipends) of all school personnel, incorporating the appropriate payroll descriptions and budgetary coding. While most school districts across the United States do not require principals to be responsible for payroll budgetary allotments and management of personnel salaries, some smaller districts, in fact, do so. Payroll is typically a fixed cost and is frequently either removed from the campus budget allocation or simply frozen at the district level. However, the process of compiling a payroll analysis via the Salary Distribution Table (see Table 6.5) does provide for a better understanding of how payroll (personnel salaries) significantly impact district and campus budgetary costs. Upward of 75% to 85% of a school district's revenue is typically required for payroll expenditure. This means that the majority of a school's budgetary funding allocation is expended even before a principal and campus SBDM team examines the campus budgetary allotment. This enormous expenditure requires principals to be effective financial stewards of the funding allotment they do receive. To coin an old phrase, money does not grow on trees—or in the case of a school, in the principal's office!

Table 6.5   Salary Distribution Table

Fund	Function	Object/Sub-object	Organization	Current School Year (CSY)	Program	Description	Total	
199	11	6119	103	CSY	11	Payroll: Regular Education Teachers (24)	$	1,140,000.00
199	11	6119	103	CSY	11	Payroll: Math/Science Stipends	$	24,000.00
199	11	6119	103	CSY	23	Payroll: Special Education Aides (4)	$	116,000.00
199	11	6129	103	CSY	11	Payroll: Secretary	$	35,000.00
199	11	6129	103	CSY	11	Payroll: Support Personnel (FEIMS)	$	29,000.00
199	11	6129	103	CSY	11	Payroll: Support Personnel (Attendance)	$	29,000.00
199	11	6129	103	CSY	11	Payroll: Support Personnel (Budget)	$	29,000.00
199	11	6129	103	CSY	11	Payroll: Support Personnel (Receptionist)	$	29,000.00
199	11	6129	103	CSY	11	Payroll: Support Personnel (At-Risk)	$	29,000.00
199	11	6129	103	CSY	11	Payroll: Support Personnel (Discipline)	$	29,000.00
199	11	6129	103	CSY	24	Payroll: Tutors (8)	$	232,000.00
						SUBTOTAL FUNCTION 11: INSTRUCTION	$	1,721,000.00
							$	
199	12	6119	103	CSY	11	Payroll: Librarian	$	47,500.00
199	12	6119	103	CSY	11	Payroll: Librarian Stipend	$	2,000.00
						SUBTOTAL FUNCTION 12: INSTR. RES. & MEDIA SRVC.	$	49,500.00
199	23	6119	103	CSY	11	Payroll: Principal	$	90,000.00
199	23	6119	103	CSY	11	Payroll: Asst. Principal	$	74,000.00

(Continued)

Table 6.5 (Continued)

Fund	Function	Object/Sub-object	Organization	Current School Year (CSY)	Program	Description	Total
						SUBTOTAL FUNCTION 23: SCHOOL LEADERSHIP	$ 164,000.00
199	31	6119	103	CSY	11	Payroll: Counselor	$ 110,000.00
199	31	6119	103	CSY	11	Payroll: Head Counselor Stipend	$ 2,000.00
199	31	6119	103	CSY	23	Payroll: Diagnostician (.5)	$ 28,500.00
199	31	6119	103	CSY	23	Payroll: Diagnostician Stipend	$ 2,000.00
						SUBTOTAL FUNCTION 31: GUIDANCE, COUNSELING	$ 1,132,500.00
199	33	6119	103	CSY	11	Payroll: Nurse	$ 47,500.00
199	33	6119	103	CSY	11	Payroll: Nurse Stipend	$ 2,000.00
						SUBTOTAL FUNCT 33: HEALTH SERVICES	$ 49,500.00
199	35	6129	103	CSY	11	Payroll: Food Services (Cafeteria Manager)	$ 22,000.00
199	35	6129	103	CSY	11	Payroll: Food Services (7)	$ 84,700.00
						SUBTOTAL FUNCTION 35: FOOD SERVICES	$ 106,700.00
199	51	6129	103	CSY	11	Payroll: Head Custodian	$ 37,000.00
199	51	6129	103	CSY	11	Payroll: Head Custodian Stipend	$ 2,000.00
199	51	6129	103	CSY	11	Payroll: Custodians (6)	$ 180,000.00
						SUBTOTAL FUNCTION 51: PLANT MAINT. & OPERATION	$ 219,000.00

199	52	6129	103	CSY	11	Payroll: Security	$	41,000.00
199	52	6129	103	CSY	11	Payroll: Security Clerk	$	29,000.00
						SUBTOTAL FUNCTION 52: SECURITY SERVICES	$	70,000.00
219	11	6119	103	CSY	25	Payroll: Bilingual Teachers (5)	$	237,500.00
219	11	6119	103	CSY	25	Payroll: Bilingual Stipend	$	10,000.00
						SUBTOTAL FUNCTION 11: INSTRUCTION (BILINGUAL)	$	247,500.00
224	11	6119	103	CSY	23	Payroll: Special Education Teachers (5)	$	237,500.00
224	11	6119	103	CSY	23	Payroll: SPED Stipend	$	10,000.00
224	11	6119	103	CSY	23	Payroll: Speech Teacher (.5)	$	26,000.00
						SUBTOTAL FUNCTION 11: INSTRUCTION (SPED)	$	273,500.00
243	11	6119	103	CSY	22	Payroll: Career/Technology Teacher	$	47,500.00
						SUBTOTAL FUNCTION 11: INSTRUCTION (CAREER/TECHNOLOGY)	$	47,500.00
		6100				TOTAL PAYROLL COSTS	$	4,080,700.00
						GRAND TOTAL	$	4,080,700.00

Final Budget Compilation—The final budget compilation is to be completed in a tabular format as dictated by the school district and on the forms (typically in electronic format) provided by the district business department. If the school district does not specify the format or provide the necessary budget compilation forms, the use of the Microsoft® Excel software program is a recommended method, although other marketed versions are readily available. The final budget compilation must utilize the fund, function, object, sub-object, organization, fiscal year, and program intent codes (see Tables 6.6–6.12 in this chapter for examples). The process of building a school budget is detailed for reader application purposes in "Case Study Application #3: The Budget Development Project."

Budget Allocations

Budgetary allocations are derived from a variety of revenue sources. These sources—federal, state, and local—provide funding dollars associated with budgetary allocations and are generally identified as governmental fund types with descriptors such as *general, special revenue, capital projects,* and *debt services.* The two most important governmental fund types insofar as the school budget allocation is concerned are *general* and *special revenue.* General funds are typically available for school allocations with minimal planned expenditure and purchasing restrictions. General funds are needed to sustain the normal operations, administration, and counseling expenditures of a school. Special revenue funds are governmental funds used to account for the proceeds of specific revenue sources that are legally restricted to expenditures for specified purposes. Examples include Title I (improving basic programs), vocational education, and food services. Dollars from these funding sources are then utilized as the basis for budgetary allocations at the school level.

School budget allocations are typically based on an ADA or an ADM formulation. ADA versus ADM is a school finance issue regarding the relationship between student attendance and financial support. Determining the allocation by ADA benefits school districts with higher attendance and penalizes those with lower levels of attendance. More students in attendance equates to more money for districts. In addition, more students in attendance equates to more learning taking place, a fact supported by test scores. Proponents of ADM as the basis for school funding cite that whether a student is in attendance on any particular day, the costs of district operations (salaries, utilities, transportation, other services, etc.) remain constant and thus the allocation of funds should recognize such (Brimley, Verstegen, & Garfield, 2015). Nevertheless, the allotment (based on either of the formulations)—along with additional dollars that may be appropriated as a result of the number of identified ELLs, gifted and talented, SPED, and at-risk students—serves as the initial basis for school allocated funds. Additional allotted monies for the school can come from grant dollars, technology funds, maintenance funds, staff development allocations, and other miscellaneous allotments. While most of these allotted dollars allow for administrators to implement and control activities authorized by the budget, certain limitations or restrictions can be placed on the budget for the following reasons:

- The budget limits the type, quantity, and quality of instruction provided at the school level, especially in an era of fiscal conservatism, which is often a result of an economic downturn.
- The public is critically interested in education and, more specifically, instruction.
- School operations are often diverse and broad in scope and, thus, important budgetary planning is necessary for effective and efficient expenditure of funds.
- School allocations provide direction for the school's future.

Restricted Funds

While budget allotments are used for a variety of services and expenditures at the school level, some are more restrictive than others. Once basic school allotments are appropriated to particular areas within the budget, function restrictions limit their use unless district approval is obtained in the form of a budget amendment or transfer.

Recall from Chapter 4 that restricted or categorical funds are often associated with Title I, bilingual education, and SPED dollars and programs. For example, many school districts carefully restrict the expenditure of funds appropriated to these particular programs on the basis of federal and state guidelines that often stipulate that funded dollars within these particular budgeted categories can only be utilized for the purpose of student-related instruction. Consider the following scenarios.

HEY, I FOUND THE MONEY!

The office secretary at Somerville School needed a new file cabinet, desk, and carpet but recognized that the general funds allocated had already been appropriated and encumbered within the budget. However, Sam Nachin, the school administrator, thought to himself, "Hey, I found the money!" noting the Title I accounts had just enough funds to be appropriated for office upgrades. Thus, in an electronic instant, the Title I dollars were encumbered and plans were made for a quick purchase of office items. No doubt, creative thinking on the part of Mr. Nachin. His actions are a reminder of the old adage, "Necessity is the mother of invention." However, the Title I funds were specifically and categorically designated for Title I–eligible students. Chances are that the justification for incorporating Title I funds for the purchase of new office equipment for the school secretary would be a real stretch of the imagination in relation to the budgeted funds utilized.

Pause and Consider

- Check with administration at your school to determine the specific guidelines regarding the expenditure of Title I funds.
- Can Mr. Nachin purchase office furniture, equipment, and carpet for his school secretary? What do your district guidelines dictate? If no, why do you think these stringent guidelines are in place?

AS GOES CALIFORNIA, SO GOES THE NATION?

Michael Fanning, instructor at the School of Continuing Education, California State University–East Bay, relates the importance of more local control and fewer restricted funds in school finance and budgeting. Dr. Fanning shares information about the California system of local control as initiated by Governor Jerry Brown and the state legislature. This initiative, recent in its manifestation, was reported as a reform movement by Margaret Weston (2011) with the Public Policy Institute of California. The project permanently extends much of the categorical funding flexibility and consolidates most categorical programs into a few larger, more equitable programs. These programs focus on broader state education goals such as the academic improvement of disadvantaged students and ELLs. The initiative provides the state of California the opportunity to prioritize educational goals, determine associated costs, and assign responsibility for greater funding and implementation at the local level. More local control, fewer restricted funds, enhanced budgeting at the campus level, and greater student achievement: As goes California, so goes the nation?

TO GAIN MORE INFORMATION, GO TO HTTP://WWW
.PPIC.ORG/MAIN/PUBLICATION_SHOW.ASP?I=1001

The concept of restricted funds brings a school leader full circle in terms of understanding the need for accounting code structures that have been determined and designated by the Governmental Accounting Standards Board (GASB). These accounting code structures ensure that a sequence of coding is uniformly applied to all schools and school districts to account for the proper appropriation and expenditure of public funds (GASB, 2016).

Coding Applications

The nationally recognized GASB prescribes that budgets for public education entities be reported on the basis of a standard operating accounting code structure (NCES, 2016d). An example of a state's operating accounting code structure is shown by fund, function, object, sub-object, organization, fiscal year, and program intent code in Table 6.6. States require a standard operating accounting code structure be adopted by every school district. A major purpose of the accounting code structure is to ensure that the sequence of codes is uniformly applied to all school districts to further account for the appropriation and expenditure of public funds (GASB, 2016).

Table 6.6   Example of a State's Operating Accounting Code Structure

199 —	11 —	6399	.00 —	001	Insert Current Year	—	11
1	2	3	4	5	6		7

1 = Fund code. How will the expenditure be financed? What is being funded?

School district accounting systems are organized and operated on a fund basis. A fund is an accounting entity with a self-balancing set of accounts recording financial resources and liabilities. There are more than 500 different types of fund codes, and examples include general fund, bilingual education, SPED, Title I, vocational education, and so forth.

2 = Function code. Why is the expenditure being made? What is the function or purpose for the expenditure?

The function code is an accounting entity applied to expenditures and expenses and identifies the purpose or function of any school district transaction. There are at least 27 different types of function codes; examples include instruction, school leadership, guidance counseling, health services, and so forth.

(Continued)

Table 6.6   (Continued)

199 —	11 —	6399	.00	—	001	Insert Current Year	—	11
1	2	3	4		5	6		7

3 = Object code. What object is being purchased?

The object code is an accounting entity identifying the nature and object of an account, a transaction, or a source. There are more than 35 different types of object codes and examples include instruction, payroll, professional and contracted services, supplies and materials, capital outlay, and so forth.

4 = Sub-object code. Which department- or grade-level purchase is being made?

The sub-object code is an accounting entity that provides for special or additional accountability and is often utilized to delineate secondary-level departments.

5 = Organization code. What unit or organization within a school system is making the purchase?

The organization code is an accounting entity that identifies the organization—the high school, middle school, elementary school, superintendent's office, and so forth. The activity, not the location, defines the organization within a school district. There are more than 900 organization codes. For example, expenditures for a high school might be classified as 001, as the organization codes for high school campuses are generally identified as 001 through 040. Middle school organization codes are typically stipulated as 041 through 100. Elementary schools fall into the organization code range of 101 through 698. For example, Cypress Fairbanks School District in Texas has 50+ elementary schools, 20+ middle schools, 15+ high schools, and 5+ alternative schools, all with differing yet independently identifiable organization codes.

6 = Fiscal year code. During what fiscal year is the purchase being made?

The fiscal year code identifies the fiscal year of any budgetary transaction. For example, during the 2025–2026 fiscal year of a school district, the numeral 26 would denote the fiscal year.

7 = Program intent code. To what student group is the instructional purchase or service being directed or intended?

The program intent code is used to designate the rationale of a program that is provided to students. These codes are used to account for the cost of instruction and other services that are directed toward a particular need of a specific set of students. There are approximately a dozen program intent codes; examples include basic educational services, gifted and talented, career and technology, SPED, bilingual education, Title I services, and so forth.

NOTE: The codification incorporated within Table 6.6 are referenced according to the NCES (2016d) and the GASB (2016). These codes are representative numbers often assigned to state operating accounting code structures. Individual state budgetary coding requirements/processes may vary. To learn more about individual state coding and budgeting requirements, contact your state education department.

States require a standard fiscal accounting code system. State coding systems are implemented and uniformly utilized by local school districts in accordance with Generally Accepted Accounting Principles (GAAP). States require that a standard fiscal accounting code system be adopted by each school district. The system must meet the minimum requirements prescribed by state boards of education and is subject to review and comment by state auditors. In addition, the accounting system utilized by states and school districts must conform to the GAAP as identified by the GASB (2016). The fiscal accounting code system ensures that the sequence of codes is uniformly applied to all school districts across a state. The budgetary accounting code system is a labeling method designed to ensure the accuracy and legality of expenditures. School budgets are tracked by state education agencies via the budgetary accounting code system.

School district accounting systems are organized and operated on a fund basis. A fund is an accounting entity with a self-balancing set of accounts recording financial resources and liabilities. A school district designates the fund's financial resources for a distinct purpose. State or federal governments, as well as the local school district, may establish the fund's purpose. Shown in Table 6.7 is an example of a state's operating accounting code structure as well as explanations that describe the specifics of each code. Table 6.8 through Table 6.12

Table 6.7 Example of a State's Operating Accounting Code Structure

199 —	11 —	6399	.00 —	001	Current Year —	11
1	2	3	4	5	6	7

Table 6.8 Categories for Fund Codes

Fund Codes—1st Digit (Nine Categories)	
100 –	Regular programs
200 –	Special or federal programs (Examples: Title I—211, bilingual education—219, special education—224, school breakfast and lunch program—240, etc.)
300 –	Vocational programs
400 –	Other state and local instructional programs
500 –	Nonpublic school programs
600 –	Adult and continuing education programs
700 –	Debt service
800 –	Community service programs
900 –	Enterprise programs
000 –	Undistributed expenditures

provide examples of categories for fund codes, function codes, object codes, organization codes, and program intent codes.

Fund codes (1) are typically mandatory for all financial transactions to identify the specific group or program to be funded. Fund codes contain three digits with the first digit identifying regular, special, and vocational programs. A second digit denotes either the grade level or particular program area or category such as the local operating fund. The third digit further defines program type in relation to student classifications, type of services, and/or student population. For example, the number 211 identifies the Title I federal fund group.

Function codes (2) are typically mandatory two- to four-digit numbers that identify the function or purpose of the expenditure (instruction = 11, for example). Function codes further designate budget program areas (see Table 6.9). Function codes represent as many as nine different categories. As noted, the most commonly used function code category within a school budget is instruction, although other areas, including school leadership, guidance counseling, and health services, are frequently incorporated.

Object codes (3) are mandatory three- to four-digit numbers identifying the particular nature or object of an account, a transaction, or a source. Object codes further describe program allocations and expenditures. Object codes represent seven different categories (see Table 6.10).

Sub-object codes (4) are two-digit numbers used as accounting entries by local school districts to delineate, for example, secondary-level departments such as English, mathematics, science, physical

Table 6.9   Categories for Function Codes

Function Codes—Nine Categories	
10–	Instruction and instructional-related services
20–	Instructional and school leadership
30–	Support services—student (pupil)
40–	Administrative support services
50–	Support services—nonstudent based
60–	Ancillary services
70–	Debt service
80–	Capital outlay
90–	Intergovernmental charges

education, and history. The sub-object code is intended to provide for special or additional accountability.

Organization codes (5) are mandatory three-digit numbers identifying accounting entries or organizations as being high school, middle school, elementary school, superintendent's office, or school board (see Table 6.11). This code readily notes which high schools in a district are the oldest or the newest. For example, Elm High School (001) is the first or oldest high school, followed by Birch High School

Table 6.10   Categories for Object Codes

Object Codes—Seven Categories	
6000–	Expenditure/expense control accounts
6100–	Payroll costs
6200–	Professional and contract services
6300–	Supplies and materials
6400–	Other operating costs
6500–	Debt service
6600–	Capital outlay—land, buildings, and equipment

Table 6.11   Categories for Organization Codes

Organization Codes—Two Categories	
001–699	Organization units—schools
700–	Organization units—administrative

Table 6.12   Categories for Program Intent Codes

Program Intent Codes—Eleven Categories	
11–	Basic educational services
21–	Gifted and talented
22–	Career and technology
23–	Special education
24–	Accelerated instruction (at-risk programs, tutoring, etc.)
25–	Bilingual education
26/27–	Nondisciplinary alternative education programs
28/29–	Disciplinary alternative education programs
30–	Title I

(002), Oak High School (003), and Hickory High School (004), and so forth. The same coding designation is true for middle and elementary schools as well.

The fiscal year (6) is a mandatory single- or double-digit code that identifies the fiscal year of budgetary transactions.

The program intent code (7) is frequently represented by two digits and designates the intent or rationale of a program provided to students. This code accounts for the cost of instruction and other services directed toward a particular need of a specific student population. The 11 program intent code categories are identified in Table 6.12.

IT DOESN'T TAKE A SECRET DECODER RING!

Learning how to use budget codes is not a difficult process. In fact, coding can be quite simple, even if the long strand of numbers looks intimidating. Noted below are four questions related to understanding the code definitions. Beyond that, the reader will find two coding activities. The correct answers are located at the conclusion of the chapter.

Pause and Consider

1. A principal seeks to purchase a printer for the school during the current fiscal year. Which code would be incorporated to describe a department the purchase is intended for?
   A. Object
   B. Sub-object
   C. Organization
   D. Program intent

2. A teacher wishes to requisition a box of 5,000 staples. Which code would best describe the item being requisitioned for purchased?
   A. Fund
   B. Function
   C. Object
   D. Sub-object

3. An assistant principal decides to secure supplies and materials for instructional uses. What code would best serve the assistant principal relative to the purpose of the purchase?
   A. Fund
   B. Function

C. Object

D. Sub-object

4. The campus nurse determines that a special medical equipment item is needed for a wheelchair-bound SPED student. What code would the nurse use to identify the specific program or type of service required to fiscally support this purchase?

    A. Fund

    B. Function

    C. Object

    D. Program intent

5. A principal determines that certain services in the way of a consultant, as related to the Title I program that targets a specific student population, must be budgetarily accounted for. Identify the particular coding required.

    A. Fund

    B. Function

    C. Object

    D. Program intent

Activity 1: Utilizing Accounting Codes

Using Tables 6.8 through 6.12 and the Accounting Codes Reference Sheet found in Resource B (pp. 293–297), determine the accounting code to be utilized to complete a school requisition form relative to the following situation. Write your answer in the blanks provided.

_____-___-_____-_____-___

The special services department has requested additional mathematics manipulatives to be utilized in several classrooms at Maple High School. These needed supplies could very well help to increase the overall mathematic test scores at the second-oldest high school in Mapletown Independent School District, as the statewide accountability system now holds all schools accountable for the academic achievement of SPED students. (Answer provided at the conclusion of this chapter.)

Activity 2: Utilizing Accounting Codes

Carefully read and assess the scenario presented and then apply the proper accounting codes by referring to the Accounting Codes Reference Sheet found in Resource B.

_____-____-_____-_____-____

Kit Monami, assistant principal at Eagletown High School, the third-oldest high school in the district, was designated as the budget manager by her principal this school year. Kit was quite competent in her new role and found working with the school budget and budget team to be quite challenging yet most interesting. In her role as budget manager, she interacted with the high school departments and their many demanding personalities. Most recently, Steven Johnson, the head football coach at Eagletown High, had asked Kit if his request for additional athletic supply funds had been included in the budget for the upcoming school year. He was particularly concerned about the need for a new digital recorder for filming the defensive line during after-school practice. "How else does the district expect us to win if I can't properly video the weekly progress of the team?" the coach inquired. Kit explained that she needed Coach Johnson to calculate the cost of the digital recorder and complete the necessary requisition form, and then she would determine if there were additional funds available in the specified account within the school budget.

In this scenario, as Coach Johnson completes the budget requisition form, consider the proper coding for each category—fund, function, object, organization code, and program intent code—and then fill in the budget accounting code found on the requisition form as noted in Form 6.1. (Answer is provided at the conclusion of the chapter.)

Specialized Electronic School Budget Worksheets

This section of the text exemplifies specialized electronic school budget worksheets in the form of screenshots. Electronic budget worksheets are typically incorporated and utilized as part of a school's budgetary reporting process. The particular screenshots, as noted in Figures 6.1–6.9, are the copyright property of Tyler Technologies, Inc. and are incorporated by the authors with permission of the copyright owners and with the assistance of Ysleta Independent School District (YISD), El Paso, Texas.

Form 6.1   Sample Requisition Form

Eagletown Independent School District

"Home of the Soaring Eagles"
100 Eagle Nest Drive
Eagletown, USA

Requisition Form

Requisition No. _____

Purchase Order No. _____

School _____   Originator _____

Budget Accounting Code _____ – _____ – _____ . _____ – _____

Stock #	Qty.	Qty. Shipped	Description	Unit Cost	Total Cost

Merchandise received by _____

Total amount $_____

Approved by _____   Date _____

Copyright © 2018 by Corwin. All rights reserved. Reprinted from *The Principal's Guide to School Budgeting*, third edition, by Richard D. Sorenson and Lloyd M. Goldsmith. Thousand Oaks, CA: Corwin. http://www.corwin.com.

Electronic budgetary worksheets are found in most school systems throughout the United States. The purpose of including these specific e-worksheets and associated descriptors is to inform practicing and prospective principals how specialized electronic budget worksheets are beneficial and productive, better ensuring quality management of the campus budget and further safeguarding against fraud and embezzlement.

Allocation summaries (Figure 6.1), sometimes referred to as *allocation statements* (see p. 233), come in differing formats that frequently identify discretionary funding distributions that could be consolidated into single revenue lines for the purpose of developing a school-based budget. Utilizing allocation summaries, the school leader and team will create line-item accounts, identified by fund, function, object, sub-object, and program intent codes and descriptors. Such line-item accounting might include the regular

Figure 6.1   Allocation Summaries

002 - High School

2017-2018 Proposed Campus Budget Allocations

Category of Allotment	Func	Prgm	SubPgrm	Basis	$Fixed$	Per Capita	Total	Allocated $
Basic Educational Services:								
Regular Program	11/13	11	001-099/400	Regular MMBR	$45,000	$100	1,571	$202,100
Magnet Program Supplement	11/13	11	001-099	Magnet MMBR	$0	$100	0	$0
Basic Education Cost to Support: All Special Education Programs (Subprogram 400)					**Total Basic Educational Services**			**$202,100**
Indirect:								
Indirect	any	any	any	Total MMBR	$25,000	$105	1,571	$189,955
Indirect Cost to Include: Office, Library, Counselor's, Nurse, Custodial, and Security Expenditures					**Total Indirect Cost**			**$189,955**
Cocurricular/Extracurricular Activities:								
Athletics	36	91	501-599	Guideline	$0	$0	N/A	$648,320
Athletics - Major Equipment	36	91	500	Guideline	$0	$0	N/A	$0
CATE Student Travel	36	99	053	Guideline	$0	$0	N/A	$30,000
Band Uniforms	36	99	603	Guideline	$0	$0	N/A	$0
					Total Cocurricular/Extracurricular Activities			**$678,320**
Gifted and Talented Program:								
Gifted and Talented Program	11/13	21	000	G/T Identified	$0	$185	79	$14,615
					Total Gifted and Talented Program			**$14,615**
Career and Technology Education:								
Career and Technology Education	11/13	22	300-399	Voc FTE's	$0	$440	361	$159,016
					Total Career and Technology Education			**$159,016**
Bilingual Education and Special Language Program:								
Bilingual Ed & SLP	11/13	25	000	BIL MMBR	$0	$50	68	$3,400
					Total Bilingual Education and Special Language Program			**$3,400**
State Compensatory Education:								
State Compensatory Education (SCE)	11/13	30	000	At-Risk Count	$0	$0	401	$20,903
					Total State Compensatory Education			**$20,903**

SOURCE: Used with permission: ©2017, Tyler Technologies, Inc. All rights reserved.

or general education allocation, supplemental programs allocation, indirect allocation (*indirect* meaning those funds for counselor, administrative office staff, or custodians, for example) which cannot be explicitly identified with direct instructional activities, cocurricular or extracurricular allocation, gifted and talented allocation, career and technology education allocation, bilingual education allocation, state compensatory education allocation, Title I allocation, and so on.

School leaders must be aware of the amount of funds, as seen in Figure 6.2, that have been committed but not yet approved for the current school year. The use of requisitions for purchases allows the price of the item requested to be encumbered against the budget while the requisition proceeds through the workflow approval process. This minimizes the risk of overspending budgeted line-item amounts.

Once a requisition has completed the approval process, it is converted to a purchase order, as noted in Figure 6.3, which, in turn, serves as the legal authority for obligating district funds. This allows the school leader or district business office to send the purchase order to the vendor to acquire the goods/services. The vendor now has a legal, binding agreement obligating the district to pay for the ordered goods/services. Much like the requisition, the purchase order encumbers the funds against the budget until the items are paid, again, minimizing risk of overspending budgeted amounts.

Figure 6.2   Purchase Requisitions

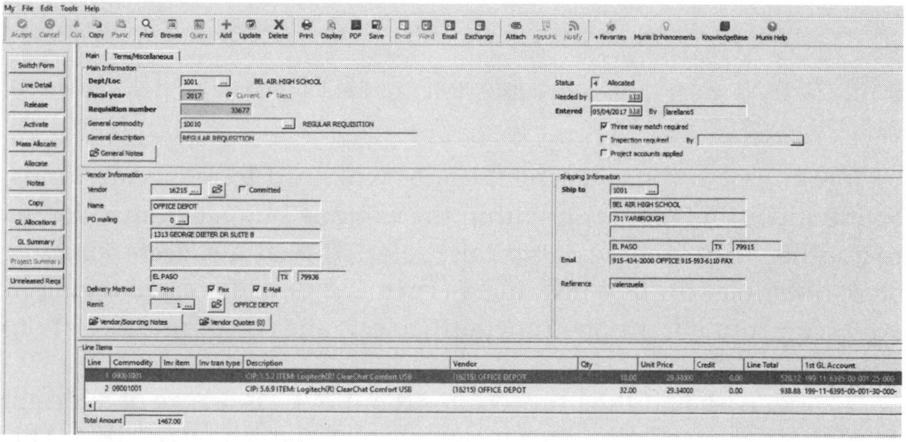

SOURCE: Used with permission: ©2017, Tyler Technologies, Inc. All rights reserved.

Figure 6.3   Purchase Orders

SOURCE: Used with permission: ©2017, Tyler Technologies, Inc. All rights reserved.

Figure 6.4   Budget Transfers and Amendments

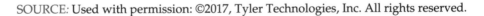

SOURCE: Used with permission: ©2017, Tyler Technologies, Inc. All rights reserved.

From time to time, a school leader will need to reallocate funds, as identified in Figure 6.4, within the campus budget from one area to another. This method is typically referred to as a *budget transfe*r or *amendment* (see pp.185–189) and as such is a process of conveying or adjusting funds from one function, object, and/or program code to another.

Proper cash handling procedures require the issuance of a receipt every time money is collected or received by the school/district. This

Figure 6.5   Cash Receipts and Deposits

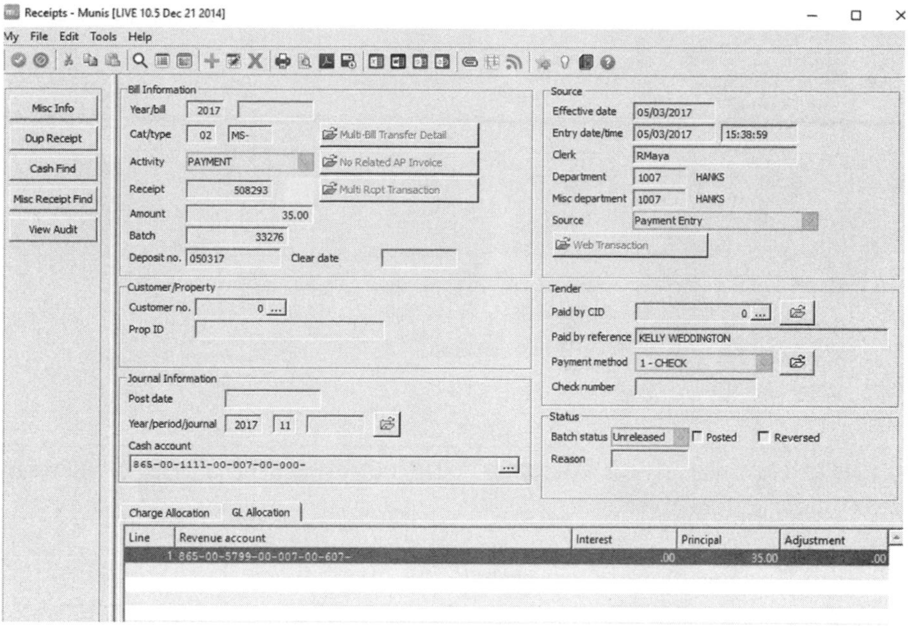

SOURCE: Used with permission: ©2017, Tyler Technologies, Inc. All rights reserved.

process, as revealed in Figure 6.5, ensures proper recording of the transaction and minimizes the risk of theft or fraudulent activities. The cash receipt will indicate how the funds are received (cash, check, or credit card), the person or company making the payment, the person collecting the payment, the reason for payment, and the correct organization to receive credit for the payment. Having an automated cash receipt system provides additional internal controls by automating the receipt numbering system and by providing reports for bank deposits reconciliation.

School systems typically require that all purchases made using federal dollars include a reference to the Campus Improvement Plan (CIP) or Campus Action Plan (CAP). The school leader or campus designee must enter the reference on the requisition in the Notes tab (see Figure 6.6). This particular screen provides a quick reference for reviewers and auditors to recognize where to look in the CIP or CAP for the goal and objective that supports the purchase. Federal guidelines require all purchases be included/documented in a CIP or CAP.

The Inventory Management/Fixed Asset e-module, as seen in Figure 6.7, allows the campus/district to maintain a subsidiary ledger

Figure 6.6   Federal Funding Accountability

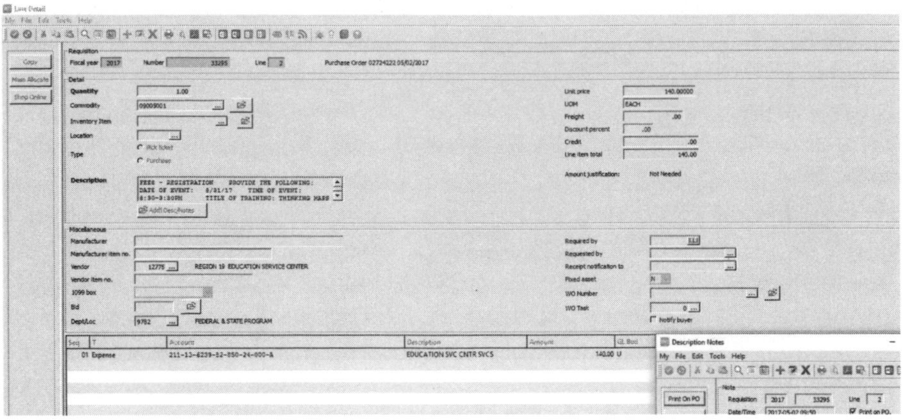

SOURCE: Used with permission: ©2017, Ysleta Independent School District (El Paso, Texas). All rights reserved.

Figure 6.7   Inventory Management

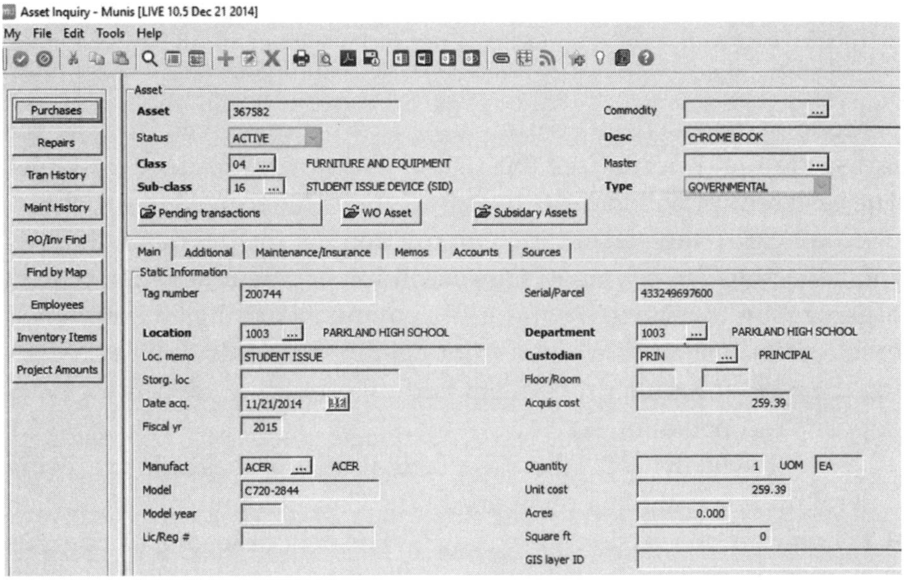

SOURCE: Used with permission: ©2017, Tyler Technologies, Inc. All rights reserved.

detailing specific capital items purchased. This ledger documents the item purchased, date purchased, tag number (if tags are used), serial number, make, model, specific location of the item, acquisition cost, and useful life and can be used to systematically calculate depreciation when necessary. The Inventory Management/Fixed

Asset e-module can be used to generate reports for the school leader to conduct annual inventories of assets and to ensure the safekeeping of the assets. The school leader and/or campus designee must accurately maintain this list to ensure the safekeeping of fixed assets and to properly record disposition or surplus of inventoried and/or unused items.

A year-to-date (YTD) budgeting report (see Figure 6.8) provides the school leader and team with a line-item analysis of available budgeted dollars, funds expended to date, and what percentage of the line-item fund has been expended and further identifies any transfers and/or amendments that have been made by the school leader. Additionally, the YTD report identifies the original campus appropriation. This is an important report to share with the site-based team when reviewing budgetary expenditures each month and when preparing to build next year's budget.

Figure 6.8   YTD Budget Reporting

SOURCE: Used with permission: ©2017, Tyler Technologies, Inc. All rights reserved.

Figure 6.9   Campus Improvement Plan Budget Report

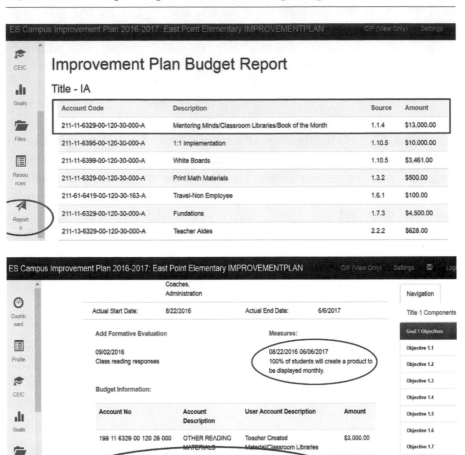

SOURCE: Used with permission: ©2017, Tyler Technologies, Inc. All rights reserved.

The CIP budget report (refer to Figure 6.9) provides the school leader and team with detail regarding purchases made and how said purchases align with district goals and campus objectives. In other words, is the school leader guiding purchases that are aligned with the action or improvement plan as developed during the SBDM process and moreover, do said purchases support student achievement?

Projecting Student Enrollment

Student enrollment information is important to schools and districts relative to declining or increasing enrollments and the corollary, revenue generation. Declining enrollments can be detrimental to a school's budget. Consider the following in relation to a decline in a school or district enrollment: reduced state aid; hiring freezes or a reduction in force (RIF); smaller class sizes, thus creating the need for fewer teachers; and redistricting of school boundaries and the possible closing of school facilities. Increasing enrollments can create overcrowded classrooms and a need for rapid staff and facilities expansion (Ubben & Hughes, 2016).

Therefore, accurate enrollment projections are vital to budgetary allotments, staff planning, and facilities utilization. Over the years, numerous methods have been incorporated by school districts to project student enrollment. The most common model to date remains the *ratio retention* or *cohort survival method*, which provides sufficiently accurate results. Today, the cohort survival method is frequently utilized by schools in the form of computer software programs developed by companies such as Ecotran Systems, Inc. of Beachwood, Ohio; Educational Data Systems of San Jose, California; and Education Logistics, Inc. of Missoula, Montana (Webb & Norton, 2012). Examples of cohort survival method worksheets and presentations (YouTube®, for example) can be examined online by utilizing the search engine descriptor *cohort survival method*. Two specific examples can be found at the following links: https://www.youtube.com/watch?v=HPSjsE3tO6s or https://www.youtube.com/watch?v=C-SA9zwe2xc.

School leaders must recognize that many district office administrators prefer to underestimate enrollment projections because the potential negative impact on cost to a school district is lower. This is important to know since under-projections can equate to less than an appropriate and necessary allocation to the school. Moreover, under-projecting student enrollment equates to understaffing a school.

It is important to note that procedures required to project student enrollments are of three types: gathering demographic data, analyzing the data for possible trends, and then projecting student enrollment on the basis of the evaluated findings. In addition, a careful review and examination of all external environment information is critical to ensure accurate enrollment projections. Listed below are several considerations as related to external environment information:

- emerging communities, including the building of new homes, rental properties such as apartment complexes, and the development of mobile home parks

- changing population patterns
- nonpublic or charter school enrollments
- open school enrollment policies
- initiation of voucher plans
- governmental reduction of federal and/or state education funds
- a significant public event such as the loss of a major community employer
- mobility rate

The cohort survival method accounts for the number of students enrolled in each grade level in a school or across a district over a specified number of years. Moreover, it requires a school to account for the number of students expected to enroll in kindergarten over the next five years. This accounting of potential kindergarten students is based on census data or housing surveys of children between birth and 4 years of age who reside in the school or district attendance zone. This information drives an average ratio calculation for each class from year to year, thus allowing for future-year enrollment projections.

Important Budget Considerations

Barbara Hutton once stated what is obvious in life and in the practice of effective and efficient budgeting: "So, you want to take it with you—well, I've never seen a Brink's truck follow a hearse to the cemetery" (AZQuotes, n.d.)! While an individual can save as much money as possible, at some point in time, those saved dollars must be spent, given away, or inherited by someone because, as Hutton implied, "You can't take it with you!" The same holds true in school budgeting—spend it or give it back. The authors suggest effective school leaders spend all the campus allocated funds but do so in the most accurate, effective, and efficient manner possible. In other words, spend wisely! With this thought in mind, consider the following top 10 school budgeting priority listings. At the conclusion of each of the 10 statements, the identification (in parentheses) of district or school site responsibility is denoted.

1. *Utilize a budget calendar*—The purpose of the budget calendar is to ensure that the budget development process is continuous. The school leader who follows the guidelines and dates associated with a budget calendar maximizes the possibility that nothing interferes

with budgetary preparation requirements or the best interest of the school and school system. (district)

2. *Identify budgetary allocations and restricted funds*—Know and understand the revenue sources and how they impact the school budgetary allotment. Recognize that allotments can be based on an ADA formulation and know how critical it is for the school leader to continuously monitor the enrollment of all students as well as those students served in special programs—for example, bilingual education, Title I, SPED, and gifted and talented. Realize that certain funds have specified restrictions associated with appropriateness of expenditures and student services. (district and school site)

3. *Project incoming and exiting student populations*—The effective school leader regularly monitors incoming and exiting student populations, as the student enrollment of a school can significantly impact the budget allocation. In addition, accomplished school leaders learn to utilize the cohort survival method as a process of projecting student population five years into the future. (district and school site)

4. *Project faculty and staff increases and reductions*—Any increase or reduction in faculty and staff strongly correlates to student enrollment. By utilizing the cohort survival method to forecast into the future, the school leader can assess how many faculty and staff will be needed to ensure personnel stability and a strong educational program. (district and school site)

5. *Conduct a needs assessment*—Efficient needs assessments allow school leaders to recognize which interventions were most effective in increasing student achievement and cost the least. (school site)

6. *Receive input from all stakeholders*—Effective school leadership incorporates collaborative strategies, which in turn generate the involvement and input from organizational followers. When collaborative decision making is implemented, visioning, planning, evaluating, and the overall budgeting process generate measurable improvements, all of which ultimately benefit students, faculty, and the organization. (school site)

7. *Project and prioritize expenditures*—Consider all line-item accounts within the budget, including supplies and materials, salaries, and capital outlay, for example, when analyzing and prioritizing budgetary expenditures. The school leader who actively monitors and regularly evaluates the budget is able to project and prioritize expenditures that focus on specified objectives, which are correlated

with the instructional program, the school action or improvement plan, and the overall vision of the learning community. (school site)

8. *Build the budget*—Exceptional budgetary leaders regularly meet with the budget development team to create a school vision, develop a plan of action, and build a budget. This level of quality leadership demonstrates the following outcomes essential in the budget development process:

- Knowledge of the complete budgetary process
- Knowledge of the amount of funding available and where the budgetary allotment is derived
- Knowledge of collaborative decision-making procedures as well as proper protocols involving the input of all stakeholders
- Knowledge of accounting codes (school site)

9. *Defend the school budget*—Skilled leadership and knowledge of the school budget permit an administrator to exercise ingenuity and competence in addressing questions, suggestions, and criticisms of the school budget at a budget defense hearing. Effectively defending the budget is an act of elucidating clear points and explicating proper justifications for budgetary decisions. Such actions in the formal budget defense hearing reveal leadership traits of credibility, transparency, and expertise. (district and school site)

10. *Amend and adjust the school budget*—Even with all the purposeful budgetary planning and careful monitoring and evaluation, no administrator can expect the school budget to remain on target without certain adjustments being made during the course of a fiscal year. Budget amendments and transfers are necessary when unexpected circumstances and situations inevitably arise. Having a working knowledge of the amendment and transfer processes will facilitate the need to move funds from one account to another without leaving an impression of budgetary incompetence or mismanagement. (district and school site)

The Budget Calendar

School administrators recognize that effective budget development is based on continuous evaluation. This recognition also brings about the need for the development of a detailed budget calendar. The budget calendar lists critical dates for the preparation, submission, review, and approval of the school budget. A variety of straightforward techniques are generally used in developing a budget calendar. While the details involved in developing a school budget are not the same in all districts, it is recommended the following steps be considered and incorporated when preparing a budget calendar:

1. Develop a master district calendar to ensure that all budgetary actions and activities are consistent and compatible across the district and from school to school.

2. Identify specified budgetary actions and activities for inclusion in the calendar and arrange them in chronological order.

3. Assign completion dates for each action and activity and note them on the budget calendar. Completion dates should be assigned by working backward through the actions and activities from legally mandated dates as stipulated by state law and local district policy.

4. Assign dates and space accordingly to ensure that sufficient time is allowed for the completion of each action and activity listed on the budget calendar.

5. Identify on the budget calendar the person(s) specifically responsible for each action or activity listed. This procedure is particularly useful to school administrators because it identifies their own detailed responsibilities and task completion dates.

Again, the budget development process and proposed calendar will vary from state to state and district to district, as fiscal year beginning dates typically start anywhere from July 1 to September 1. School officials who fail to establish a budget calendar or who procrastinate the budget-development process are making a serious mistake, because the avoidance of approaching deadlines will definitely interfere with conscientious budget-building efforts (Brimley et al., 2015).

Outlined in Table 6.13 is a proposed budget calendar with specified considerations as related to the budget development process.

The development and utilization of a budget calendar assists in the formulation of an integrated plan of fiscal operations and further provides a means of communication between the various levels of the organization. Finally, the budget calendar effectively provides each administrator within the organization with appropriate information and deadlines necessary to perform specified budget development duties and responsibilities.

Table 6.13 Proposed Budget Calendar

Schedule	Procedure
Prior to February 1	The superintendent of schools establishes the budget planning format and schedule for preparation of the next fiscal year budget. *Person Responsible:* Superintendent
February 1	A budget request by function and object form should be distributed to school administrators for completion by March 1. Columns for *Actual Previous Year* and *Estimated Current Year* should be completed prior to the form being disseminated to the administrators responsible. *Person Responsible:* Associate superintendent for finance
February 15	Projected student enrollments should be developed. *Person Responsible:* Associate Superintendent for District Administration in collaboration with school leaders
March 1	School administrators should return the completed budget request by function and object form to the district administrator responsible for the initial review and consideration of school needs. The school budget preparation process begins with the involvement of the budget development team. *Person Responsible:* School leaders and SBDM team members.
April 1	Completed school budgets should be submitted to the district administrator responsible for the consolidation of the organizational budget. *Person Responsible:* School leaders
April 15	The district administrator should submit the overall organizational budget to the superintendent of schools for review, along with suggested revisions prior to consolidation into a total district budget. *Person Responsible:* Associate superintendent for finance

Schedule	Procedure
May 15	The accepted budget for the entire school district should be prepared and ready for adoption in its final form. *Person Responsible:* Associate superintendent for finance and superintendent
June 1	The superintendent of schools should have completed the review of the accepted budget in its final form. *Person Responsible:* Superintendent
Months of June/July	Budget workshops are scheduled for school board members. *Person Responsible:* Superintendent and school board
No later than August 15	The district budget should be submitted to the local school board for public hearings and final approval. This final date will vary from district to district. However, the final approval date is typically prescribed by state law, as any district and school budget must be approved prior to the expenditure of public funds. *Person Responsible:* School board, superintendent, and associate superintendent for finance
No later than August 31	Budget adopted *Person Responsible:* School board

The Budget Hearing and Defense

Many districts require school leaders, department directors, and other school personnel responsible for the development of budgets to formally meet and independently defend their budgets. This process can be quite stressful if the administrator has not properly prepared the budget. Preparation for the budget hearing and defense requires the school leader to devise an interesting and informative manner of presenting the fiscal and budgetary facts. This is often accomplished with visual aids presenting the necessary budgetary points and justifications. The school leader must comprehend the budgetary components (accounting codes and descriptors), have been intimately involved in the budget development process, and understand the rationale for the monetary requests accompanying the proposed budget. Some districts require the school leader to meet with the superintendent or a designee, and, in some instances, a committee of supervisors or peers. In any case, the process typically includes the necessary justification of questioned budgetary items, with final approval coming only after adjustments or revisions have been made to the proposed budget.

Finally, it is advised that the school leader follow this useful adage: The best defense is a good offense. In other words, work hard at developing an effective budget, do the necessary homework associated with the budgetary tasks, and be prepared to expect the unexpected when defending the budget.

Final Thoughts

The effective school leader understands the importance of budgeting, especially as schools and school districts realize that the function of a budget is more than mechanics and mathematics. The development of a school budget today, especially in this era of fiscal constraint and accountability, requires strong leadership skills, a vision with a purpose, and an action plan for the future. The development of an effective school budget necessitates teamwork, dedicated efforts, and proper coding. Budget development demands budgetary applications whereby major budgeting considerations increase opportunities for all stakeholders to play an active role in defining school issues and addressing problems. This process generates appropriate decisions and solutions.

Effective leadership enables a school administrator to develop a budget that projects the school's vision and academic action plan. Moreover, the effective school leader informs the general public regarding the direction of the school program and provides the framework for appropriate accounting and wise expenditure of educational dollars—all for the benefit of students. While no budget is ever perfect, proper visioning, regular planning, and continuous evaluation transform a common ledger of revenue and expenditures into a supportive document, leading students to academic success and fulfilling the campus and district visions or missions.

Building a school budget is never an easy task. Budgeting provides the necessary framework to help make a school's vision a reality. With the institutionalization of site-based decision making in schools today, educational leaders have the opportunity and the obligation to engage the learning community in the budget development process by working collaboratively with all stakeholders to incorporate visioning and planning as necessary components in better budgets for better schools. By applying proven budgetary theory and techniques, administrators today—working with an attitude of "all of us are smarter than any one of us"—can utilize budgeting applications whereby the final budget compilation can positively impact the overall educational program and, most importantly, increase student achievement.

Discussion Questions

1. What is the purpose of the accounting code system?

2. How have the total quality movement and the SBDM process impacted the development of budgets in public schools?

3. Identify stakeholders in the budget development process and explain how the concept of "all of us are smarter than any one of us" can serve to ensure better budgets for better schools.

4. Who must be responsible for student enrollment projections—school district administration or school principals? Explain your answer.

5. How might the school budget applications detailed within this chapter serve the school leader at the budget defense hearing?

6. Why are certain budget allotments more restrictive than others? Explain your answer by providing examples.

7. You are in the second semester of your first year as a school leader, and the budget season is hastily approaching. You know your school enrollment has been rapidly growing over the past three years. The associate superintendent for finance informs you that your budget allotment will be less for the upcoming fiscal year because the school district needs extra funds for a new facilities improvement effort. Your current enrollment is 815 students. Last school year, the campus enrollment was 796. The year prior, the enrollment was 779. Three years ago, the enrollment was 761. For previous years 4, 5, and 6, student enrollment was 761, 757, and

(Continued)

(Continued)

752, respectively. How should you address the possibility of a decrease in your budgetary allotment? What methods would you apply and specifically utilize to resolve this budgetary issue at the upcoming budget defense hearing? Apply your answer(s) in writing.

8. Why is the incorporation and utilization of a budget calendar important in building an effective school budget?

Case Study Application #1: Shifting Paradigms With Changing Times

The application of a case study or case studies as related to campus visioning, planning, and budgeting is presented at the conclusion of each chapter to provide applicable and relevant workplace scenarios so the reader can apply, in a practical manner, the knowledge acquired through textual readings.

Note: This case study is a continuation of the one introduced in Chapter 3. The reader will recognize the characters portrayed and will further apply accounting codes to the budgetary allotments designated in Table 3.4 on pages 112 and 113 of Chapter 3 within the PBHS Nonprioritized Identified Needs chart.

Part IV: The Budget—Coding the Budgetary Allotments

The Situation

Dr. Hector Avila, principal, and Ms. Abigail Grayson, assistant principal, at Pecan Bay High School sat down the next Tuesday afternoon with the SBDM committee to review the prioritized needs listing as related to the next fiscal year school budget. It was obvious there were more needs than dollars at Pecan Bay High School. Dr. Avila thought to himself, "Isn't that always the case!" Nevertheless, the decisions had been made in the best interests of the students at PBHS. Dr. Avila was proud of the committee's efforts. Ms. Grayson was more than impressed with the progress that had been made and with how much she had learned from an outstanding instructional leader. While funding every need would be impossible based on the $100,000 allotment, the next step in the visioning, planning, and budgeting process was to integrate the needs with budgetary descriptors and accounting codes. This would be a learning experience for not only Ms. Grayson but also the entire SBDM committee. What Dr. Avila really appreciated about the SBDM initiative was the fact every aspect of the budget was being considered, assessed, evaluated, and approved in a public forum where all would recognize there were no hidden agendas or secret principal "slush" funds.

Following a short period of greetings and welcoming committee members to the conference room, the business of coding the differing needs began in earnest. Troy Allens, one of the initial opponents to the SBDM process and good friend of Ed Feeney, was present, smile on his face, and excited to be a part of a group who had bought into the concept of "all of us are smarter than any one of us!" Even old Ed was slowly but surely coming along and had sat in on a SBDM meeting for Troy a few weeks ago when Troy had to take his daughter to a softball game.

Thinking It Through

Now that you have prioritized the differing needs at Pecan Bay High School and constructed an abridged action plan, it is time to consider all line-item accounts within the school budget in relation to the fund, function, object, sub-object (utilize 00 for this exercise), organization, fiscal year, and program intent codes. Review the ten steps to budgeting success from Chapter 4 and then determine what the committee has accomplished to (1) determine the allotment, (2) identify any fixed expenditures, (3) involve all parties, (4) identify potential expenditures, (5) cut back as is necessary, (6) avoid any debts, (7) develop a plan of action, (8) set goals, (9) evaluate the budget, and (10) abide by the budget.

Where are you and your team in the 10-step process?

Turn to the Accounting Codes Reference Sheet located in Resource B. Use this document to complete the Budget Spreadsheet exhibited in Table 6.14 by listing the correct accounting codes as associated with the prioritized needs previously selected. To better assist, an example indicating the proper accounting code for health services (nurse or clinic) has been provided and listed on the first row of the Budget Spreadsheet. Note that the description category of the Budget Spreadsheet is associated with the Function and Object code descriptors. Remember, accounting codes may vary from state to state and from district to district. The process utilized in this text is simply an example. Seek your own state or school district version of the accounting code process to complete this task.

Case Study Application #2:
Requisition Season at Kay Carter Middle School

Donna Arnold, assistant principal at Kay Carter Middle School, has been given the responsibility of serving as budget manager. Donna has been an assistant principal at Kay Carter for three years. She has really come to like the old school, the first one built in the school district well over 60 years ago. One of Donna's specified tasks associated with the role of budget manager is to review all campus requisitions and assign the appropriate accounting codes.

Table 6.14　Budget Development Spreadsheet

Fund	Function	Object/ Sub-Object	Year	Program Intent	Organization	Description	Total
199	33	6399.00	Current date	11	002	Health Services (Nurse)	$1000.00
						Grand Total	$

NOTE: This form also appears in Resource A.

This evening, after a long day at school, Donna sits down and begins analyzing a stack of requisitions placed on her desk. As she examines each requisition, she realizes how important it is to learn the differing accounting codes in order to save time. While Donna thumbs through the stack of requisitions, she notes out loud what is being ordered and then speculates as to the appropriate code for entry in the fund account blank.

Requisition #1: Janice Minsky orders the director's cut of the 1960 video production *Alamo*, starring John Wayne, to show to her Title I social studies class.

_____-___-_____.___-___-___-_____

Requisition #2: Dolores Chavez needs one grand prize trophy and several ribbons for placing as well as certificates of achievement for the gifted and talented students participating in the annual National Geography Bee.

_____-___-_____.___-___-___-_____

Requisition #3: Henri Adams, librarian, requests several new book titles for the school library, as the bilingual teachers strongly desire books in the native languages of their ELLs.

_____-___-_____.___-___-___-_____

Requisition #4: Betty Sanchez, the school nurse, is requesting she be permitted to attend the National Conference for Wellness Programs to be held in Chicago, Illinois.

_____-___-_____.___-___-___-_____

Requisition #5: Julie Aikman requests a set of colored transparencies to aid her SPED students with visual-reading perception problems.

_____-___-_____.___-___-___-_____

Requisition #6: Larry Nolton, building principal, is seeking to renew the subscriptions to *The Journal of Principal Leadership* for all of his administrative team members.

_____-___-_____.___-___-___-_____

Application Questions

1. Using Tables 6.6 through 6.12 within the chapter as well as the Accounting Codes Reference Sheet in Resource B, indicate the fund, function, object, sub-object (utilize 00 for this exercise), fiscal year, program intent, and organization codes for each of the requisition submissions noted above. Place your answer in the blanks below each requisition number. (Answers are provided at the conclusion of this chapter.)

2. Contact your business department administrator or school superintendent or state finance person to obtain a copy of the state's Operating Accounting Code structure. How is this structure similar to or different from the examples utilized in Chapter 6?

3. Exceptional school leaders have been described as showing and sharing love, joy, peace, kindness, forbearance, goodness, gentleness, self-control, gratitude, strength, wisdom and knowledge, skill application, high-expectations, tenacity, perseverance, and understanding. These descriptors have been documented as attributes of a successful leader and a successful life. Which of these attributes do you believe are most applicable to excellence in budgetary management? Other attributes not noted? Explain your answer(s).

Case Study Application #3: The Budget Development Project

The Budget Development Project provides the reader with a comprehensive examination of a fictitious school and school district. The school will be known as Mountain Vista Elementary School, and the district will be called Mesa Valley Independent School District (ISD).

Mesa Valley ISD serves a major suburban area just north of a large urban center. The school district has earned an outstanding reputation over the years for its strong academic and extracurricular programs, its effective school leadership, and its financial stability. The district's tax base, while more than adequate, remains most interestingly diverse, with local revenues generated from the agribusiness industry, which includes pecan growing, milk and dairy products, cotton farming, and cattle ranching, as well as an infusion of high-tech industries that ultimately attracted the now-famous computer software company, Styl-USA, Inc. With a diverse tax base also comes a diverse population with socioeconomic levels representative of the poor agribusiness workers, the medium-income urban-flight families, and the independently wealthy CEOs—all of whom now reside in what has become known as Technology Valley.

Mesa Valley ISD serves 25,502 students. The district has three high schools, five middle schools, and 15 elementary schools. Mountain Vista Elementary School is the fifth oldest elementary school in the district, with a population of 818 students enrolled for the current school year. Listed in Table 6.15 are total student enrollments for the previous five school years.

The campus has a free and reduced-price lunch population of 87% and is thus considered a Title I schoolwide project. The ADA is 90%. Mountain Vista has a unique student population ranging from high socioeconomic background to high-poverty status. The school is also home to a large English

Table 6.15   Student Enrolment

School Year	Student Enrollment
Previous Year #1	831
Previous Year #2	845
Previous Year #3	850
Previous Year #4	826
Previous Year #5	808

language learner (ELL) population, since many of the families living within the attendance zone are resident or migrant farm workers employed by the numerous agribusinesses.

Mountain Vista Elementary School houses prekindergarten through Grade 5, with a student population of 80% Hispanic, 10% Anglo, 5% African American, and 5% Asian American. Gifted and talented students make up 4% of the population, 5% of the student body is identified as special education, and 25% is served in the bilingual education program. The school has 42 teachers, one counselor, one nurse, one nurse assistant, one instructional facilitator, one librarian, 13 instructional aides, two clerical aides, one secretary, one attendance clerk, one assistant principal, and one principal.

Each of the grade levels at Mountain Vista Elementary School has six sections of students with the exception of prekindergarten (two sections—one bilingual and one monolingual), Grade 2 (five sections), and Grade 4 (five sections). Every grade level has one section of bilingual students and one section of special education inclusion–monolingual students (except prekindergarten), with the remaining sections serving monolingual students. Each section of bilingual students at every grade level is served by one teacher and one instructional aide. The prekindergarten sections are served by one teacher and one instructional aide each. Finally, the special education students are served by two teachers and five instructional aides.

Mountain Vista Elementary School also employs one gifted and talented teacher (half time) and one speech therapist (half time) as well as a full-time physical education teacher, music teacher, and Title VI aide. There are four custodians and five food services employees. Finally, both faculty and administration agree that Mountain Vista Elementary School is in need of a full-time campus diagnostician and hope to convince the superintendent during the budget defense hearing of this educational need.

The Mesa Valley ISD associate superintendent for finance has indicated that each elementary school will be provided a per-pupil campus budget allocation of $2,537 for the next school year. This allocation is to support the school's academic programs, salaries, any supplemental stipends ($2,000) for special education teachers, bilingual teachers, math and science teachers, testing coordinators, and head librarian, counselor, nurse, custodian, and grade-level chairs. Table 6.16 lists the annual salaries of all school personnel.

Table 6.16   Salaries

Personnel Position	Salary per Year ($)
Teachers, nurse, librarian	47,500
Principal	101,000
Assistant principal	87,000
Counselor	55,000
Diagnostician	57,000
Instructional facilitator	60,000
Speech therapist	52,000
Testing coordinator	49,000
Security officer	41,000
Secretary	35,000
Instructional and clerical aides	31,000
Nurse assistant	31,000
Custodian (head)	37,000
Custodians	30,000
Food services	12,000
Consultant(s) per day	2,500

Mountain Vista Elementary School has been experiencing problems with reading achievement and, consequently, low problem-solving skills in the area of mathematics as measured by the State Assessment of Essential Skills (SAES). This problem encompasses most of the content areas since reading is the primary factor for academic success. The SBDM committee believes that the promotion of literacy at school and within the community should be a campus priority. Other academic considerations are included within the proposed CAP for the next school year. However, a needs assessment and priority analysis have not been conducted in relation to the action plan. Identified on subsequent pages is the Mountain View Elementary School's CAP or CIP.

Finally, the school has recently experienced a turnover in campus leaders. The prior principal replaced a strong and effective instructional leader who had gained the trust, confidence, and respect of the learning community. However, this principal—Mr. Belton Dwanes—has since retired after leading the school to the highest accountability rating according to the State Education Agency. Mr. Dwanes's replacement for the previous two years had been a less-than-effective instructional leader, and both he and his assistant principal resigned to pursue other educational interests. During the two years after Mr. Dwanes's retirement, the instructional program at Mountain Vista

Elementary School had suffered and, just this school year, Dr. Jenda Taft and her assistant, John Steven Leakey, assumed the roles of principal and assistant principal. Both realized that they had their work cut out for them, but both are ethical and moral professionals with excellent credentials and reputations. Both leaders, after reviewing the State Academic Performance Report (SAPR), certainly understood the charge that had been issued to them by Dr. Leroy J. Thedson, the Mesa Valley ISD superintendent: "Turn Mountain Vista around and get those scores back on track. I expect all of your test groups and sub-population scores to be at 90% and higher in the next two years!"

Directions: To best complete the Budget Development Project, the following format is suggested. Carefully read, in sequence, each information guideline along with supporting materials and then complete the noted tasks before moving on to the next set of instructions. Refer to, read, and follow Information Guideline #4 only after completing the first three directives and activities.

This particular project has been an extremely successful activity and is often considered the most popular aspect of our budget course teaching and learning, as it permits the prospective school leader to gain significant and practical insights and experiences into building a school budget.

While no clinical practicum can ever be as true to life as the on-site experience, the processes detailed within the Budget Development Project are intended to present the reader and student of the budgeting process with a meaningful and relevant perspective that is as close as possible to the actual budgetary practices of a real school and school district.

1. Follow the Sorenson-Goldsmith Integrated Budget Model, as identified in Chapter 3, which showcases the eight components necessary to define and select the appropriate stakeholders, conduct a needs assessment, analyze the data presented, prioritize needs, set goals and objectives, and develop an action or improvement plan.

2. Review all information and data provided (including the Mountain Vista Elementary School Action Plan and SAPR) to determine if the information and data are being appropriately, effectively, and efficiently utilized. If not, make any and all necessary changes.

3. Develop a campus budget for Mountain Vista Elementary School by reflecting upon the budgetary applications detailed in this chapter. Your completed budget project should include a descriptive narrative, programmatic identifiers, a mission statement, student enrollment projections, an analysis of the academic action plan, a needs assessment and priority analysis, a teacher/student distribution table, a faculty apportionment table, a forecast of population trends utilizing the cohort survival method, any above-basic personnel requests and justifications, an allocation statement, and salaries for personnel table, along with the final budget compilation utilizing accounting codes, descriptors, and dollar totals.

Begin the Budget Development Project

Good luck and good visioning, planning, and budgeting!

4. Finally, after completing Information Guides 1, 2, and 3 (noted above), you may turn to the Mesa Valley ISD Memorandum found at the conclusion of this case study. Remember, that this memorandum is to be read and complied with only after you have completed the first three information guidelines.

Campus Action Plan

Mountain Vista Elementary School

Mesa Valley Independent School District CAP

SBDM Committee

Belinda Del Monte, preschool teacher	Jaye Minter, music teacher
Karla Billingsly, Grade 1 teacher Leslie Lovington, Grade 2 teacher Dianna Sanchez, Grade 3 bilingual teacher	Phyllis Canton, instructional aide Suzan Rollins, parent–teacher association president
Barbara Axleson, Grade 4 Title I teacher	Molly Corlioni, parent
Susie Wigington, Grade 5 teacher	Flo Cortez, parent
Norma Garcia, special education teacher	Lisa Nachin, parent
Randy Woodson, Chief of Police, community member	John Steven Leakey, assistant principal

Dr. Jenda Taft, Principal

Mission Statement

Mountain View Elementary School will provide a safe environment for all students by fostering productive citizens for a better tomorrow.

Goal I: Increase student achievement after a review and analysis of SAES data.

Objective 1: By student population—gender, ethnicity, educationally disadvantaged (at risk), and instructional setting teacher—develop strategies that will increase student achievement.

Strategy 1: Target specific instructional objectives.

Action(s)/ Implementation(s)	Responsibility/ Staff Assigned	Timeline Start/End	Resources (Human, Material, Fiscal)	Audit (Formative)	Reported/ Documented
Identify instructional areas of strength, areas needing improvement, and areas of weakness with regard to specific SAES objectives.	Principal and teachers	August–May (current year)	SAES English language arts reading objectives and measurement specifications booklet; SAES mathematics objectives and measurement specifications booklet; Mesa Valley ISD curriculum guides; instructional resource center materials; teacher-made materials; SAES disaggregated data Mountain Vista SAES booklet time on target criterion-referenced pretests	Disaggregated data information sheets, SAES ATTACK skills worksheets, diagnostic and screening results, and lesson plans	Principal's office

Evaluation (Summative): All disaggregated student groups will obtain 90% or greater mastery on SAES.

Goal II: Provide a curriculum that addresses higher-order thinking skills to increase student academic performance.

Objective 1: Explore and implement programs that will increase overall student achievement.

Strategy 1: Continue current instructional programs.

Action(s)/Implementation(s)	Responsibility/ Staff Assigned	Timeline Start/End	Resources (Human, Material, Fiscal)	Audit (Formative)	Reported/ Documented
Develop staff development programs for Grade 4 process writing. Enhance the reading program by implementing: —— phonemic/phonetic instruction —— increased reading time per day —— learning centers —— subgrouping —— integrated units —— reading styles inventories Continue cross grade-level planning during the first six weeks of school.	Principal and teachers, director of elementary education	August–May (current year)	Integrated reader library books and software; Phonetic readers teaching resources; SOAR With Knowledge instructional materials; Maria Carlo Reading Styles Inventory; and teacher-made resources	Integrated Reader participation charts and printout reports, as well as lesson plans, Teacher observation of student performance, Principal visitation and participation in classroom	Principal's office; lesson plans, and library circulation records

Evaluation (Summative): All disaggregated student groups will obtain 90% or greater mastery on SAES.

Goal II: Provide a curriculum that addresses higher-order thinking skills to increase student academic performance.

Objective 1: Explore and implement programs that will increase overall student achievement.

Strategy 1: Continue current instructional programs.

Action(s)/Implementation(s)	Responsibility/ Staff Assigned	Timeline Start/End	Resources (Human, Material, Fiscal)	Audit (Formative)	Reported/ Documented
Continue the *On to Math* program. Develop a math curriculum cross-referenced guide incorporating *On to Math*, *Maxim Math*, and *Math This Way* instructional programs. Design math diagnostic tests to be administered in Grades 1–5. Integrate science and social studies into the math instructional program with the extensive implementation of *SOAR With Knowledge*. Plan lessons to incorporate the Living Science Center into the instructional program at least twice every six weeks throughout the school year.	Principal, teachers, resource center coordinator, and the director of elementary education	August–May (current year)	*On to Math* and *Maxim Math* teaching resources, Mesa Valley ISD curriculum guides, library books, classroom libraries and readers, periodicals, newspapers, other reading materials, and teacher-made resources	Software printout reports as well as lesson plans, teacher observation of student performance, principal visitation and participation in classrooms	Principal's office and lesson plans, library circulation records

Evaluation (Summative): All disaggregated student groups will obtain 90% or greater mastery on SAES.

Goal III: Develop methods and strategies to assist at-risk students in achieving academic success.

Objective 1: Identify and serve students in at-risk situations in order to have them obtain 80% or greater mastery on SAES.

Strategy 1: Extend learning opportunities and intervention programs for at-risk students.

Action(s)/Implementation(s)	Responsibility/ Staff Assigned	Timeline Start/ End	Resources (Human, Material, Fiscal)	Audit (Formative)	Reported/ Documented
Follow guidelines for identification of at-risk students as mandated by the State Education Agency and the Mesa Valley ISD at-risk plan. Continue tutoring, counseling, special education, and 504 referral programs and interagency involvement referrals. Enhance the student mentoring program between Grades 3 and 4 at-risk students and Grades PreK–2 at-risk students. Implement Title I contacts to encourage parental involvement and awareness as well as increase student achievement and teacher responsibility.	Principal, teachers, counselor, instructional aides, and security officer	August–May (current year)	Principal and counselor, at-risk coordinator, and the campus at-risk committee	At-risk student activity and identification sheets	Principal's office

Evaluation (Summative): All disaggregated student groups will obtain 90% or greater mastery on SAES.

Goal III: Develop methods and strategies to assist at-risk students in achieving academic success.

Objective 1: Identify and serve students in at-risk situations in order to help them obtain 90% or greater mastery on SAES.

Strategy 2: Offer parent training and information sharing opportunities.

Action(s)/ Implementation(s)	Responsibility/ Staff Assigned	Timeline Start/End	Resources (Human, Material, Fiscal)	Audit (Formative)	Reported/ Documented
Conduct a parent classroom orientation program during the first six weeks of the school year. Provide for a Parent University each school year. Survey parents to determine needs to be addressed during the Parent University program.	Principal, counselor, at-risk coordinator and committee, and teachers	August–May (current year)	Newsletters, meeting notices, and parent survey and evaluation forms; child care; phone bank; and door prizes	Parent newsletters, parent training workshop notifications, parent classroom orientation sign-in sheets, and parent evaluation forms	Principal's office

Evaluation (Summative): Parent training opportunities and orientations will be held in order that all disaggregated student groups will obtain 90% or greater mastery on SAES.

STATE ACADEMIC
PERFORMANCE REPORT (SAPR)

Campus Report

DISTRICT NAME: MESA VALLEY ISD
CAMPUS NAME: MOUNTAIN VISTA ES
CAMPUS NUMBER: 105
ACCOUNTABILITY RATING: MET STANDARD

Met Standard

Improvement Required

Not Rated

Distinction Designations:

Academic Achievement in Science

State Education Agency

District Name: Mesa Valley ISD
Campus Name: MOUNTAIN VISTA
ES Campus #: 105

SAPR Campus Accountability Rating:
Met Standard

Total Enrollment: 831 Grade Span PreK-5
School Type: Elementary

Indicator:	*State, %*	*District, %*	*Campus, %*	*African American, %*	*Hispanic, %*	*Anglo, %*	*Asian American, %*	*Economic Disadvantage, %*
SAES % Passing *Grade 3*								
Reading	71.3	78.9	74.2	75.6	69.7	80.5	83.2	67.4
Math	74.6	79.2	73.8	65.7	61.7	84.2	86.3	63.7
SAES % Passing *Grade 4*								
Reading	78.7	81.0	70.7	70.2	61.5	78.6	81.2	60.9
Math	68.3	71.6	62.3	58.4	57.7	66.0	71.3	40.0
Writing	78.6	84.7	75.2	70.7	69.6	80.6	83.2	60.7
SAES % Passing *Grade 5*								
Reading	75.5	77.2	60.1	57.6	52.9	69.3	72.4	40.0
Math	77.3	78.0	67.3	58.6	47.6	70.2	73.5	47.2
Science	74.7	83.4	84.7	81.2	79.0	95.1	93.2	77.0
Attendance	94.5	95.6	90.1	88.5	85.3	95.4	98.7	82.3

Student Information

Total Students: 831

Students by Grade:	Prekindergarten	32
	Kindergarten	124
	Grade 1	121
	Grade 2	102
	Grade 3	123
	Grade 4	105
	Grade 5	181
	Special Education	43

Retention Rates by Grade, %:

	State	*District*	*Campus*
Kindergarten	1.7	0.7	2.2
Grade 1	4.7	3.9	5.1
Grade 2	1.7	0.7	1.9
Grade 3	1.1	0.6	1.3
Grade 4	0.9	0.7	1.2
Grade 5	0.8	0.3	0.9

Budgeted Operating Expenditure Information

Budgeted Operating Expenditure Information

	Campus	Pct.	District	Pct.	State	Pct.
Total Campus Budget	$2,108,247	100	$116,168,713	100	$12,711,996,407	100
By Function						
Instruction	$1,486,314	70.5	$88,520,559	76.2	$9,559,421,298	75.2
Administration	$215,041	10.2	$8,596,486	7.4	$953,399,731	7.5
Other Campus Costs	$406,892	19.3	$19,051,668	16.4	$2,199,175,378	17.3

Budgeted Instructional Operating Expenditures by Program

	Campus	Pct.	District	Pct.	State	Pct.
Regular Education	$1,142,975	76.9		86.9		86.8
Special Education	$84,720	5.7		11.4		11.2
Title I Education	$219,974	14.8		15.0		14.9
Bilingual Education	$11,891	0.8		4.7		3.6
Gifted/Talented Ed.	$26,754	1.8		1.3		0.6

Memorandum

Mesa Valley Independent School
District

Committed to
Excellence in Education

TO: Dr. Jenda Taft, Principal
                    Mountain Vista Elementary School and
                    The Budget Team Members
FROM: Dr. Leroy J. Thedson, Superintendent of Schools
DATE: Spring (Current Year)
SUBJECT: Budgetary Constraints and Reductions

Due to the recent closure of the Mountain Stream Manufacturing Plant, a significant loss of district revenue has occurred. To ensure that the district budget and reserves remain solvent, all schools and departments are being asked to include a nine percent (9%) reduction (see specified accounts) within their organizational budgets for the upcoming fiscal year.

    Specified line item accounts by code/description:

199-11/13-6112.00	*Substitutes*
199-11/13-6118.00	Extra Duty Pay
199-11/23-6269.00	Rentals—Operating Leases (copiers)
199-11/13/23/31/33-6411	Travel

Please note the school district, along with the board of trustees, remain genuinely concerned about this temporary financial setback. However, be aware all areas of the district budget are being reduced and expected revenue to be generated from the Mesa Vista Valley Packing Company—which is scheduled to open within the next two years—will hopefully compensate for this unexpected budgetary reduction. Your continued commitment to the students of this school district is most appreciated.

Chapter 6 Answers

Noted below are the answers to the activities in this chapter.

Answer to Form 6.1: Sample Requisition Form

199-36-6399.00-91

Answers to Activity 1 and Activity 2: Utilizing Accounting Codes

#1 200-10-6300-002-23
#2 199-36-6399-003-91

Answers to "It Doesn't Take a Secret Decoder Ring!"

#1   B. Sub-Object

#2   C. Object

#3   B. Function

#4   A. Fund

#5   D. Program Intent

Answers to Application Questions

Requisition #1: 199-11-6399.00-Current School Year-11-101
Requisition #2: 461-11-6399.00-Current School Year-21-101
Requisition #3: 219-12-6669.00-Current School Year-25-101
Requisition #4: 199-33-6411.00-Current School Year-11-101
Requisition #5: 199-11-6329.00-Current School Year-23-101
Requisition #6: 199-23-6329.00-Current School Year-11-101

Resource A

Selected Forms

Budget Development Spreadsheet

Fund	Function	Object, Sub-Object	Year	Program Intent	Organization	Description	Total
						Grand Total	$

Copyright © 2018 by Corwin. All rights reserved. Reprinted from *The Principal's Guide to School Budgeting*, second edition, by Richard D. Sorenson and Lloyd Milton Goldsmith. Thousand Oaks, CA: Corwin. http://www.corwin.com.

This form is also available for viewing and printing purposes at the following Corwin web link: http://resources.corwin.com/schoolbudget.

Strategy Page

Goal 1:

Objective 1:

Strategy 1:

Actions	Responsibility	Timeline Start/End	Resources (Human, Material, Fiscal)	Reported/Audit (Formative)	Documented

Evaluation (Summative):

Copyright © 2018 by Corwin. All rights reserved. Reprinted from *The Principal's Guide to School Budgeting*, second edition, by Richard D. Sorenson and Lloyd Milton Goldsmith. Thousand Oaks, CA: Corwin. http://www.corwin.com.

This form is also available for viewing and printing purposes at the following Corwin web link: http://resources.corwin.com/schoolbudget.

Resource B

Experiential Exercises

The Budgeting Codes Activity

Directions: Carefully read and assess each scenario presented and then refer to the Accounting Codes Reference Sheet (pp. 293–297) to complete the activity. Fill in the blanks with the proper accounting codes. For the purpose of this exercise, utilize the current school year for fiscal year coding and 00 for the sub-object code.

Note: Accounting codes vary from state to state and from district to district. The codes utilized in Resource B represent one particular example.

1. Smyler Grogan, assistant principal at Desert Valley Elementary School, had been given the responsibility of budget manager and was working with the budget development team to prepare the school budget for the next fiscal year. In the course of the budget preparation process, Grogan was genuinely contemplating which accounting codes would best correlate with the budgetary decisions made by him and the team. He knew that the school's guidance counselor, Mrs. Vestal Umberger, needed a new filing credenza for her office. Desert Valley was built in 1962 and was the third elementary school in the district at the time; and Mr. Grogan realized that much of the furniture in Mrs. Umberger's office had never been replaced.

Fill in the blanks with the proper coding:

_____-___-_____.___-___-___-_____

2. Consuelo Estringel, principal at the Mission Hills Alternative Center for Education, was reviewing the monthly budget report when she realized that she had not budgeted for the additional $2,000 that would be needed to pay for the honorarium to be provided to the staff

development presenter who was coming next week. Quickly, she began completing a district budget amendment and transfer form to ensure that the budgeted dollars would be available in the correct account. The presenter was a known expert in the area of teaching methodologies as associated with effective alternative school settings. Dr. Estringel finished the budget amendment, thus making certain that the appropriate funds were budgeted for this summer school program. She then called the presenter to verify his acceptance of the district contract.

Fill in the blanks with the proper coding:

_____-____-_____.____-____-____-____-_____

3. Tim Spedman, site-based committee chair at Western Ridge Middle School, was just finishing his lunch when Letty Muñoz—the school secretary—came by and told Tim that he needed to provide her with an accounting code for a recent purchase he had made. Letty always had to track down Tim each time he spent money out of the school's activity account for items associated with the journalism department. She knew that Tim was an exceptional teacher, but he had to be more responsible when it came to keeping up with activity fund expenditures.

Letty, being quite frustrated at the moment, thought to herself, "This old school (the second middle school built in the district) is really getting to me!" She then told Tim that he needed to allocate funding for the copy machine that the department was leasing from the Whatacopy Shop. In fact, she bluntly told him to "finish that deviled-egg sandwich and get me those account codes right away!"

Fill in the blanks with the proper coding:

_____-____-_____.____-____-____-____-_____

_____-____-_____.____-____-____-____-_____

4. Bayou Elementary School was the newest elementary campus in Pecan Grove Independent School District. It had just opened four months ago to accommodate the growing population of students in the greater Hudston metropolitan area. The seven other elementary schools were highly rated according to the statewide accountability standards. Susan Dianes knew that she had a task on her hands as she assumed the role of the school's first principal. Nevertheless, Dr. Dianes had been a strong assistant principal for four years at Enchanted Path Elementary School and had been an outstanding special education teacher for seven years in a nearby school district. However, today, she had to work with the site-based team, and some difficult decisions had to be made.

Dr. Dianes had received word earlier in the week that the school budget was about to be cut in the area of student field trips. Student travel had become a school board issue, and starting next semester, any new student travel requests would be denied. Dr. Dianes knew that the fourth-grade class always made a major end-of-the-year trip to Seaside Kingdom down on the coast. Monies must be encumbered now or any attempt next semester to fund the trip would be met with stiff resistance from central office administration, not to mention the school board.

Later that afternoon, Dr. Dianes and the site-based team met, and all agreed that funds must be amended from other budgetary accounts. Thus, Dr. Dianes and the team reviewed the budget and determined where the cuts would come from, and then Dr. Dianes completed the necessary budget amendment/transfer forms.

Fill in the blanks with the proper coding:

_____-____-_____.____-____-____-_____

Accounting Codes Reference Sheet

State education codes across the nation require a standard fiscal accounting system be adopted by each school district. A major purpose of any accounting code structure is to ensure that the sequence of codes uniformly applies to all school districts. Utilize this coding structure when responding to the scenarios presented in Chapter 6 of this text and to the Resource B: Experiential Exercises.

199—11—6399.00—001—Current Year—11

1   2   3   4   5   6   7

1. Fund Code (500+)*

185 = State Compensatory Education
199 = General Fund
204 = Title IV (safe and drug-free schools)
205 = Head Start
211 = Title I (funding for low-achievement students in high-poverty schools)
212 = Title I (funding for migrant students)
219 = Bilingual Education

---

*The number in parenthesis represents the total number of differing accounting codes that might be utilized when developing a school budget. The codes listed within the accounting codes reference sheet, which is most commonly utilized at the school site level.

224 = Special Education
243 = Vocational Education (career and technical/techprep)
255 = Title II (funding to hire, train, and retain quality educators)
461 = Campus Activity Fund

2. Function Code (27)

11 = Instruction
12 = Instructional Resources and Media Services
13 = Curriculum and Staff Development
21 = Instructional Leadership (instructional specialist/district office directors)
23 = School Leadership (administration)
31 = Guidance Counseling and Evaluation Services
32 = Social Work Services
33 = Health Services (nurse)
35 = Food Services
36 = Extracurricular (stipends and travel—athletics, drama, choir, band, etc.)
51 = Maintenance and Operations (custodial supplies)
52 = Security
53 = Computers/Maintenance and Repair (students/teachers)
61 = Community Services

3. Object Code (35)

6100 = Payroll Costs
6110 = Teachers and Other Professional Personnel
6112 = Salaries or Wages for Substitute Teachers
6117 = Extra Duty Pay—Professional (expenditures for professional development/curriculum writing as related to Function 12)
6118 = Professional Personnel Stipends and Extra Duty Pay
6119 = Salaries or Wages—Teachers and Other Professional Personnel (summer/evening classes, for example)
6121 = Paraprofessional Personnel/Extra Duty Pay (overtime)
6129 = Salaries for Support Personnel (paraprofessionals, etc.)
6200 = Professional and Contracted Services
6219 = Other Professional Contracted Services (architecture, landscaping, engineering, etc.)
6239 = Contracted Services (education service centers, for example)
6249 = Maintenance and Repair
6269 = Rentals/Operating Leases (copiers, etc.)
6291 = Consulting Services

6300 = Supplies and Materials

6321 = Textbooks

6325 = Magazines and Periodicals

6329 = Reading Materials

6339 = Testing Materials

6395 = Technology Supplies/Equipment Under $5,000 (per-unit cost)

6396 = Technology Furniture and Equipment Under $5,000 (per-unit cost)

6398 = Technology Site Licenses

6399 = General Supplies (everything from paper clips to staples to postage)

6400 = Other Operating Costs

6411 = Travel/Subsistence (employees)

6412 = Travel/Subsistence (students)

6494 = Transportation (buses)

6498 = Hospitality Expenses

6600 = Capital Outlay—Equipment

6636 = Technology Equipment Over $5,000 (per-unit cost)

6637 = Computer Labs

6639 = Furniture and Equipment Over $5,000 (per-unit cost)

6649 = Furniture and Equipment Under $5,000 (per unit cost)

6669 = Library Books

4. Sub-Object Code

This code is often used to delineate, for example, local departments. (For the purpose of the exercises and activities within this book, utilize 00 for the sub-object code).

5. Organization Code (School) (900)

001–040 = High School Campuses

041–100 = Middle School Campuses

101–698 = Elementary School Campuses

699 = Summer School Organizations

6. Fiscal Year Code

18 = 2017–2018

19 = 2018–2019

20 = 2019–2020

21 = 2020–2021

22 = 2021–2022
23 = 2022–2023
24 = 2023–2024
25 = 2024–2025, etc.

7. Program Intent Code (13)

11 = Basic Educational Services
21 = Gifted and Talented
22 = Career and Technology
23 = Special Education
24 = Accelerated Instruction
25 = Bilingual Education
28 = Disciplinary Alternative Education Placement (AEP) Services
30 = Title I (schoolwide programs/projects)
91 = Athletics
99 = Undistributed (charges not distributed to specific programs, i.e., employee allowance for cell phones, as well as band, choir, drama, other extracurricular programs)

ADDITIONAL FUND CODE INFORMATION

It is not unusual for differing programs and/or specified service agreements to be categorized by code funding numbers that are sequentially based. Listed below are several examples. Your state coding may be identical to the examples identified. However, to best ensure accuracy in coding, it is always recommended that school leaders and prospective school leaders check with their school systems and/or state education department for absolute coding accuracy.

200–289 = Federal Programs(examples include Title I, 211; bilingual education, 219; special education, 224; school breakfast and lunch programs, 240; etc.)

290–379 = Federally Funded Shared Services Agreement[1] (examples include a rural special education co-op or idea and Part B Discretionary Deaf shared services, 315)

---

[1]A *federally funded* shared services agreement/arrangement exists when two or more school systems enter into an agreement for the performance and administration of a program. School systems who enter into a written contract to jointly operate, for example, their special education programs as a shared services agreement and must follow procedures developed by the U. S. Department of Education.

380–429 = State Programs (examples include adult basic education, 381; successful schools program, 393; life skills programs, 394; advanced placement incentives, 397; state reading initiative, 414, etc.)

430–459 = State-Funded Shared Services Agreement[2] (examples include Regional Day School for the Deaf, 435, etc.)

460–499 = Local Programs (examples include a high school culinary arts program, 481, etc.)

---

[2] A *state-funded* shared services agreement/arrangement exists when a school system enters into an agreement with another school system or other state-funded institutions for the performance and administration of a program. Schools systems may enter into a written contract to jointly participate in a Regional Day School for the Deaf, for example, as part of a state shared services agreement and therefore must follow procedures developed by the state department of education.

Resource C

Budgeting Checklist for School Administrators

School administrators have numerous tasks and responsibilities that are related to the school budget and other bookkeeping procedures. This checklist is intended to assist the school leader in mastering those tasks and responsibilities. Furthermore, it is anticipated that each of these checklist items will further serve to ensure a successful budgetary year as well as the overall success of those individuals involved in a most demanding yet essential process.

Bookkeeping Tasks and Responsibilities

❑ Review all receipt books.
❑ Reconcile all bank statements on a monthly basis.
❑ Account for petty cash funds and reconcile these accounts on a monthly basis.
❑ Ensure each month that all checks have been signed with proper signatures.
❑ Visit on a regular (weekly) basis with the bookkeeping clerk regarding all budgetary considerations.
❑ Ensure that all bookkeeping personnel are bonded.
❑ Monitor all payments of bills and potential discounts for early or timely payments.
❑ Review any bookkeeping or budgetary issues that require your approval or signature. Examples include the following:
    ❑ checks
    ❑ purchase orders

□ financial reports
□ fundraising requests
□ amendments
□ field trip requests

Budget Manager Tasks and Responsibilities

□ Examine and review the budget on a monthly basis.
□ Ensure that all requisitions that are prepared; specifically list and identify the quantity ordered, the proper accounting code(s), the description of the item(s) ordered, and the unit cost per item(s) ordered. Ensure that subtotals and grand totals are reflected on the requisition, the originator is identified, and the approval signature is noted.
□ During the requisition or budget season, ensure that all requisition forms are prepared by faculty and staff and submitted on a timely basis.
□ Ensure that all accounts have been properly audited by authorized outside accounting firms.
□ Update the faculty handbook annually regarding any fiscal and/or budgetary topics or issues.
□ Hold a faculty meeting prior to the budget development and requisition season to ensure that all parties understand the allocations provided as well as the proper procedures associated with requisition supplies, materials, and all other budgetary considerations.
□ Develop a school academic action or improvement plan and integrate the plan with the school budget.
□ Review the different budget accounts each month. Do not allow over-expenditures to roll forward from one month to the next.
□ Amend the school budget as is necessary and in accordance with the school academic action or improvement plan.
□ Be aware of all district guidelines and deadlines associated with the school budget.
□ Spend all school funds wisely, appropriately, legally, timely, and with a student-centered approach/application.

Fundraising and Crowdfunding Considerations

□ All fundraising and crowdfunding must comply with local board policy and/or administrative regulations.

❏ All fundraising and crowdfunding requests/projects must be monitored and approved prior to initiating any student-focused efforts.

❏ Crowdfunding, as an alternative method of raising funds, is a means of enhancing schools and classrooms in terms of supplies and materials and can also be utilized for more creative projects such as start-up funding for student films, music, small business ventures, and field trips, for example.

❏ See Chapter 5 (pp. 174–176) for further insight and information regarding fundraising and crowdfunding.

❏ What additional outside sources of revenue (Adopt-A-School businesses, grants, foundation dollars, etc.) can further facilitate and enhance the budgetary allotment?

Site-Based Team and Budget Development

❏ The budget development season begins each January with a meeting with the site-based team to initiate discussions about issues and considerations that will impact the budget proposed for the next school year.

❏ Establish a budget calendar and begin regular meetings for the purpose of developing the school budget.

❏ Plan to spend the time necessary for proper budget development. In most cases, this will require several after-school meetings, at least two half-day sessions, and at least one full-day meeting.

❏ Provide the site-based team with the proper accounting codes and categories to begin the school budget development process.

❏ Establish all revenue and expenditure targets for the next fiscal-year budget with the team. Enter all revenue and expenditure funds on the appropriate school form to be submitted to the district business department.

❏ Examine any budgetary concerns that might have been problematic during the previous year budget cycle. Review the budget on an account-by-account basis.

Important Budgetary Questions

❏ What is the budgetary allotment for the next fiscal year?
❏ What is the basis for the upcoming budgetary allotment?

❑ What is the projected student enrollment for next year and what is the per-pupil allotment?

❑ Are there any money or budgetary concerns or considerations to be aware of this week?

❑ Are any employees not following proper fiscal procedures as related to the budget or bookkeeping management, receipts, purchase orders, reimbursements, or financial reports, to include bank reconciliation?

❑ Do any checks or purchase orders need approval and/or authorized signature?

❑ Are daily bank deposits being made?

❑ Are there any other items related to the school budget or bookkeeping procedures that need to be discussed or examined?

❑ What bookkeeping or budgetary improvements need to be made?

❑ When do I get a well-deserved vacation?

Copyright © 2018 by Corwin. All rights reserved. Reprinted from *The Principal's Guide to School Budgeting, second edition*, by Richard D. Sorenson and Lloyd Milton Goldsmith. Thousand Oaks, CA: Corwin. http://www.corwin.com.

References

Adams, C., Forsyth, P., & Mitchell, R. M. (2009). The formation of parent–school trust: A multilevel analysis. *Educational Administration Quarterly, 45*(1), 4–33.

Alexander, K., & Alexander, M. D. (2012). *American public school law* (8th ed.). Belmont, CA: Wadsworth, Cengage Learning.

Allen, D. (2001). *Getting things done: The art of stress-free productivity*. New York, NY: Penguin Books.

American Association of School Administrators (AASA). (2002). *Using data to improve schools: What's working*. Alexandria, VA: AASA.

American Society of Civil Engineers. (2017). *2017 Infrastructure report card*. Retrieved June 18, 2017, from http://www.msn.com/en-us/money/markets/us-infrastructure-is-falling-apart-%e2%80%93-heres-a-look-at-how-terrible-things-have-become/ss-BBCM3Aq?li=BBnb7Kz&ocid=iehp#image=14

Anderson, L. (1997). *They smell like sheep*. West Monroe, LA: Howard.

AZQuotes. (n.d.). Retrieved March 1, 2017, from http://www.azquotes.com

Banks, C. M. (2000). Gender and race as factors in educational leadership. In M. Grogan (Ed.), *The Jossey-Bass reader on educational leadership* (pp. 217–256). San Francisco, CA: Jossey-Bass.

Banks, T., & Obiakor, F. E. (2015). Culturally responsive positive behavior supports: Considerations for practice. *Journal of Education and Training Studies, 2*(2), 83–90.

Barth, R. S. (2001). *Learning by heart*. San Francisco, CA: Jossey-Bass.

Be the Change Group. (2017). *Learn to change the world*. Cambridge, MA: Harvard Graduate School.

Beckner, W. (2004). *Ethics for educational leaders*. Boston, MA: Pearson Education.

Borja, B. R. (2005). Ethics issues snare school leaders. *Education Week, 24*(18), 1 4.

Bracey, G. W. (2002). *The war against America's public schools: Privatizing schools, commercializing education*. Boston, MA: Allyn & Bacon.

Brady, K. P., & Pijanowski, J. C. (2007). Maximizing state lottery dollars for public education: An analysis of current state lotter models. *NORMES, 7*(2), 20–37.

Brainy Quote. (2001–2017a). *Samuel Johnson quotes*. Retrieved May 7, 2017, from https://www.brainyquote.com/quotes/authors/s/samuel_johnson.html

Brainy Quote. (2001–2017b). *Baruch Spinoza*. Retrieved May 7, 2017, from https://www.brainyquote.com/quotes/authors/b/baruch_spinoza.html

Brewer, E. W., & Achilles, C. M. (2008). *Finding funding: Grant writing from start to finish, including project management and internet use.* Thousand Oaks, CA: Corwin.

Brimley, V., Jr., Verstegen, D. A., & Garfield, R. (2015). *Financing education in a climate of change* (12th ed.). Upper Saddle River, NJ: Pearson Education.

Burke, M. A. (2002). *Simplified grantwriting.* Thousand Oaks, CA: Corwin.

Carroll, L. (1993). *Alice's adventures in Wonderland* (Dover Thrift ed.). New York, NY: Dover Publications. (Originally published in 1865)

Celio, M. B., & Harvey, J. (2005). *Buried treasure: Developing an effective guide from mountains of educational data.* Seattle, WA: Center on Reinventing Public Education.

Center for Public Education. (2009). *The challenges ahead.* Retrieved March 20, 2017, from http://www.centerforpubliceducation.org/Main-Menu/Public-education/An-American-imperative-Publiceducation-/The-challenges-ahead-.html

Childress, M. (2014, May–June). Building teacher capacity. *Principal*, 8–12.

Cizek, G. J. (1999). *Cheating on tests: How to do it, detect it, and prevent it.* Mahwah, NJ: Lawrence Erlbaum.

Clover, C., Jones, E., Bailey, W., & Griffin, B. (2004). Budget priorities of selected principals: Reallocation of state funds. *NASSP Bulletin, 88*(640), 69–79.

Columbia Records. (1969). *Johnny Cash at San Quentin.* Los Angeles: Author.

Cooper, T. L. (2012). *The responsible administrator: An approach to ethics for the administrative role.* San Francisco, CA: Jossey-Bass.

Council of Chief State School Officers (CSSO). (2016). *The Professional Standards for Educational Leaders (PSEL) 2015 and the Interstate Leaders Licensure Consortium (ISLLC) standards 2008: A crosswalk.* Retrieved May 7, 2017, from http://www.gtlcenter.org/sites/default/files/PSEL_ISLLC_Crosswalk.pdf

Cover, D. (2017). *There is always hope.* Unpublished interview, Department of Educational Leadership and Foundations, The University of Texas at El Paso, El Paso, TX.

Covey, S. R. (2004). *The seven habits of highly effective people.* New York, NY: Simon & Schuster.

Creighton, T. (2006). *School and data: The educator's guide to improve decision making* (2nd ed.). Thousand Oaks, CA: Corwin.

Darling-Hammond, L., & McLaughlin, M. W. (1995). Policies that support professional development in an era of reform. *Phi Delta Kappan, 76*(8), 597–604.

Data Quality Campaign. (2009). *The next step: Using longitudinal data systems to improve student success.* Retrieved June 19, 2009, from http://www.Data qualitycampaign.org/files/nextstep.pdf

Dayton, J. (2002). Three decades of school funding litigation: Has it been worthwhile and when will it end? *School Business Affairs, May,* 7–9.

Deal, T. E., & Kennedy, A. A. (1982). *Corporate cultures: The rites and rituals of corporate life.* Reading, MA: Addison-Wesley.

Deal, T. E., & Peterson, K. D. (1998). How leaders influence the culture of schools. *Educational Leadership, 56*(1), 28–30.

Deal, T. E., & Peterson, K. D. (2009). *Shaping school culture: Pitfalls, paradoxes, and promises* (2nd ed.). San Francisco, CA: Jossey-Bass.

Debate.org. (2017). *Do the pros of school privatization outweigh the cons?* Retrieved July 23, 2017, from http://www.debate.org/opinions/do-the-pros-of-school-privatization-outweigh-the-cons

Deming, W. E. (2000). *Out of crisis.* Cambridge, MA: MIT Press.

DePree, M. (2003). *Leading without power: Finding hope in serving community.* San Francisco, CA: Jossey-Bass.

Desimone, L. M., Porter, A. C., Garet, M. S., Yoon, K. S., & Birman, B. F. (2002). Effects of professional development on teachers' instruction: Results from a three-year longitudinal study. *Educational Evaluation and Policy Analysis, 24*(2), 81–112.

Devaney, L. (2016). *6 ways to support computer science education.* Retrieved February 24, 2017 from http://www.eschoolnews.com/2016/06/02/6-ways-to-support-computer-science-education/?

Dove, M. K. (2004). Teacher attrition: A critical American and international education issue. *Delta Kappa Gamma Bulletin, 71*(1), 8–15.

DuFour, R., & Eaker, R. (1998). *Professional learning communities at work.* Bloomington, IN: Solution Tree.

Dunn, L. A. (1999). Transforming identity in conflict. In C. Fchrock-Shenk & L. Ressler (Eds.), *Making peace with conflict: Practical skills for conflict transformation* (pp. 38–46). Waterloo, Ontario, Canada: Herald Press.

Earl, L. (1995). Moving from the political to the practical: A hard look at assessment and accountability. *Orbit, 26*(2), 61–63.

Earl, L., & Katz, S. (2005). Painting a data-rich picture. *Principal Leadership, 5*(5), 16–20.

Edmonds, R. R. (1979). Effective schools for the urban poor. *Educational Leadership, 37*(2), 15–24.

Eliot, T. S. (1935). *Murder in the cathedral.* San Diego, CA: Harcourt Brace.

Elmore, R. F. (2002). *Bridging the gap between standards and achievement.* Washington, DC: Albert Shanker Institute.

Erekson, O. H., DeShano, K. M., Platt, G., & Zeigert, A. L. (2002). Fungibility of lottery revenues and support for public education. *Journal of Education Finance, 28*(2), 301–311.

Essex, N. L. (2015). *School law and the public schools: A practical guide for educational leaders.* Upper Saddle River, NJ: Pearson Education.

Ferlazzo, L. (2011). Involvement or engagement? *Educational Leadership, 68*(8), 10–14.

Fisher, R., Ury, W., & Patton, B. (1991). *Getting to Yes: Negotiating agreement without giving in* (2nd ed.). New York, NY: Penguin Books.

Fullan, M. G., & Miles, M. (1992). Getting reform right: What works and what doesn't. *Phi Delta Kappan, 73*(10), 745–752.

Fullan, M. G., & Stiegelbauer, S. (1991). *The new meaning of educational change.* New York, NY: Teachers College Press.

Garrett, T. A. (2001). Earmarked lottery revenues for education: A new test of fungibility. *Journal of Education Finance, 26*(3), 219–238.

Gleason, S. C., & Gerzon, N. J. (2014). *Growing into equity: Professional learning and personalization in high-achieving schools.* Thousand Oaks, CA: Corwin.

Goldsmith, L. M., & Sorenson, R. D. (2005). Ethics, integrity and fairness: Three musts for school vision and budgeting. *Texas Study of Secondary Education, 15*(1), 7–9.

Gordon, M. F., & Louis, K. S. (2009). Linking parent and community involvement with student achievement: Comparing principal and teacher perceptions of stakeholder influence. *American Journal of Education, 116*(1), 1–32.

Gorton, R., Schneider, G., & Fisher, J. (1988). *Encyclopedia of school administration and supervision.* Phoenix, AZ: Oryx.

Governing Data. (2016). *Education spending per student by state.* Retrieved December 07, 2016, from http://www.governing.com/gov-data/education-data/state-education-spending-per-pupil-data.html

Governmental Accounting Standards Board (GASB). (2016). *Codification of governmental accounting and financial reporting standards.* Norwalk, CT: Author.

Green, L. (2016). *Booster club embezzlement: Legal issues, preventive strategies.* Retrieved March 3, 2017, from https://www.nfhs.org/articles/booster-club-embezzlement-legal-issues-preventive-strategies/

Green, R. L. (2013). *Practicing the art of leadership: A problem-based approach to implementing the ISLLC standards* (4th ed.). New York, NY: Pearson.

Greenberg, E., Dunleavy, E., & Kutner, M. (2007). *Literacy behind bars: Results from the 2003 national assessment* (NCES 200-473). U.S. Department of Education, National Center for Education Statistics. Retrieved July 23, 2017, from http://nces.ed.gov/pubs2007/2007473.pdf

Greenleaf, R. K. (2002). *Servant leadership: A journey into the nature of legitimate power and greatness.* Mahwah, NJ: Paulist Press.

Guernsey, L., & Levine, M. H. (2016). Nurturing young readers: How digital media can promote literacy instead of undermining it. *American Educator, 40*(3), 23–28, 44.

Guthrie, J. W., Hart, C., Hack, W. G., & Candoli, I. C. (2007). *Modern school business administration: A planning approach.* Boston, MA: Allyn & Bacon.

Hadderman, M. (2002). School-based budgeting. *Teacher Librarian, 30*(1), 27–30.

Hallinger, T., & Heck, R. H. (2010). Collaborative leadership and school improvement: Understanding the impact on school capacity and student learning. *School Leadership and Management 30*(2), 95–110.

Halsne, C., & Koeberl, C. (2016). *Denver public schools crack down on employee credit card use.* Retrieved on February 10, 2017, from http://kdvr.com/2016/03/02/dps-cracks-down-on-employee-credit-card-use/

Halverson, R., Prichett, R., Grigg, J., & Thomas, C. (2005). The new instructional leadership: Creating data-driven instructional systems in schools. WCER Working Paper No. 2005-9. *ERIC Digest.* Retrieved from ERIC Data Base (ED497014)

Hansen, R. C. (2016). Professional Standards for Educational Leaders presentation. Indianapolis, IN: Indiana Association of School Principals. Retrieved May 21, 2017, from http://www.iasp.org/wp-content/uploads/Hansen.-PSEL-2016-17-.pdf

Harris, S. (2004). Strategies to meet the challenge of the age of accountability. *Insight, 18*(3), 25–28.

Henderson, A. T., Marburger, C. L., & Ooms, T. (1986). *Beyond the bake sale: An educator's guide to working with parents.* Columbia, MD: National Committee for Citizens in Education.

Henrichson, C., & Delaney, R. (2012). *The price of prisons: What incarceration costs taxpayers.* Vera Institute of Justice, Center on Sentencing and Corrections. Retrieved July 23, 2017, from https://www.vera.org/publications/price-of-prisons-what-incarceration-costs-taxpayers

Holcomb, E. L. (2004). *Getting excited about data: Combining people, passion; and proof to maximize student achievement* (2nd ed.). Thousand Oaks, CA: Corwin.

Hopkins, D., & West, M. (1994). Teacher development and school improvement: An account of improving the quality of education for all (IQEA) project. In D. R. Wallings (Ed.), *Teachers as leaders: Perspectives on the professional development of teachers* (pp. 179–199). Bloomington, IN: Phi Delta Kappa.

Hoy, W. K., & Miskel, C. G. (2012). *Educational administration: Theory, research, and practice.* Boston, MA: McGraw-Hill Humanities/Social Sciences/Languages.

Hughes, R. L., Ginnett, R. C., & Curphy, G. J. (2015). *Leadership: Enhancing the lessons of experience.* Boston, MA: McGraw-Hill Education.

Iger, A. L. (1998). *Music of the golden age, 1900–1950 and beyond: A guide to popular composers and lyricists.* Westport, CT: Greenwood.

Independent School Management (ISM). (2017). *Strategies for strengthening ties with feeder schools.* Retrieved May 21, 2017, from https://isminc.com/e-letters/advancement/vol-15/no-4/strategies-for-strengthening-ties-with-feeder-schools

Johnson, C. E. (2017). *Meeting the ethical challenges of leadership.* Thousand Oaks, CA: SAGE.

Johnson, L. (2007). Rethinking successful school leadership in challenging U.S. schools: Culturally responsive practices in school–community relationships. *ISEA, 35*(3), 49–57.

Johnson, R. S. (2002). *Using data to close the achievement gap: How to measure equity in our schools* (2nd ed.). Thousand Oaks, CA: Corwin.

Jones, T. H., & Amalfitano, J. L. (1994). *America's gamble: Public school finance and state lotteries.* Lancaster, PA: Technomic.

Just Ask Publications and Professional Development. (2017). *Yesterday & today: Where we've been and where we're going.* Retrieved May 7, 2017, from http://www.justaskpublications.com/just-ask-resource-center/e-newsletters/professionalpractices/operations-and-management/

KFOX 14 Television. (2011, August 2). *Update: EPISD superintendent Lorenzo Garcia arrested.* Retrieved February 20, 2012, from http://www.kfoxtv.com/news/news/update-episd-superintendent-lorenzo-garciaar-reste/nDTLn/

Khalifa, M. A., Gooden, M. A., & Davis, J. E. (2016). Culturally responsive school leadership: A synthesis of the literature. *Review of Educational Research, 86*(4), 1272–1311.

Knowles, C. (2002). *The first-time grantwriter's guide to success.* Thousand Oaks, CA: Corwin.

Kouzes, J. M., & Posner, B. Z. (2007). *The leadership challenge* (4th ed.). San Francisco, CA: Jossey-Bass.

Laffee, S. (2002, December). Data-driven districts. *The School Administrator, 59,* 6–15.

Lai, E. (2014). Principal leadership practices in exploited situated possibilities to build teacher capacity for change. *Asia Pacific Education, 15,* 165–175.

LaMorte, M. W. (2011). *School law: Cases and concepts.* Boston, MA: Allyn & Bacon Educational Leadership.

Lazear, J. (1992). *Meditations for men who do too much.* New York, NY: Fireside/Parkside, Simon & Schuster.

Leachman, M., Albares, N., Masterson, K., & Wallace, M. (2016). Most states have cut school finding, and some continue cutting. *The Center on Budget and Policy Priorities.* Retrieved December 9, 2016, from http://www.cbpp.org/research/state-budget-and-tax/most-states-have-cut-school-funding-and-some-continue-cutting

Learning Point Associates. (2004). *Guide to using data in school improvement efforts: A compilation of knowledge from data retreats and data use at Learning Points Associates.* Retrieved April 2, 2012, from http://www.learningpt.org/pdfs/datause/guidebook.pdf

Leithwood, K. (1990). The principal's role in teacher development. In B. Joyce (Ed.), *Changing school culture through staff development: 1990 yearbook of the Association for Supervision and Curriculum Development* (pp. 71–90). Alexandria, VA: ASCD.

Levin, H. M. (2011, Summer). Waiting for Godot: Cost-effectiveness analysis in education. *New Directions for Evaluation, 90.* San Francisco, CA: Jossey-Bass.

Lewis, J. D., & Weigert, A. (1985). Trust as a social reality. *Social Forces, 63,* 967–985.

Linder, D. (n.d.). *Regulation of obscenity and nudity.* Retrieved September 6, 2004, from http://law2.umkc.edu/faculty/projects/ftrials/conlaw/obscenity.htm

Loeb, S., & Plank, D. N. (2007). *Continuous improvement in California education: Data systems and policy learning.* Berkeley: Policy Analysis for California Education (PACE), University of California–Berkeley.

Lunenburg, F. C., & Irby, B. J. (2006). *The principalship: Vision to action.* Belmont, CA: Wadsworth.

Maeroff, G. I. (1994). On matters of body and mind: Overcoming disincentives to a teaching career. In D. R. Walling (Ed.), *Teachers as leaders: Perspectives on the professional development of teachers* (pp. 45–57). Bloomington, IN: Phi Delta Kappa.

Mandinach, E., & Jackson, S. (2012). *Transforming teaching and learning through data-driven decision making.* Thousand Oaks, CA: Corwin.

Martinez, A. (2017, June 14). *Murphy details role in cheating plan.* Retrieved from http://www.elpasotimes.com/story/news/crime/2017/06/13/defense-episd-case-says-inquiry-politically-motivated/393867001/

McCloskey, W., Mikow-Porto, V., & Bingham, S. (1998). *Reflecting on progress: Site-based management and school improvement in North Carolina.* ERIC Document Reproduction Service ED 421766.

Miranda, A. (2012). Excellent leadership in budgeting strategies. Unpublished interview, Department of Educational Leadership and Foundations, The University of Texas at El Paso, El Paso, TX.

Mutter, D. W., & Parker, P. J. (2012). *School money matters: A handbook for principals.* Alexandria, VA: Association for Supervision and Curriculum Development (ASCD).

Nash, R. J. (1996). *"Real world" ethics: Frameworks for educators and human service professionals.* New York, NY: Teachers College Press.

National Center for Education Statistics (NCES). (2016a). *Digest of education statistics.* Retrieved December 03, 2016, from http://nces.ed.gov/pubs2016/2016006.pdf

National Center for Education Statistics (NCES). (2016b). *Stats in brief: Trends in public and private school principal demographics and qualifications: 1987–88 to 2011–12.* Retrieved February 28, 2017, from https://nces.ed.gov/pubs2016/2016189.pdf

National Center for Education Statistics (NCES). (2016c). *Fast facts: What is Title I and what type of student does it serve?* Retrieved December 07, 2016, from https://nces.ed.gov/fstfacts/display.asp? id=158

National Center for Education Statistics (NCES). (2016d). *Financial accounting for local and state school systems.* Retrieved December 03, 2016, from https://nces.ed.gov/pubsearch/pubsinfo.asp? pubid=2015347

National Conference of State Legislatures. (2011). *State budget update: Fall 2011.* Retrieved December 03, 2016, from http://ncsl.org

National Conference of State Legislatures. (2016). *School finance.* Retrieved December 3, 2016, from http://www.ncsl.org/research/education/school-finance.aspx

National Education Association. (2016). *Rankings and estimates: Rankings of the states and estimates of school statistics 2016.* Atlanta, GA: Author.

National Policy Board for Educational Administration (NPBEA). (2015). *Professional standards for educational leaders.* Retrieved May 7, 2017, from http://www.npbea.org/wp/wp-content/uploads/2014/11/ProfessionalStandardsforEducationalLeaders2015forNPBEAFINAL-2.pdf

National Staff Development Council. (2001). *Standards for staff development* (rev. ed.). Oxford, OH: Author. Available at http://www.nsdc.org/educator index.htm

Negron, S. (2006). *Kinky Friedman: A Texas twister of a candidate.* Retrieved February 14, 2012, from http://newspapertree.com/view_article.sstg?c=4caab8c666334633

Nelson, A., & Toler, S. (2002). *The five secrets to becoming a leader.* Ventura, CA: Regal Books.

New Jersey School Board Association (NJSBA). (2007). *Financing special education in New Jersey.* Retrieved March 15, 2017, from http://www.google.com/url? sa=t&rct=j&q=&esrc=s&source=web&cd=7&ved=0CFoQFjAG&url=http%3A%2F%2Fwww.njsba.org%2Fspecialeducation%2FExecutiveSummary.pdf&ei=TMCNT6PfMMbF2QXyjeH_Cw&usg=AFQjCNFiOT YoASaOvvIsKvJBox7v1ZGK1w

Newman, F. M., Smith, B., Allensworth, E., & Bryk, A. S. (2001). Instructional program coherent: What it is and why it should guide school improvement policy. *Educational Evaluation and Policy Analysis, 23*(4), 297–321.

Northouse, P. G. (2015). *Leadership: Theory and practice.* Thousand Oaks, CA: SAGE.

Norton, M. S. (2005). *Executive leadership for effective administration.* Boston, MA: Pearson Education.

O'Donnell, L., & Sorenson, R. D. (2005). *How sex and money ruined Dr. Ed U. Kator's career.* Manuscript submitted for publication.

Odden, A., & Archibald, S. (2001). *Reallocating resources: How to boost student achievement without asking for more.* Thousand Oaks, CA: Corwin.

Odden, A., & Wohlstetter, P. (1995). Making school-based management work. *Educational Leadership, 52*(5), 32–36.

Office of Management and Budget. (2005). *Preventing embezzlement.* Washington, DC: Author.

Oliva, P. (2005). *Developing the curriculum* (6th ed.). Boston, MA: Pearson.

Omarsson, I. (2017). *14 things that are obsolete in 21st century schools.* Retrieved May 7, 2017, from http://ingvihrannar.com/14-things-that-are-obsolete-in-21st-century-schools/

Osborne, J., Barbee, D., & Suydam, J. A. (1999). FBI is asked to examine CCISD. *Corpus Christi Caller-Times.* Retrieved June 17, 2005, from http://www.caller2.com/1999/october/06/today/local_ne/1147.html

Ovsiew, L., & Castetter, W. B. (1960). *Budgeting for better schools.* Englewood Cliffs, NJ: Prentice Hall.

Owings, W. A., & Kaplan, L. S. (2013). *American public school finance.* Belmont, CA: Wadsworth, Cengage Learning.

Park, S., Hironaka, S., Carver, P., & Norgstrum, L. (2013). Continuous improvement in education. *Carnegie Foundations for the Advancement of Teaching*. White Paper.

Patterson, K., Grenny, J., McMillan, R., & Switzler, A. (2002). *Crucial conversations: Tools for talking when stakes are high*. New York, NY: McGraw-Hill.

Peterson, S. L. (2001). *The grantwriter's internet companion: A resource for educators and others seeking grants and funding*. Thousand Oaks, CA: Corwin.

Poston, W. K., Jr. (2011). *School budgeting for hard times: Confronting cutbacks and critics*. Thousand Oaks, CA: Corwin.

Property Tax Division of the Texas Comptroller's Office. (2017). *Window on state government: More challenges facing Texas education today*. Retrieved on January 13, 2017, from http://www.window.state.tx.us/comptrol/wwstand/wws0512ed

Razik, T. A., & Swanson, A. D. (2010). *Fundamental concepts of educational leadership and management*. Boston, MA: Allyn & Bacon.

Reagan, R. (1987). *Remarks on signing the intermediate-range nuclear forces treaty, December 8, 1987*. Retrieved February 20, 2012, from http://www.reagan.utexas.edu/archives/speeches/1987/120887c.htm

Roe, W. H. (1961). *School business management*. New York, NY: McGraw-Hill.

Ronka, D., Lachat, M. A., Slaughter, R., & Meltzer, J. (2009). Answering questions that count. *Educational Leadership, 66*(4), 18–24.

Ryan, K., & Cooper, J. (2004). *Those who can teach* (10th ed.). Boston, MA: Allyn & Bacon.

Schaffhauser, D. (2016). *Report: Education tech spending on the rise*. Retrieved February 24, 2017 from https://thejournal.com/articles/2016/01/19/report-education-tech-spending-on-the-rise.aspx

Schladen, M., & Kappes, H. (2012, February 4). *El Paso ISD's former superintendent Lorenzo Garcia sets trial date of June 18*. Retrieved from http://www.elpasotimes.com/news/ci_19890821

Sergiovanni, T. J., Kelleher, P., McCarthy, M. M., & Fowler, F. C. (2009). *Educational governance and administration*. Boston, MA: Allyn & Bacon.

Severson, K. (2011, July 6). Systematic cheating is found in Atlanta's school system. *New York Times*. Retrieved from http://www.nytimes.com/2011/07/06/education/06atlanta.html

Shapiro, J. P., & Stefkovich, J. A. (2016). *Ethical leadership and decision making in education: Applying theoretical perspectives to complex dilemmas*. New York, NY: Routledge.

Shaw, P. L. (2012). *Taking charge: Leading with passion and purpose in the principalship*. New York, NY: Teachers College Press.

Slaikeu, K. A. (1996). *When push comes to shove: A practical guide to mediating disputes*. San Francisco, CA: Jossey-Bass.

Snopes. (2017). *If 99.9 percent is good enough, then . . .* Retrieved May 05, 2017, from http://msgboard.com/cgi-bin/ultimatebb.cgi? ubb=get_topic;f=47;t=000474;p=0

Sorenson, R. D. (2007, Winter). How sex and money ruined Dr. Ed U. Kator's career. *Leadership in Focus 6*, 6–10.

Sorenson, R. D. (2008, Winter). Principal effectiveness: A twelve-step approach to leadership success. *Principal Matters: Journal for Secondary School Leaders, 75,* 6–8.

Sorenson, R. D. (2010). Making sense of dollars and cents. School management. *NAESP Principal, 90*(1), 10–15.

Sorenson, R. D., & Cortez, M. T. (2010). The principal's role and responsibility in analyzing the campus improvement plan and conducting a needs assessment. *Instructional Leader, 23,* 11–14.

Sorenson, R. D., & Goldsmith, L. M. (2004, July). The budget–vision relationship: Understanding the interwoven process. Paper presented at the annual Texas Association of Secondary School Principals New Principals Academy, Trinity University, San Antonio, Texas.

Sorenson, R. D., & Goldsmith, L. M. (2006). Auditing procedures and ethical behaviors: Cures for the common scheme. *TEPSA Journal, Winter,* 10–14.

Sorenson, R. D., & Goldsmith, L. M. (2007). The budget–vision relationship: Understanding the interwoven process. *Journal of School Business Management 19*(1), 27–29.

Sorenson, R. D., & Goldsmith, L. M. (2009). *The principal's guide to managing school personnel.* Thousand Oaks, CA: Corwin.

Sorenson, R. D., Cortez, M. T., & Negrete, M. A. (2010, Spring). What makes for an ideal principal? A framework for leadership development and organizational success as perceived by lead teachers. *Leadership in Focus, 19,* 46–49.

Sorenson, R. D., Goldsmith, L. M., & DeMatthews, D. E. (2016). *The principal's guide to time management: Instructional leadership in the digital age.* Thousand Oaks, CA: Corwin.

Sorenson, R. D., Goldsmith, L. M., Méndez, Z. Y., & Maxwell, K. T. (2011). *The principal's guide to curriculum leadership.* Thousand Oaks, CA: Corwin.

Stansbury, M. (2016). *Students say campus technology needs major overhaul—but why?* Retrieved June 30, 2016, from http://www.ecampusnews.com/technologies/students-campus-technology/? print

Starr, L. (2008). *Show me the money: Tips and resources for successful grant writing.* Retrieved February 19, 2012, from http://www.educationworld.com/a_curr/profdev/profdev039.shtml

Stein, J. (Ed.). (1967). *The Random House dictionary of the English language* (Unabridged ed.). New York, NY: Random House.

Stokes, B. (2011). *America's first deflationary depression: Is a bigger one ahead?* Retrieved on February 15, 2012, from http://www.elliottwave.com/freeupdates/archives/2011/11/01/America-s-First-Deflationary-Depression-Is-a-Bigger-One-Ahead.aspx

Strauss, V. (2012, March 30). Mega millions: Do lotteries really benefit public schools? *The Washington Post.* Retrieved December 8, 2016 from https://www.washingtonpost.com/blogs/answer-sheet/post/mega-millions-do-lotteries-really-benefit-public-schools/2012/03/30/gIQAbTUNlS_blog.html? utm_term=.f70e58041303

Strauss, V. (2017, May 24). Analysis: Five startling things Betsy DeVos just told Congress. *The Washington Post*. Retrieved May 25, 2017, from https://www.washingtonpost.com/news/answer-sheet/wp/2017/05/24/five-startling-things-betsy-devos-just-told-congress/?utm_term=.f22282af510f

Tanner, D., & Tanner, L. (2006). *Curriculum development: Theory into practice*. Englewood Cliffs, NJ: Prentice Hall.

Tempel, E., Seiler, T., & Aldrich, E. (Eds.). (2015). *Achieving excellence in fundraising*. San Francisco, CA: John Wiley & Sons.

Texas Education Agency (TEA). (2017a). *TEA correspondence*. Austin, TX: Author.

Texas Education Agency (TEA). (2017b). *13 components of the campus improvement plan*. Austin, TX: Author.

Texas Taxpayers and Research Association (TTARA). (2017). *An introduction to school finance in Texas*. Retrieved January 13, 2017, from http://www.ttara.org

Thinkexist. (2017). Dwight Eisenhower. Retrieved February 09, 2017, from http://thinkexist.com/quotes/dwight_david_eisenhower/

Tschannen-Moran, M. (2014). *Trust matters: Leadership for successful schools* (2nd ed.). San Francisco, CA: Jossey-Bass.

U.S. Bureau of Labor Statistics. (2011). *Education pays*. Retrieved July 23, 2017, from https://www.bls.gov/careeroutlook/2010/summer/oochart.pdf

U.S. Bureau of Labor Statistics. (2016). *Unemployment rate and earnings for educational attainment, 2016*. Retrieved July 23, 2017, from https://www.bls.gov/emp/ep_chart_001.htm

U.S. Census Bureau. (2016). *Public education finances: 2014*. U.S. Department of Commerce, U.S. Census Bureau. Retrieved July 23, 2017, from https://www2.census.gov/govs/school/14f33pub.pdf

Ubben, G. L., & Hughes, L. W. (2016). *The principal: Creative leadership for excellence in schools*. Boston, MA: Pearson Education.

Urban, W. J., & Wagoner, J. L. (2014). *American education: A history*. New York, NY: Routledge.

Vamos, M., & Jackson, S. (Eds.). (1989, May 29). The public is willing to take business on. *Business Week/Harris Poll, 3107*, 29.

Walton, M. (1986). *The Deming management method*. New York, NY: Perigee.

Warner, M. (n. d.). Using a Sphero BB-8 droid in the classroom. *Teaching ideas*. Retrieved August 5, 2017, from http://www.teachingideas.co.uk/control-technology/using-a-sphero-bb-8-droid-in-the-classroom

Warren, M. R., Hong, S., Rubin, C. L., & Uy, P. S. (2009). Beyond the bake sale: A community-based relational approach to parent engagement in schools. *Teachers College Record, 111*(9), 2209–2254.

Webb, L. D., & Norton, M. S. (2012). *Human resources administration: Personnel issues and needs in education*. Boston, MA: Pearson Education.

Weston, M. (2011). *Public Policy Institute of California: Just the facts, financing California's public schools*. Retrieved March 1, 2017, from http://www.ppic.org/main/publication_show.asp?i=1001

Wilhour, J. (1998). I teach. Unpublished interview, Department of Educational Leadership and Foundations, The University of Texas at El Paso, El Paso, TX.

Wilkins, A. L., & Patterson, K. J. (1985). Five steps for closing culture-gaps. In R. H. Kilmann, M. J. Saxton, & R. Serpa (Eds.), *Gaining control of the corporate culture* (pp. 351–369). San Francisco, CA: Jossey-Bass.

Will, G. (2005, February 17). These bones protected by muscle. *Abilene Reporter-News*, p. 4AA.

Wilmot, W. W., & Hocker, J. L. (2007). *Interpersonal conflict*. (7th ed.). New York, NY: McGraw-Hill.

Worrell, D. (2011). *Fraud: 5 simple steps to prevent embezzlement and theft*. Retrieved on February 20, 2012, from http://www.allbusiness.com/finance/accounting-budgeting/16653461-1.html

Worth, J. (2015). *4 ways to protect your business against employee fraud and theft*. Retrieved on February 10, 2017, from http://www.entrepreneur.com/article/244607

YARN. (2005–2017). *Citizen Kane film clip/quote*. Retrieved May 7, 2017, from https://getyarn.io/yarn-clip/ad8ddd36-e9a9-41da-894e-64420505a6bd

Yeagley, R. (2002). A forum for becoming data savvy. *The School Administrator, 59*(11), 13.

Yukl, G. A. (2012). *Leadership in organizations* (8th ed.). Upper Saddle River, NJ: Pearson Education.

Zane, E. B. (2016). *Writing proposals: A handbook of what makes your project right for funding*. Seattle, WA: Amazon Digital Services.

Index

CORWIN LEADERSHIP

Simon T. Bailey & Marceta F. Reilly
On providing a simple, sustainable framework that will help you move your school from mediocrity to brilliance.

Edie L. Holcomb
Use data to construct an equitable learning environment, develop instruction, and empower effective PL communities.

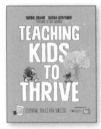

Debbie Silver & Dedra Stafford
Equip educators to develop resilient and mindful learners primed for academic growth and personal success.

Peter Gamwell & Jane Daly
A fresh perspective on how to nurture creativity, innovation, leadership, and engagement.

Steven Katz, Lisa Ain Dack, & John Malloy
Leverage the oppositional forces of top-down expectations and bottom-up experience to create an intelligent, responsive school.

Lyn Sharratt & Beate Planche
A resource-rich guide that provides a strategic path to achieving sustainable communities of deep learners.

Peter M. DeWitt
Meet stakeholders where they are, motivate them to improve, and model how to do it.

To order your copies, visit **corwin.com/leadership**

Leadership that Makes an Impact

Also Available

Charlotte Danielson
Harness the power of informal professional conversation and invite teachers to boost achievement.

Liz Wiseman, Lois Allen, & Elise Foster
Use leadership to bring out the best in others—liberating staff to excel and doubling your team's effectiveness.

Eric Sheninger
Use digital resources to create a new school culture, increase engagement, and facilitate real-time PD.

Russell J. Quaglia, Michael J. Corso, & Lisa L. Lande
Listen to your school's voice to see how you can increase engagement, involvement, and academic motivation.

Michael Fullan, Joanne Quinn, & Joanne McEachen
Learn the right drivers to mobilize complex, coherent, whole-system change and transform learning for all students.

A SAGE Publishing Company

Helping educators make the greatest impact

CORWIN HAS ONE MISSION: to enhance education through intentional professional learning. We build long-term relationships with our authors, educators, clients, and associations who partner with us to develop and continuously improve the best evidence-based practices that establish and support lifelong learning.

Solutions you want. Experts you trust. Results you need.

AUTHOR CONSULTING

Author Consulting

On-site professional learning with sustainable results! Let us help you design a professional learning plan to meet the unique needs of your school or district. www.corwin.com/pd

INSTITUTES

Institutes

Corwin Institutes provide collaborative learning experiences that equip your team with tools and action plans ready for immediate implementation. www.corwin.com/institutes

ECOURSES

eCourses

Practical, flexible online professional learning designed to let you go at your own pace. www.corwin.com/ecourses

READ2EARN

Read2Earn

Did you know you can earn graduate credit for reading this book? Find out how: www.corwin.com/read2earn

Contact an account manager at (800) 831-6640 or visit **www.corwin.com** for more information.